Death by Journalism?

One Teacher's Fateful
Encounter with Political
Correctness

Jerry Bledsoe

Down Home Press, Asheboro, N.C.

ISBN 1-878086-93-6

Library of Congress Control Number 2001-
129226

Printed in the United States of America

Book design by Beth Hennington

Down Home Press
P.O. Box 4126
Asheboro, N.C. 27204

Down Home Press books are distributed by
John F. Blair, Publisher
1406 Plaza Dr.
Winston-Salem, N.C. 27103

How easy it is to make people believe a lie, and how hard it is to undo that work again!

—Mark Twain

Contents

Foreword vii

Prologue ix

Part 1: Heritage & History 11

Part 2: War in North Carolina 35

Part 3: Civil Wrongs 91

Part 4: Aftershocks 189

Epilogue 231

Afterword 239

Foreword

This book is about innocent people going about innocent activities who come under assault by a newspaper and not only find themselves the object of nationwide vilification, but thwarted in getting out the truth by the very media that condemned them.

It happened in mid-November, 1998, in the North Carolina county in which I live. The newspaper that started it, the *News & Record* of Greensboro, was one I had loved, one where I worked as reporter and columnist for more than twenty years. I knew the editors and publisher involved, and I found myself in disbelief at what they allowed to occur.

I missed the controversy when it broke. I had left the newspaper years earlier to write books and was on a promotion tour. I didn't get home until nearly three weeks afterward. I first heard about it when I had lunch with friends from the paper. It was the main topic of conversation.

A few days earlier, I learned, an expensive ad appeared claiming that the controversy—which revolved around an adult Civil War course at Randolph Community College—was contrived, the reporting false. As my friends discussed the ad and the articles that evoked it, I was without details sufficient to participate.

After lunch, curious, I sat down with a stack of back issues at the library. I was astonished at what I read. Not only was the reporting sensational and provocative, it was patently shoddy in other ways, and I was dismayed that it appeared in a newspaper that once had been recognized as one of the finest of its size in the country. Yet, despite these obvious flaws, and denials from students and lecturers, the newspaper's editors insisted that the articles were accurate and fair.

The final class had been cancelled because of the angry and overwhelming response, and students were waiting to hear whether they would be allowed to complete their studies.

Political censorship had become a very real possibility in my county, and my passions for free speech, truth, and honest journalism wouldn't allow me to sit by quietly.

I wrote a lengthy open letter questioning the credibility of the reporting and challenging the *News & Record*'s publisher to present proof of its claims. After the college permanently cancelled the final class and dropped the course, I wrote to my hometown newspaper, the *Courier-Tribune* of Asheboro, saying that this abrogation of the First Amendment shouldn't be allowed and the course should be restored.

Although the *News & Record* publicly ignored my letter, it was published in an alternative newspaper, causing the course's instructor, Jack Perdue, to write to me. We subsequently had telephone conversations, one quite lengthy, during which I took extensive notes.

I had no intention or time to pursue the matter further, but when Jack Perdue died suddenly a few weeks later, I changed my mind. I had believed all along that behind this controversy lay a bigger, more important story about free speech, academic freedom, political correctness, racial politics, and journalistic ethics and responsibility, all of which came together at the same time in Jack Perdue's life.

This is that story.

Prologue

No reporters attended Jack Perdue's funeral. No indignant editorial writers, angry columnists, or frothing radio and TV talk show hosts. Nobody from CBS, NBC, ABC, CNN, BBC, AP, or UPI showed up, although only weeks earlier, all had been clamoring to get to Jack.

But the world's news media had lost interest and moved on. Jack was no longer of use to them. He was yesterday's story. His death was not their concern.

If any reporters had chosen to attend, they might have found his funeral of interest, if for no other reason than it reflected a different time.

A Confederate battle flag, a flag Jack revered, adorned the wall at the front of the chapel behind a table bearing photographs and memorabilia from his life. On the table, too, was a decorative canister with a Civil War battle scene wrapping its corners. In it were Jack's ashes.

As the service began, a uniformed honor guard of Confederate Army re-enactors marched solemnly to seats across the aisle from the family. They were followed by women of the Confederate Order of the Rose, their faces veiled, wearing the long, black mourning dresses of the 1860s.

The music, too, was of that period. "Buffalo Gals, Won't You Come Out Tonight" served as prelude. And the mourners would exit the chapel with the strains of "Dixie," the anthem of the Old South, reverberating in their heads.

Some in this congregation said later that they were disappointed that no reporters came, for they would have been curious to see their reactions when one of the ministers denounced the news media—and the *News & Record* and its reporter in particular—another aspect of this funeral that made it distinctive.

The condemnation prompted a muttered chorus of "Amen," for

many in the congregation believed that a single fabricated article in the *News & Record*, and all that resulted from it, had contributed to Jack's death, if not having been directly responsible for it, as his mother, his wife, and others felt certain.

Jack Perdue, many of his mourners thought, was a Southern casualty of the Civil War 135 years after the fact, little different from men who had fallen on the battlefield. The only difference in their minds was that he had been felled by lies, distortions and the awesome power of the press and political correctness instead of by grapeshot, bayonet, or miniè ball, brought down not for taking up arms against troops invading his homeland but for teaching the history of those who did.

Part I

Heritage & History

Like many Americans, I long to know the past. There's a sense of loss in America today, a feeling of disconnectedness. We're no longer quite sure who we are or how we got here. More and more of us are rummaging in the attic, trying to retrieve our history. We draw genealogical charts and hang old quilts on the wall. We seem to hope that if we can find out our family stories and trace our roots and save the old cookie jars and coal scuttles, we just might rescue ourselves and be made whole.
—Bobbie Ann Mason

One

If the beginning of any story truly can be known, this one may have started on a sunny Saturday in May, 1993. It did in Annie Laura Perdue's mind anyway, perhaps because events eventually would bring her back full-circle to this day.

It was not unusual for Annie Laura to be prowling another cemetery with her husband, Jack. They often rode back roads together, their eyes alert for church graveyards or tiny family burial grounds. Annie Laura sometimes felt as if she'd been in every cemetery in North Carolina, but they always managed to find more. Her husband loved cemeteries—they were so filled with history, he liked to say, held so many curiosities, had so much family lore to offer—and she had come to share his enthusiasm for them.

On this morning they had examined every tombstone in the cemetery of a small, country Baptist church called Oak Level, not far from the town of Stokesdale, barely inside the Rockingham County line. A distant cousin, only recently discovered, directed Jack there in the hope of fulfilling a long quest for kin.

Indeed, Jack had found a cluster of Perdue graves, not to mention a pod of Pegrams, who also were in his family line. He photographed all the stones. The names on them, along with the birth and death dates, would go into the big family history on which he had been working for decades.

Yet, despite these rewards, Jack was disappointed. He hadn't come upon the graves that were his object this day, the graves that had taken him and Annie Laura on many futile hunts, those of his great, great grandparents, Jehu Jackson Perdue and his wife, Eliza Jane.

What he knew of them was scant, the details of their lives eluding him as surely as their graves. He did know that Jehu was born around 1828 and may have been the son of Jehu and Susannah Ham Perdue.

Eliza, born in 1830, was the daughter of William A. and Nancy Perdue. Records showed that Eliza and Jehu married in Rockingham County in September, 1848. Jack didn't know if they were related, because he couldn't confirm Jehu's parentage, but it wasn't unusual for cousins to marry in that time and place. Eliza had five children, two sons and three daughters, between 1850 and 1860.

On March 11, 1862, at age thirty-three, Jehu enlisted in the Madison Greys, Company D, 45th Regiment, North Carolina Troops. His brother-in-law, John C. Perdue, joined with him, both getting a $100 enlistment bonus. They went off with sixty-six of their neighbors for training at Camp Magnum near Raleigh, then were quickly pressed into service against Federal forces that had invaded the state's coast. Within a year, half of the Madison Greys were dead of disease or wounds, including Jehu and John Perdue, both victims of "camp fever" (probably typhoid), John dying less than two months after his enlistment, Jehu on February 1, 1863.

But where Jehu's grave lay, Jack never had been able to discover, although he knew that he had been sent home to die and surely was buried somewhere in what Jack called "Perdue Country" in southwestern Rockingham County.

He had hoped that the little cemetery at Oak Level Church might hold that answer and was disappointed that it didn't. He and Annie Laura were heading back toward the Guilford County line when Annie Laura spotted something.

"Honey, I think I saw a tombstone back there in those weeds," she said.

Jack stopped the car and backed up. Sure enough, just a hundred yards or so from the church, on the opposite side of the road from the cemetery, barely visible through the weeds, saplings, and briers, stood two lonely granite gravestones.

After picking their way through the tangled growth, Jack and Annie Laura discovered that the most recently placed stone had been there for nearly fifty years. Jack grew excited when he read the inscription:

Bettie Jane Perdue, Wife of W.A. York
Dec. 24, 1873, Feb. 15, 1944

The other stone marked the grave of Bettie Jane's husband, who was born in 1861, the year the Civil War began, and died nearly twenty-five years before her, on May 3, 1919, at age fifty-eight.

Jack knew that Bettie Jane was the daughter of William Saunders Perdue, his great-grandfather, the eldest son of Jehu.

His excitement and wonder grew even greater when he realized that what appeared to be piles of rock in the nearby underbrush had patterns. Closer examination convinced him that these were raised graves, several as much as a foot and a half high, bordered by stacked field stones, graves unlike any he had seen. He counted at least eighteen, most unmarked. A few had upended field stones at one end. Jack noticed crudely carved inscriptions, barely discernible, on two, standing side-by side. One was a huge, irregularly-shaped slab of rock nearly five feet tall. On it was this:

B 1796   D 1861
M P

The smaller stone was flatter and stood only about three feet high. On it was this:

B 1795   D 1856
N P

Later, back at home, poring through his research materials, Jack matched the birth and death dates on the stones with those of William A. Perdue, the father of Eliza, and William's first wife, Nancy. The only problem was that the *M P* on the larger stone didn't match William's initials. Actually, what he had taken for an "M" appeared to be two inverted Vs so close together that the joining lines crossed like swords. Had somebody been trying to carve a "W" and gotten it upside down? Did the unmarked graves under these nearby piles of stone also hold other Perdues, perhaps Jehu and Eliza? Jack was sure that finding the answers was just a matter of time.

Two

That Jack became so engrossed in family history was no surprise to anybody who had known him very long. History—any kind of history—had fascinated him since childhood.

Born on December 17, 1938, in High Point, N.C., where his father was working as a machinist, he was the first child of Lewis and Mary Katherine Perdue, who moved to nearby Greensboro when their son was six months old. Lewis Perdue went to work at Newman Machine Company in Greensboro, where his father, Martin, spent his entire career until retirement, and where Lewis eventually would rise to be vice president. Jack, too, would work there during summers while he was in high school and college.

Jack and his sister, Betsy, two years younger, grew up in pleasant houses in two close-by, middle-class neighborhoods, first on Spring Garden Street, then on Springwood. The house on Springwood had a white-columned front porch, magnolias in the yard—Lewis Perdue loved magnolias—and a tool-filled workshop out back, where Jack often puttered around with his father, learning woodworking and machining skills. The family moved to this house when Jack was in fifth grade, Betsy the third, and there they lived until both finished college and married. The family faithfully attended College Place Methodist Church.

Jack was a shy, quiet and exceptionally well-behaved child, family members recalled, serious by nature. He always did what was expected without protest and was never a problem. Even at a young age, Jack seemed mature, with an innate sense of morality, totally honest and straightforward. "Most people are searching to find values," Betsy said, "but it was like Jack came with them."

The past was ever present in his childhood. His mother loved antiques and her husband bought them for Christmas and every birth-

16

day and anniversary. On weekend trips and summer vacations, the family toured historic sites, including Civil War forts and battlefields, piquing Jack's early interest in that bloody conflict.

Few weekends passed that the family didn't visit Jack's and Betsy's grandparents, Martin and Elizabeth Perdue, who lived in a log house on a twelve-acre farm just south of Greensboro. They had a barn, a cow for milk, and a horse named Fannie, trained to the plow. Through all his coming years, Jack would look back fondly on the many hours he spent there searching for arrowheads and other relics, creating a life-long fascination with the natives who roamed North Carolina for thousands of years before the arrival of European settlers.

Jack loved family gatherings, and even as a child preferred sitting and listening to adults recall family stories to playing outside. It was in such sessions that he first heard about his great, great uncle, William A. Perdue Jr., who went off to fight the Yankees and was wounded first at Chancellorsville, again at Gettysburg, before deserting and returning to Rockingham County, where he lived in hiding in the woods, hunted by the home guard, surviving on food slipped to him by family.

His mother told others that from the time Jack learned to read, his nose was stuck in some book. Likely as not, it was a book about history, particularly the Civil War. So voracious was his appetite for the written word that by the time he graduated from Lindley Park Junior High, he had read every volume of the family's set of encyclopedias—and retained an amazing amount of the information. "Jack just absorbed everything immediately," his sister said.

Betsy was a reader, too, but she preferred fiction, especially romantic and historical fiction about the South. She loved *Gone With the Wind*, both the book and movie, as did her brother, and read everything written by North Carolina novelist Inglis Fletcher. As a child, she had pictures above her bed of Old-South plantation balls, and later she would have her own pink, Old-South ball gown made to wear to a high school dance.

Jack's shyness and studiousness kept him out of popular social circles at Greensboro Senior High, but he had a small group of close friends. He played trombone in the concert band, even though he was tone deaf. He dated occasionally, but never had a steady girlfriend. By his senior year, he had his own car, an old Nash Rambler, bought with money he'd saved from working at Newman Machine Company. Unlike classmates who spent weekends cruising the Boar & Castle Drive-In on West Market Street, Jack was more apt to be at a coin shop adding to his extensive collection, in his father's workshop figuring out how some gadget worked, or in his room, which was decorated with a portrait of Robert E. Lee, reading about the Civil War.

After his graduation in 1957, Jack went off to the University of North Carolina in Chapel Hill, but for the first time his grades, usually high, didn't live up to his family's expectations. His father thought he was playing too much and studying too little. After his freshman year, Jack returned home to his old upstairs bedroom. He joined the National Guard and entered Guilford College, a small Quaker school on Greensboro's western edge. His mother's family was Quaker. Under his father's watchful eye, Jack spent more time with his textbooks, and his grades improved considerably.

Although his interest in history remained keen, it offered little prospect of a lucrative future, and at his father's suggestion, Jack chose economics as his major, history as his minor, reasoning that such a plan would offer more job possibilities later. But the course his life would take was about to be determined by something other than his fascination with history or his studies. His sister was to see to that.

As Jack began his second year at Guilford in the fall of 1959, his sister was beginning her first year at Woman's College (later the University of North Carolina at Greensboro) within walking distance of their home. Betsy planned to study American history and hoped to become a high school teacher. (She would get her bachelor's degree in history, but her master's would be in counseling, and her career would be as a public school counselor.)

She became quick friends with a dorm mate named Annie Laura Blackwelder, with whom she shared chemistry lab. Annie Laura was from the historic town of Hillsborough, about forty miles east of Greensboro, where her father worked as a supervisor at a cotton mill. She was petite and slender, with long brown hair, flashing dark eyes, a quick laugh and an ebullient personality. Her plan was to study biology and become a high school science teacher. She intended to attend Appalachian State Teachers College in Boone but changed her mind at the last minute, a decision she later saw as fateful.

That winter, Jack broke up with his first serious girlfriend, whom he had been dating for more than a year. At about the same time, Annie Laura quit seeing the boy she dated in high school. When a morose Jack called with news of his breakup, Betsy told him, "I've got the perfect girl for you."

But she had little luck with her initial efforts in matchmaking. That changed when the movie *South Pacific* came to the Carolina Theater. Annie Laura was dying to see it.

"Betsy was pestering me to go out with Jack," she recalled, laughing. "I think he was dating his way through the whole dorm, and I wasn't much interested. But when that movie came around, I said, 'Betsy, you tell your brother I will go out with him if he will take me to see *South Pacific.*'"

Jack soon called and offered to do just that. Annie Laura loved the movie and had a great time. Jack was a nice guy after all, she realized, smart and witty, and at the end of the evening, when he invited her to attend church the following day, she accepted.

Annie Laura had been a whiz in home-ec classes in high school, had sewn her entire college wardrobe. One dress she made was special. It was startlingly red, and she was wearing it when Jack picked her up for church the next morning. Through the rest of his days, Jack would say that it was that red dress that did it. Before a week was out, he was telling Annie Laura that they were destined to be married, and his reasoning was straight from *South Pacific*: "Once you have found her, never let her go."

They were inseparable from that point, and they made a striking couple. Jack was lean and lanky, six-feet-three, while Annie Laura barely topped out at five feet. "He said he was looking for a tall, long-legged blonde, but he tripped over me," she said.

Their senses of humor meshed as well as their interests. Annie Laura, too, grew up respecting family and the past and spent vacations touring historic sites with her parents and sister, Frances, two years younger.

Jack and Annie Laura were not married until February 10, 1962, nearly two years after they met. Jack had gotten his degree from Guilford College in December. The wedding took place at First Presbyterian Church in Hillsborough.

After the reception, the newlyweds returned to Greensboro to the tiny apartment they rented for sixty-five dollars a month in Sunset Hills, not far from Jack's family home. It would be six months before they took a brief honeymoon to Charleston, where they toured old plantations and other historic sites, with an obligatory first stop at Fort Sumter.

By the time of their honeymoon, Jack had taken a job as a sanitarian with the Guilford County Health Department. He worked out of the Greensboro office for two days each week, and for the rest out of the High Point office, of which he eventually would be in charge. Annie Laura still had a year of college to go, but before classes began that fall, she discovered that she was pregnant and dropped out. Both were ecstatic about becoming parents.

One Sunday morning when she was seven months pregnant, Annie Laura stayed home when Jack went to church because her family was coming for Sunday dinner, bringing a cradle for the baby. But as she worked in the kitchen, her placenta separated. Panicked, she sought help from a neighbor, who called an ambulance. The baby was delivered still-born the next day.

Annie Laura went into depression. "That was a rough, rough time," she remembered.

Three other young women in nearby apartments, all acquaintances, had been pregnant at the same time, and all had healthy babies, making Annie Laura's loss even more difficult. One of those women asked Annie Laura to care for her child while she worked, and she eagerly accepted. That baby became her surrogate child for a year.

Searching for ways to ease his wife's pain, Jack turned their attention to the house they dreamed of building. They already had collected stacks of plans and photographs from magazines. Their brains burgeoned with ideas far more grandiose than they could afford.

First, though, they had to find a place to put it. Because of his job, Jack wanted the house to be convenient to High Point and Greensboro, so he concentrated his search around Jamestown, the oldest town in Guilford County, although it was not much larger than a village, long since far outgrown by the cities between which it was situated.

By the end of summer, Jack had found the perfect site. The lot once had been part of a wildlife preserve where wealthy northerners came to hunt. It sat on an incline at the end of a cul-de-sac in a new development a couple of miles northwest of Jamestown. Heavily wooded, it backed up to High Point's watershed along the Deep River, which was restricted to development. The woods behind them would remain untouched. Both Jack and Annie Laura were nature lovers, and that had great appeal.

By fall, the lot was theirs, and they hired a contractor willing to work from hand-sketched plans and magazine photographs. The house was to be more or less southern colonial in style—"phony co-lony," Jack always called it. It was to have two stories with a full basement, including a garage in one end. It would be built of old bricks that Jack found, and it would have a narrow front porch with tall white columns. They placed it well back from the street among the trees, giving instructions that no tree was to be cut unless absolutely necessary.

That winter proved to be a bad one, slowing construction, and it was not until the following June that they moved into the house. They didn't have furniture enough to furnish it—some rooms would remain empty for years—but they were joyous just to be in a house of their own. Jack's father brought a tiny magnolia to plant next to the street in the front yard.

Annie Laura and Jack wanted to show their thankfulness with a house dedication, and they held it just before Thanksgiving. Annie Laura had taken a job as a secretary at Lindley Park Baptist Church in Greensboro to help make house payments, and she asked the minister, Monty Bishop, to join their own minister from Muirs Chapel Methodist Church, John Sills, in conducting the service. Jack and Annie Laura filled the empty living room with borrowed folding chairs and invited all their family and friends to help dedicate their house to God, to the love they found in each other, and to the children with whom they hoped to someday share their love and new home.

As it turned out, their family wouldn't begin with their own issue. Jack joined the Jamestown Jaycees, which one day would name him Man of the Year. The parents of the chaplain of that group worked at the Methodist Children's Home in Winston-Salem, twenty miles away. They told their son of a boy there, eleven years old, who was angry and bitter. They were fearful that he might be headed for trouble. Would the Jaycees take on the boy as a project, attempt to change his attitude and mold his future? Billy Joe Hill was the boy's name, and the group held a get-acquainted cookout for his twelfth birthday.

Jack and Annie Laura were taken with Billy Joe from the moment they met him. His mother died at his birth, they learned, his father two years later. He had been placed with a foster parent, an older woman who kept him until she no longer was able, and he was sent to the children's home. He felt cheated, abandoned by his foster mother, and deeply resentful.

Billy Joe didn't become a Jaycee project. That wasn't necessary, because Jack and Annie Laura soon were going to Winston-Salem almost every weekend to get him. He began spending summers with them as well. To Jack, Annie Laura, and their families, Billy Joe became family, too. They couldn't have loved their own child more.

On March 16, 1968, not quite four years after moving into their new house, Annie Laura gave birth to a healthy daughter. They named her Laura Katherine. Throughout her childhood Laura would think that Billy Joe was her older brother. Two years and not quite two months after Laura's birth, on May 2, 1970, the size of the family took an unexpected jump. Annie Laura had twin boys, Jack Lewis Jr., and Charles Lewis. Later, when the twins were four, Annie Laura would lose a fifth child after carrying it full term from the same problem that had cost her the first.

By the time the twins were born, Billy Joe had finished high school and decided to attend High Point College so he could live with Jack and Annie Laura. He loved taking care of Laura and the twins.

"I'd come home and he'd be in the rocking chair rocking all three to an Elvis record," Annie Laura recalled. "The boy rocked constantly. He wore out two rocking chairs and wore a hole in the floor rocking. He loved Elvis. Elvis and hamburgers. He'd eat hamburgers three meals a day if he could get away with it."

Three

Jack developed an interest in genealogy in college, and after his marriage he joined the Guilford County Genealogical Society and became engrossed in family history.

"It became like a treasure hunt," Annie Laura recalled. "He'd find some little nugget he'd been looking for for a long time, and he'd be so excited, just like a kid on Christmas morning."

Family research was only one aspect of Jack's continuing devotion to history. He loved taking his children to historic sites and developed a passion for preserving old structures.

Jack began his preservation efforts in Jamestown, a town rife with history. Settled in the last half of the eighteenth century by Quakers from Pennsylvania and Massachusetts, the community became a center of gold mining and gunmaking. Quaker gunsmiths along the Deep River turned out long, graceful, muzzle-loading weapons that became known throughout the nation as Jamestown rifles.

Jack immersed himself in Jamestown's history and took a particular interest in the town's gunsmiths, researching them intensively. Over the next twenty years he became the acknowledged authority on Jamestown rifles and the men who made them. He published a monograph, "The Gunmakers of Jamestown," and supplied material for the book *Gunsmiths of the Carolinas 1660-1870*.

A love of maps caused Jack to search out early maps of Jamestown and the surrounding area. He worked closely with local cartographer and amateur historian, Fred Hughes, and assisted Hughes in creating an historical map for Guilford County, which appeared in 1980. Many of the maps Jack discovered would be published in 1997 in the book *Roads to Jamestown* by C. Yvonne Bell Thomas.

In 1974, Jack and others organized the Historic Jamestown Commission. He became the group's second president in 1975 and served through 1977. (Annie Laura, too, later would be president.) Among the commission's early goals were creating a historic district for the town and saving and restoring a local landmark called Mendenhall Plantation. Jack would be instrumental in achieving both.

Mendenhall Plantation wasn't a plantation of the stereotypical Old South variety with a big-columned mansion and cabins for slaves who tended extensive fields of cotton, tobacco, or marshes of rice. It was a family farm, the home of Richard Mendenhall, a tanner, son of Jamestown's founder. He started building it in 1811 in anticipation of his marriage. The house was still under construction when he moved into it with his bride a year later. An opponent of slavery, Mendenhall prospered, opened a free school for all races, and founded a manumission society. It was believed that he helped slaves to freedom during the years of the Underground Railroad, from 1830 to 1860. After his death, the farm passed to his daughter, Minerva, eventually ending up in other hands, deteriorating with the years, until 1951 when Mary Elizabeth Ragsdale, the wife of a local industrialist and county commissioner, learned that it might be torn down. She talked her husband into buying the farm to save it.

As the nation's 200th birthday approached, Guilford County established a bicentennial commission to plan the county's celebration. Anita Schenck was appointed its director in 1974. Schenck had been a volunteer at Blandwood, a historic site in Greensboro, the home of former Governor John Motley Morehead. She set up an office in a two-room log house called the Potter cabin near Mendenhall Plantation. She soon met Jack and they formed a working partnership that would last for many years. She admired his extensive knowledge, his integrity, his enthusiasm, his willingness to work hard and long without payment except for the satisfaction of knowing that history was being served.

"He was a real historian," she recalled, "just steeped in Guilford County history. He loved Guilford County, and he loved history. When it came to history, he was almost like a kid, he'd get so excited about things."

Jack worked with Schenck on several aspects of the county's bicentennial celebration, but his primary goal was to make Mendenhall Plantation part of it.

Historic Jamestown arranged with Mary Elizabeth Ragsdale, who was on its board of directors, to donate the farm to the society to become a historic site, if the society could raise money to restore it. That was a long-term project, but Jack wanted to open the house temporarily to the public for the first time on the big Independence Day weekend.

He, Annie Laura and the children joined other volunteers to get the house ready, and hundreds of people showed up on a rainy Saturday, July 3rd, for the opening. On that day and the next, more than 1,800 people filed through. Jack's family never would forget how excited and proud he was.

The following year, the Historic Jamestown Society made the house its headquarters, and Jack headed the committee that raised the money to restore it. In 1985, the farm was deeded to the society, and Jack later served as chairman of the board that oversaw its direction. Not until 1990 was the plantation fully restored and opened as an historic site offering visitors a glimpse into the "other South" of the nineteenth century, the South that treasured education, opposed slavery, and worked to defeat it.

Jack's interest in historic sites was not limited to Jamestown. He became concerned about an old grist mill on Beaver Creek near Oak Ridge in northwestern Guilford County. An earlier mill known as Dillon's Mill had been constructed on the site between 1767 and 1769, and according to undocumented reports had been seized by British troops under the Command of General Charles Cornwallis in 1781. That mill was abandoned early in the nineteenth century. Construction of a new mill with an overshot wheel began just downstream in 1819 and was completed in 1822. It remained in service until 1975, when miller Lloyd Lucas died.

Jack and Annie Laura loved the old mill. They went there regularly to buy flour, cornmeal, and grits. When it closed, Jack worried about it.

In the fall of 1976, Charlie Parnell, an engineer and native of Scotland, came across the old mill while visiting friends in North Carolina and quickly bought it.

Jack didn't know the mill had been sold until Parnell sought a septic tank permit. He drove out to perform the necessary soil tests and learned Parnell's plans for reopening the mill. They hit it off immediately, and Jack soon brought Annie Laura to meet Parnell. Jack volunteered to help with renovations, and the next thing Annie Laura knew, she was shoving around heavy equipment.

After the mill reopened in the spring of 1977, Jack wrote a booklet about its history, *The Old Mill of Guilford*, still sold at the mill. Jack accepted no information without documentation, and he wrote all the documented facts in upper case type, all the stories and lore in lower case so readers could easily tell the difference. Later, Annie Laura took a job at the mill, and in 1983, Parnell left her in charge, went to Florida on vacation, and returned married for the first time at age sixty-four. Charlie and Heidi Parnell became almost like another set of parents to Annie Laura and Jack.

Meanwhile, Jack and Anita Schenck were working on a more lasting contribution to Guilford County's history—a commission to oversee historic properties.

"Jack really became the leader in pressing the idea of having a joint historic properties commission," Schenck remembered.

He worked countless hours to establish the commission in 1980. He became its chairman, a non-paying position he held for seven two-year terms. Schenck served with him for eight years.

"He was a very realistic man," she recalled, "a rational man, an honorable man, a truthful person. The truth as he saw it was very important to him. He was a real straight shooter. Always said what he thought. He could be rather blunt at times, even a little abrasive. But he mellowed as years went on, learned to be more diplomatic. I think he began to understand that other people cared about history, too, and maybe would go about things in a different way. But he did know a whole lot. He really knew Guilford County history."

Just as the historic preservation commission was getting started, Jack's personal life took an unexpected turn. He had been with the Guilford County Health Department for eighteen years, had become deeply involved with environmental matters and worked on developing the county's first air pollution control plan. When the job of chief environmental officer came open, he thought he might get it, but it went to an outsider. Although he never spoke about it, his disappointment was obvious to Annie Laura, and he soon became unhappy at work. When he was instructed to attest to a charge against a colleague that a supervisor wanted to have fired, a charge he believed to be untrue, he resigned instead.

Things were difficult for a while. Jack started a land consultant business. When that didn't work out, he took real estate classes. He and Annie Laura were quickly going through their savings and Jack's retirement funds. Annie Laura, who hadn't worked for several years, took a job as a teacher's aide at Florence Elementary School, where her sons were students, where she earlier had served as a volunteer and Jack had helped fourth grade teachers develop their Guilford County social history curriculum.

Within a year, Jack found a job with a small real estate agency. He later became an appraiser and turned his basement garage into an office. By 1989, he was president of the High Point Board of Realtors. During his term, he proposed organizing the computerized listing services of Realtor boards in High Point, Greensboro, Winston-Salem and Thomasville into a single entity, and became president of the Triad Multiple Listing Service in 1990.

Through all the turmoil and change, Jack's dedication to genealogy, to history and to historic preservation never wavered. In addition to continuing work with Mendenhall Plantation, he turned his attention to another Jamestown landmark.

The Jamestown Public School, built in 1915, was the town's most impressive structure before it was abandoned in 1982. It had become an eyesore and the school board was talking of tearing it down when a former teacher started a campaign to save it and turned to Jack and other community leaders for help. The building was restored in 1987. It opened the following year as Jamestown Public Library.

By 1989, Jack had written his first family history. He had traced some lines of his family for many generations. But not his primary line of Perdues. He knew that he had sprung from Huguenots, French protestants driven from their homeland late in the seventeenth century by religious persecution. Most Perdues in this country were believed to have descended from John Perdue—Ol' John, he was called—who migrated from England and received a land grant in Amelia County, Va., in 1741. Ol' John sold his land twenty years later and moved to Warren County, N.C., where he died in 1768. Jack, however, couldn't make a connection to Ol' John because of gaps starting with his great, great grandfather, Jehu.

If he could find Jehu's grave, he thought he might verify that he was the son of Jehu and Susannah Ham Perdue and get other clues to lead him through his ancestry. Early in the 1990's, he wrote to family members asking for information. Several responded but were of little help.

In 1992, however, he found two allies to join his hunt. The first was Elizabeth Pardue Bryant, the wife of a Baptist minister in Rocky Mount, Va. Bryant had gotten interested in family history after her father's death in 1987. The death of her mother in 1992 prompted her to action. She had no idea how to begin, but a relative told her about Jack. Her father and Jack's had been first cousins. She called Jack and he enlisted her in his campaign. She became an enthusiastic researcher, spending so many hours at it that she sometimes forgot to eat or to cook supper for her husband. She and Jack talked at least twice a week by telephone and exchanged information by mail. "He was so respectful of me," Bryant remembered, "such a gentleman."

Jack's second enlistee was Todd Southard, only twenty years old, a student at Rockingham Community College in Wentworth, who like Jack, had been fascinated with history and the Civil War since childhood. A teacher got him interested in genealogy and a relative told him about Jack, to whom, he discovered, he was related. Southard wrote to him and got a quick response. Southard went on to become a high school history teacher before taking a job as house manager at Blandwood, the Greensboro historic site where Jefferson Davis' wife, Varina, took tea as she fled from Richmond ahead of her husband at the end of the Civil War.

It was Southard who came up with the information that Jehu and Eliza Perdue might be buried at Oak Level Baptist Church in Rockingham County.

Well before Jack got that tip from Southard, he conceived another tool for garnering family information: a monthly newsletter called the *Perdue News*. The first four-page edition was already in the mail when he and Annie Laura drove to Oak Level Church in May, 1993. In it he included a short article under the headline, "Where are they buried?" It asked for help in finding the graves of Jehu and Eliza.

The following month's edition contained photographs of the unusual gravestones he and Annie Laura found.

"Please ask around and see if anyone can shed any light on this mystery," he wrote.

That fall, Jack was one of the organizers of a family reunion held at Stokesdale United Methodist Church. More than sixty people attended, bringing photos, letters and family Bibles. Jack brought a copier so he could add all the materials to his records.

By the time of the second family reunion a year later, Jack had learned who owned the property where the old cemetery lay and had gotten permission to attend to its upkeep.

Early in 1995, Jack finished an analysis of the cemetery and devoted the February issue of the *Perdue News* to it. He had learned that it contained the remains of forty-eight people, many children and infants. The occupants of only seven graves had been positively identified. Jack had diagrammed the cemetery, numbering each grave and offering a description of each.

Two side-by-side columns offered his findings. One was marked, "What we know," the other, "What we surmise."

What he knew was that William A. Perdue once owned the land where the cemetery lay, as well as most of the land for a good distance around it, and that it was divided and passed on to his four surviving children after his death in 1861, one of them Eliza.

Jack surmised that William's wife, Nancy, was the first person buried in the cemetery and that William himself likely was the second, five years later. He ascertained the names of several children and grandchildren of William and Nancy who were buried there and tentatively identified their graves.

Still, he only could surmise that the cemetery also was the resting place for Jehu and Eliza. That conclusion seemed likely, because he had found no deeds showing that Jehu owned property. It seemed reasonable that he and Eliza lived on land owned by her father until she inherited it.

Since other of William's and Nancy's children were known to be buried in the cemetery, it seemed likely that John Perdue, who joined the Confederate Army with Jehu and died two months later, was buried near his parents. It seemed likely, too, that Jehu was buried there when he died in 1863, and that his wife, who never remarried, would be laid beside him at her death in 1900. After all, their graves hadn't been found in any other known cemetery, and Jack and Annie Laura had searched all in the area. Although these conclusions were plausible, Jack remained vexed that he couldn't prove them.

On a Sunday morning in the spring of 1995, Jack was in his office laboring over his genealogy charts, when Annie Laura, in the kitchen above, heard a great whoop erupt. She hurried down to see what had happened and met Jack coming out of his office, his face a picture of happiness. He was so excited that it took her a few moments to grasp what he was saying: he'd just discovered a family connection to Robert E. Lee. This was no nugget in his long treasure hunt, she knew; this was a mother lode.

"It just absolutely thrilled him no end."

The first person Jack called to tell about his discovery was his daughter, Laura, in Atlanta. Laura was close to her father and talked to him regularly by phone. She knew how deeply he admired Lee and how much this meant to him.

Jack had read every book he could find about Lee, but he most admired Douglas Southall Freeman's biography. Later, he wrote about his connection to Lee on the opening page of each copy of his four-volume set of Freeman's work:

> Gen. Robert E. Lee was married to my 5th cousin, 3 times removed, Mary Ann Randolph Custis, through the Pegram-Macon line of my father. Robert E. Lee's children were my 6th cousins, twice removed.

Rahlo Fowler got to know Jack when both served on the board to save Jamestown School. A reserved, soft-spoken man, Fowler, a field engineer with National Cash Register Company, grew up in Jamestown. In 1990, he saw a notice in the newspaper about an organizational meeting for a local camp of Sons of Confederate Veterans. He'd always been interested in the Civil War and went to the meeting out of curiosity. He didn't know if he had ancestors who served in the war, but soon after the meeting, an uncle told him that his great grandfather, William Ren Fowler, was captured at Petersburg and spent the remainder of the war at the notorious federal prison at Point Lookout, Md.

Fowler became one of twelve charter members of the Lt. F.C. Frazier Camp 688, named for an adroit artilleryman from Randolph County, when it organized in 1991. The following year, he became the camp's second commander, a position he held for four years. That same year, he ran into Jack and invited him to a meeting. Jack accepted, joined the camp in October, and he and Fowler became close friends. "He almost felt like a brother to me," Fowler said.

Jack was not one to undertake anything half-heartedly, and that was true as well of his membership in the SCV. "Some members sit back and watch things happen," Fowler said. "You've got some people who make things happen, and Jack was one of those."

The SCV doesn't stage battle re-enactments, but some members, a minority, belong to groups that do. Fowler and Jack joined such groups so they could participate in living history demonstrations and honor comrades at memorial services.

Fowler was one of the first people Jack told after learning about his relationship to Robert E. Lee in 1995, and the discovery seemed to increase his dedication to the SCV. Soon afterward, Jack called Fowler and said he had something to show him. He came to his house with a mockup for a new camp newsletter.

"I said, 'Jack, this is fantastic,'" Fowler recalled. "He just took over the newsletter, made it colorful, made it interesting, wrote all kinds of articles for it."

Jack was still publishing his family newsletter, which by this time had increased in size. He also had made the acquaintance of two other avid genealogists who were tracing different lines of the family.

The first was Sherman Pardue, an architect from Charlotte. He got a copy of *The Perdue News* from a relative and wrote to Jack to compliment him on it. The two soon were exchanging information, talking regularly by telephone and corresponding through e-mail.

"He was a grand fellow," Pardue said. "He was a very intense man. I guess that overworked word 'passion' is the one that is most appropriate to Jack. He was a very passionate man."

Pardue introduced Jack to another family researcher, Norman C. Pardue, an engineer from Falls Church, Va. Norman Pardue had started the *Pardue Times and Historical Gazzette* in 1990, and his records were considered the most extensive on the family. Jack invited both genealogists to the third annual family reunion at Stokesdale United Methodist Church in October, 1995, and both accepted.

But in late August, Norman Pardue and two of his four children were killed when the family mini-van was struck by a train. Nobody was certain what would become of his records and newsletter. But by the time of the reunion, Sherman Pardue had taken over the *Pardue Times and Historical Gazzette*. (Later he also would see that Norman's records were rescued from his outdated computer and preserved.) He attended the reunion as planned, meeting Jack for the first time.

Jack began the fourth year of the *Perdue News* with the February issue, 1996. In it, he acknowledged his frustration at not being able to learn more about Jehu and Eliza and again appealed for help. This proved to be the final issue of the *Perdue News*. By the next issue in April, Jack had merged it with the newsletter Sherman Pardue was producing.

The new publication became The *Perdue News & Pardue Gazette*. The first issue included a photograph of the graveyard at Oak Level with the news that Todd Southard had applied to the Veterans Administration for markers for the graves of Jehu and John Perdue and that an appropriate ceremony would be held when they arrived.

That ceremony didn't take place until more than a year later, May 19, 1997. More than fifty family members attended. Jack, dressed in his Confederate uniform, was the primary speaker. He told of the effect of war on the family of William A. Perdue, two of whose daughters were left widows, two of whose sons went to battle, only one surviving, he being twice wounded before deserting. Jack recited what was known of the lives of the two men being remembered. They had been buried "without the benefit of a military ceremony to honor their service to their state and country," he noted. "We are here today, over one hundred and thirty-four years later, to provide them with that ceremony and to dedicate markers which recognize and preserve for future generations their service and sacrifice."

Re-enactors from the 14th N.C. Troops presented the colors and fired a three-round volley from their muskets in salute. Jack's daughter, Laura, placed flowers at Jehu's stone, Liz Bryant at John's. Both stones had been placed at the front of the cemetery, because the actual gravesites remained unknown.

At a reunion of several branches of the Perdue and Pardue families in Atlanta in July, 1997, Jack and Sherman Pardue announced that their work and other activities had grown so heavy that they would be giving up the editorship of the newsletter at the end of the year. Two new editors were selected.

That fall, Jack put together elaborate family histories for each of his three children and two grandchildren: Liam, who was two, the son of Lewis and his wife, Jenny; and Kenny, who was born the previous October, son of Laura and her husband, Keith Goodman. He included charts and relationship tables for each of their family lines, along with many photos. He put the histories in heavy binders with the Perdue coat of arms on the cover. In the front of each he wrote:

> *I have prepared this family history for you so that*
> *you may have a record of your heritage. You are a product of*
> *all the ancestors in this book and others that I have not been*
> *able to yet identify.... I hope you will cherish this record of*
> *your family, update as your family grows and pass it on to*
> *generations to come.*
>
> *Love,*
> *Dad*

He did the same for Betsy's two children, and presented all as gifts at Christmas.

The Christmas edition of the *Perdue News & Pardue Gazette*—twenty-eight pages—was its last. The new editors never produced an issue.

An unsigned short story about the death of a Civil War soldier, written by a family member in South Carolina, began on the front page and wove throughout the issue. Above it was an editor's note:

> *A foreboding hangs in the air day after day that is*
> *not washed away with the fresh rain, nor tempered by the*
> *changes of season. It curls with the first Fall smoke from the*
> *cabin chimney, it can be seen in the long shadows on the*
> *ground, it rides among the clouds high in the late summer*
> *sky, some say, like soldiers on horseback.*

That could have been written for Jack, for the coming new year would be troublesome and trying, and before another autumn passed his passion for history would sweep him into a nightmare beyond his imagination.

Part II

War in North Carolina

As an American liberal, I would like to say that political correctness is going to kill American liberalism if it is not fought to the death by people like me who see it for the dangers it represents to free speech, to openheartedness. Political correctness is a form of both madness and maggotry that has already begun to silence the voices of writers...across the land.
—**Pat Conroy**

Four

Rhonda Winters was browsing crafts booths at the Bush Hill Heritage Festival in Archdale, N.C.—an event celebrating the town's Quaker beginnings—in September, 1997, when she unexpectedly came upon an acquaintance, Darla Barber.

Winters was the director of Randolph Community College's only satellite branch, which was in Archdale, originally known as Bush Hill, a town of some 9,000 people in the fast-growing northwestern sector of mostly rural Randolph County, adjoining the furniture-making city of High Point in Guilford County.

Barber, a former teacher, was an occasional instructor in RCC's continuing education program, which offered inexpensive nighttime adult classes as a means of community outreach. She taught signing for the deaf. On this day, she was helping her husband, Charles, called Tuck, who as a hobby created figures of Civil War soldiers and Civil War chess sets. Her husband had been a member of the Sons of Confederate Veterans for several years.

As Winters admired Tuck Barber's work, she remarked that she had been thinking about adding a class on the Civil War to her continuing education program. It seemed to be a popular subject, she noted.

"You need to talk to Jack Perdue," Darla Barber told her. "He's a walking history book when it comes to that war."

Winters knew Jack. He had taught real estate appraisal courses in the continuing education program since 1995. He was an enthusiastic, well-prepared instructor, she knew, his classes usually well attended. But she wasn't aware of his interest in the Civil War.

In the spring of 1998, as she began planning her continuing education program for the fall, Winters remembered her conversation with Darla Barber and called Jack.

"I said, 'Jack, how would you like to teach a Civil War class for me?' He kind of laughed. He said, 'Well, I might be willing to teach one on the War for Southern Independence. But there was nothing civil about that war.'"

Winters was aware that the war was an exceedingly broad subject for a one-night-a-week course of ten weeks duration. She thought the scope should be limited to North Carolina's role. Jack agreed. So much had happened right in this area, he told her, and so few people knew anything about it.

But he wanted to think about the offer first.

Jack had been in an uncharacteristic funk that spring, and Annie Laura was sure that it had to do with the death of his brother-in-law, Jim Twiford, the husband of her sister, Frances. A retired North Carolina wildlife officer, Twiford lived on Albemarle Sound in eastern North Carolina and had taken up crabbing, the trade of his ancestors. He fell from his boat and drowned while checking test traps on the last day of February. Jack and Twiford had been close. They looked forward to seeing each other at family gatherings, spent time together at the beach each year, talked frequently by telephone.

"They were a lot alike," Annie Laura recalled. "Both were strong-willed men of principle. They had good senses of humor, always carrying on some kind of foolishness."

When Annie Laura heard about the course Rhonda Winters proposed, she thought it was just the thing to bring Jack out of the doldrums. She saw that he was excited about the idea. She always thought he should have been a history teacher. She knew how much he enjoyed talking to school children about native Americans and regional history, an activity that he continued long after their own children were grown. She knew that he loved taking part in living history demonstrations at area schools. She knew, too, that he believed that public school students were not taught enough about the war that fascinated him from childhood. He told her that if the course at RCC came about, he wanted to aim it at eighth-grade teachers, who taught North Carolina history. Perhaps some would attend, he said, and be inspired afterward to tell their students more. He wanted the class to become an annual event.

Jack told this to Rhonda Winters, too, when he called her back. He said his Sons of Confederate Veterans camp would like to co-sponsor the course. He also wanted the instructor's fee to be used to create a history essay writing contest for area eighth graders. Winters didn't see any problem with that, but she didn't know much about the SCV and wanted to learn more before making a commitment. Jack invited her to attend the camp's next meeting, on the second Tuesday of May.

Jack introduced Winters and she spoke briefly about her hopes for the course. Jack said that he'd be calling on members for help.

Jack already had prepared a tentative plan for the course. He wanted to use guest lecturers for different aspects of it. He had earned a reputation for bringing many compelling speakers to camp meetings, and he hoped to recruit some of them.

He sketched out the topics he wanted to cover, marked some for specific lecturers, asked for volunteers with others, then sent a proposal to Winters, who routinely forwarded it to the main campus for approval. She expected no problems and none arose. The class was set to begin on September 17—if a minimum of ten students signed up. It was titled "North Carolina History: Our Role in the War for Southern Independence." The fee was forty dollars. Fees would pay the costs of the course, which was the rule for personal interest and hobby classes. Other courses offered at the Archdale campus at the time included getting out of debt, gold prospecting, quilt making, and taxidermy.

Jack spent much of the summer gathering material, studying and writing in preparation for the course. In July, he was elected commander of the Frazier Camp for a two-year term. He was sworn in on the second Tuesday in August. He asked a friend and fellow history buff, Larry Hill, to be his first lieutenant commander. Todd Southard, who joined the Frazier Camp eighteen months earlier without knowing that Jack was a member, became adjutant. Herman White, an Archdale minister, was named chaplain.

Less than two weeks after becoming lieutenant commander, Larry Hill, a Baptist minister who had undergone two heart bypass operations, fell ill and was admitted to the hospital. He died five days later on August 29 at age fifty-nine. Jack served as pallbearer at his funeral. Hill's death cast him back into the same morose mood into which he had fallen after his brother-in-law's drowning in the spring.

His mood was darkened further when death struck close again in September. Annie Laura's uncle, Ned Blackwelder, brother of her father, who had been dead nearly eight years, died at seventy-three in Hillsborough. Her sister, Frances, wasn't sure that she could go through another funeral so soon after her husband's death. "I can't take this," she cried, and bolted from the service, with Jack and Annie Laura following. Jack found himself walking the streets of Hillsborough trying to console his distraught wife and sister-in-law.

On the day of Larry Hill's funeral, September 1, an article appeared in the *High Point Enterprise* about the impending course. Reporter Steve Huffman had interviewed Jack the week before, and Jack told him that current history presented the war as being fought only over slavery.

"Slavery is not why North Carolina was involved," he said. "But kids these days aren't being taught that in the classroom. What they teach about the war is not very much and what they do teach is not all correct."

He went on to say, "We want to present factually documented history, not propaganda."

He stressed that to his lecturers as well, they later said. He didn't want them spouting opinions or getting into politics. He wanted everything they taught to be documented, and he wanted copies of reference materials and bibliographies prepared for his approval.

The *Enterprise* article attracted several students. Within a week Rhonda Winters called to tell Jack that enough had signed up for the course to proceed.

Five

Of the eleven students who turned out for the first class at 6:30 on Thursday evening, September 17, six were male, five female. The youngest was twenty-one, the eldest seventy-five. Two were mother and son. Two others were ex-teachers who wanted to keep their certification current. Two were new members of the Sons of Confederate Veterans. Two were friends of Jack. Most were Civil War buffs.

The class was held in a laboratory filled with faceting machines because all the regular classrooms were occupied.

"We're going to have fun," Jack said, going on to lay out his plan for the course and describe the lecturers the students would be hearing. "We want to learn from you, want you to learn from us. Feel free to participate; feel free to ask questions."

He had passed out thick, spiral binders with an illustration on the cover of North Carolina's first flag, adopted after the state seceded in 1861. The binders were to hold the many source materials that would be handed out during the classes. For the first class, the binders already held copies of original historical documents, illustrations of all the flags of the Confederacy, an article by Jack about the weapons North Carolina soldiers carried, even a copy of an area recruiting poster seeking "intelligent, active young men" to join Confederate forces.

Jack read from an introduction as he began the class, speaking from a table-top lectern in front of a green chalk board, taking off his suit coat as he talked.

"It is time for a balanced view of the history of this era to be presented," he read. "It should no longer be acceptable to make young North Carolinians feel ashamed of their ancestors, white, black, Hispanic and Native American, who fought for North Carolina and the Confederacy."

He went on to speak briefly about the SCV, explaining that the group had camps all over the United States, in Europe and Brazil, with membership that included Presidential candidates, U.S. senators, governors and people from many other walks of life.

"We are a heritage organization," he said. "We are not a hate group and will not knowingly accept members who belong to hate groups. Blacks, Hispanics and Native Americans served honorably in Confederate service and their descendants are welcome in the SCV."

Much of the material in this class would be original to the period, he noted.

"It is important that we try to look at this subject from the viewpoint of the eighteen-sixties and not from the dawn of the twenty-first century. It's easy to say with twenty-twenty hindsight that a lot of what went on back then was wrong. But you need to look at what went on back then from the times back then and not judge what people did in the eighteen hundreds by the way we live now.... A lot of the history we're going to be presenting will have been written by people from that period who lived it, not by Ph.D.s looking back and criticizing from today's viewpoint."

The war that erupted in 1861 was not truly a civil war, Jack told the class. A civil war involves two factions fighting for control of the same government. In this case, states had chosen to leave a government which forced them back with military power. The War of Rebellion had been the U.S. War Department's official description. Many had called it The War Between the States. Jack, like many SCV members, preferred The War for Southern Independence.

Understanding North Carolina's role in the war required going back before the American Revolution, he explained. He directed the students' attention to the Mecklenburg Declaration of Independence in their notebooks.

This document supposedly was adopted in Mecklenburg County in May, 1775, more than a year before the Continental Congress approved the far better known declaration drafted by Thomas Jefferson. Whether it actually existed was in question, Jack noted, because the original supposedly was destroyed in a fire in 1800 and later was reconstructed from memory. Still, real or not, it represented the way North Carolinians felt about liberty.

When the Treaty of Paris (copies of which were in each student's binder) was signed in 1783, it was between Britain and thirteen free and independent states, the former colonies, which at that time were bound in a confederacy. But when a new constitution was signed in

1787 and ratified in 1788, North Carolina and Rhode Island held out.

No North Carolinians voted for George Washington, Jack noted, because they weren't eligible.

"We were a free and independent country," he said, "and so was Rhode Island."

Both states ratified the constitution late in 1789, after the Bill of Rights was proposed. But Rhode Island, like New York before it, included a clause stating that "the powers of government may be resumed by the people whenever it shall become necessary to their happiness."

Clearly, Rhode Islanders and New Yorkers wanted to establish the possibility of secession, Jack noted. And in coming years, on several occasions, northern states threatened to secede over issues that included the War of 1812, and nobody questioned their right to do so.

The original confederacy of states was described as a "perpetual union," meaning that no state could withdraw, Jack pointed out, but the constitution changed that.

"One nation, under God, indivisible, is not in the constitution," he said. "There is nothing in the constitution that says this nation is indivisible." It was, instead, a union of free states.

Even Abraham Lincoln appeared to believe that, Jack told the class. In a speech to Congress in 1848, he said: "Any people anywhere, being inclined and having the power, have the right to rise up and shake off the existing government, and form a new one that suits them better."

Lincoln's opinion had changed, however, by the time he was elected President and Southern states began to secede.

Current common knowledge says that the Civil War was fought only to end slavery, Jack said, but the reality was far more complex, the reasons many. They included economics; tariffs (War over a tariff dispute was barely averted in 1832.); the right of states to determine their own destinies; whether slavery would be allowed in the new western states, a matter that could change the base of power between the industrial North and the far-less-populated, agricultural South; and the question of whether the constitution was to be enforced.

He directed attention to Article IV, Section 2 of the U.S. Constitution, a copy of which was in each student's notebook: "No person held to Service or Labour in one State, under the Laws thereof, escaping into another, shall, in Consequence of any Law or Regulation therein, be discharged from such Service or Labour, but shall be delivered up on Claim of the Party to whom such Service or Labour may be due."

This applied not only to slaves but to any indentured servant, no matter race or nationality, Jack pointed out. It had been bolstered by fugitive slave acts in 1793 and 1850, which had been upheld by the Supreme Court. But when Northern states refused to abide by the law, and it went unenforced, Southern states claimed that a compact had been broken and they had a right to leave the Union.

Many people in the South wanted to end slavery, he said, and many of those were in North Carolina.

"Slavery was wrong. I don't think that any right thinking person in today's society would dispute that. But the fact remains that for almost the whole history of mankind up until this century slavery existed, and in some places in Africa today it still exists.

"And it was not normally a racial thing. The Egyptians had slaves, the Greeks had slaves, the Romans had slaves, the Jews had slaves. And usually these slaves were people of their own race. They usually resulted from war. Many free blacks in the South had slaves. American Indians had slaves. They would make slaves of blacks, other Indian tribes they had wars with and whites that they captured.... The slaves brought to America were captured in Africa by other blacks. Many whites came to this country as indentured servants. They were not free to leave their masters during the period of servitude."

In the states of the Deep South, sustaining slavery was a major reason for secession, Jack said, but in others it was less so. Some slave states—Delaware, Maryland, Kentucky and Missouri—remained in the Union and slavery continued in those states until the ratification of the Thirteenth Amendment after the war. Slaves worked to complete the new capitol in Washington during the war, and some Union officers held slaves throughout the war.

North Carolina did not secede over slavery, Jack said. It was a rural state made up largely of small farmers, craftsmen and shopkeepers. Only a single town, Wilmington, had more than 10,000 citizens. Less than a fourth of North Carolina families owned slaves, and only a small percentage of those had more than twenty. (The census of 1850 showed that out of some six million Southern whites, only 347,525 owned slaves.)

"We weren't worried about (maintaining) slavery," Jack said. "We would never have seceded over slavery.... North Carolina believed in the Union, and North Carolina was a strong Union state."

When seven Deep South states seceded at the beginning of 1861, North Carolina did not join them. An attempt to hold a convention of delegates elected by voters to consider secession failed. Not until Ft. Sumter was fired upon and Lincoln issued a call for North Carolina to field troops to put down the rebellion in South Carolina did the pro-Union sentiment change. North Carolina would not invade a fellow southern state. Another convention was called to consider secession, and this time it convened.

The only debate of any consequence was whether the state was rebelling and joining a revolution, or was simply revoking its ratification of the constitution, Jack noted. The delegates chose the milder approach, and on May 20, 1861, unanimously voted for a resolution declaring "that the union now subsisting between the state of North Carolina and the other states under the title of 'The United States of America,' is hereby dissolved, and that the state of North Carolina is in full possession and exercise of all those rights of sovereignty which belong and appertain to a free and independent state." The convention then ratified the Provisional Constitution of the Confederate States of America.

Counting the home guards, North Carolina sent some 125,000 men to war, about a sixth of all Confederate forces, nearly 10,000 more men than ever voted in an election in the state. All but 20,000, who were conscripted in 1862 or later, were volunteers, and fewer than fifteen percent had any connection to slavery. The state suffered a full fourth of the South's battlefield deaths.

If the war had begun to end slavery, why would so many North Carolinians who had no personal interest in slavery be so willing to go to battle? In many cases, their own words provided that answer. They saw themselves as fighting to protect their families, their homes, their lands from invaders, as well as to maintain their liberty and their right to a government of their own choosing. Preserving slavery was not a motivation for the great majority.

The U.S. Congress passed a resolution in July, 1861, stating that the war was being fought to preserve the Union, not abolish slavery. And though adamantly opposed to slavery, which he saw as evil, President Lincoln repeatedly stated that the purpose of the war was to preserve the Union. As far into the war as August 25, 1862, he wrote to newspaper editor Horace Greeley, "My paramount object in this struggle is to save the Union, and neither to save or destroy slavery. If I could save the Union without freeing any slave, I would do it."

"He was not going to preside over the dissolution of the Union, so the war ensued," Jack said. "And it did not ensue over slavery."

Union troops didn't march off to battle to end slavery, but to maintain the Union. Not until Lincoln published the Emancipation Proclamation in an effort to keep Britain from siding with the South (less than a month after his letter to Horace Greeley) did he change the focus of the war to slavery, Jack told the class. That proclamation didn't free all persons held as slaves as of January 1, 1863, as is falsely proclaimed in the textbook used to teach North Carolina eighth graders about the war, Jack pointed out. He asked his students to turn to the proclamation in their notebooks and read it for themselves. It freed no slaves in Maryland, Kentucky, Delaware, Missouri, Washington, D.C., or in any part of the seceding states that were then occupied by Union forces, he pointed out. It only freed slaves where it had no effect, in areas over which Lincoln had no control.

The class was scheduled to last until nine, and Jack had been talking for nearly an hour and a half. "Okay, let's take about a fifteen-minute break," he said.

He went outside with some of the students who smoked and fired up his pipe.

More than half an hour into the class, as Jack had been describing the four flags of the Confederacy and how they came about, a tall, lean young man slipped into the laboratory, settled into a seat near the door, and started taking notes. Class members who noticed assumed that he was just another student arriving late.

As Jack smoked during the break, the young man approached.

"The first words out of his mouth to me were, 'Why are you being allowed to teach such a controversial course?'" Jack recalled.

A man of courtesy and good manners, he was a little taken aback by a question so brusque and assumptive from a stranger. He took a moment to answer.

"There's nothing controversial about it," he replied. The college asked him to teach about North Carolina's role in the war, he explained, and that was what he was doing.

The young man, Jack learned, was Ethan Feinsilver. He was the Randolph County reporter for the *News & Record* of Greensboro. He requested an outline of the course, Jack said, and he provided one, along with other materials he handed out that night.

Herman White, the Frazier Camp chaplain who later would be a lecturer, came outside during the break and saw Jack talking to the young man.

"I heard Jack say to him, 'You need to learn some history,'" he recalled.

Later, White said, Jack told him that the young man was a reporter who wanted to write about the class, but when he questioned him about the war he didn't even know the names of major battles, didn't know that Virginia had been the site of most of the fighting, and that

North Carolina had seen relatively little action.

Jack told several people that night that a reporter had been present, including his friend Rahlo Fowler, who was videotaping the class. Fowler got the feeling that Jack was pleased that a story might be written. Rhonda Winters, the campus director, got the same impression when Jack told her about it a week later. Jack thought it might attract more people and allow them to have the course annually, she remembered.

During the last forty-five minutes of the class, Jack talked about a subject dear to his heart: how North Carolina had armed itself—and the weapons its soldiers carried into battle.

He had several types of muskets, all replicas, including one he'd made himself. He described in detail their strengths and shortcomings and demonstrated how they worked.

He talked about how North Carolina's troops had been regimented, about the camps where they had trained, including one in High Point, before bringing the class to a halt.

"We've hit our stopping time, according to the clock," he said. "Next week we're going to have the gals here, showing off their costumes, and their underwear, and everything else. Going to be an interesting program, talking about civilian life during the war. We're going to be down the hall in another room. You'll just have to look for the signs when you get here. 'Preciate it."

Six

Nearly two dozen volunteers took part in the next two classes.

Darla Barber, who had recommended Jack to teach this course, was guest lecturer for the class about life on the home front. She recruited ten women, most wives of Sons of Confederate Veterans, to assist her. Some were in period costume, as was Barber. Some brought items common to the period to talk about.

Barber spoke of home and community life before the war, and how war brought unimagined hardship, leaving women, children and old men to fend for themselves, often without necessities, while worrying about the men who had gone off to fight. She told of the resourcefulness of the families left behind, and offered excerpts from diaries written by women during the war as vivid testimony.

When students arrived for their third class, they had no question about where they were supposed to be. A naval jack, the rectangular version of the battle flag, snapped in gusts from a short staff beside a white tent in a grassy area adjoining the campus main building. Muskets were stacked before the tent and a replica cannon sat nearby. Half a dozen men in different Confederate uniforms were completing a campsite to demonstrate how North Carolina troops lived in the field.

Rahlo Leonard, first sergeant of the 21st N.C. Troops, a re-enactment group representing eight Piedmont counties, was in charge of the first half of this class.

Most North Carolina troops were farmers, country boys, many of whom never had ventured more than twenty miles from home, he told the students. Thrown together in camps, more died from infection than battle wounds. Treatment, he noted, was limited. "Biggest thing they knew how to check you for was regularity. If you were tight, they knew how to loosen you up. If you were loose, they knew how to tighten you up. Other than that, it was pretty much amputation."

Leonard and his fellow re-enactors went on to show students the gear troops carried into battle and how it was used. They demonstrated arms commands and facing commands, and as darkness fell, they lined up and fired their muskets, flames dancing from the long barrels.

The second half of this class was conducted inside by Bob White, who had taught sociology and been assistant dean of students at Guilford College before illness forced his retirement. He was a lieutenant colonel in the 26th Regiment of N.C. Troops, the largest Civil War re-enactment group in the nation, and an authority on Confederate uniforms.

He brought many different uniforms to show the students, and told them that North Carolina troops were by far the best uniformed in the Confederacy because the output of the state's textile plants equalled that of all the rest of the Southern states. The problem was logistics—getting the uniforms to the constantly moving troops in the field.

Jack was pleased with the response to this night's class, but he was concerned about something that happened as it began. As the students were arriving at the campsite, he noticed a man with cameras hanging from his neck and shoulders. He introduced himself and learned that the man was Joseph Rodriquez of the *News & Record*, assigned to take photos for a future story. He was not accompanied by a reporter and Jack had heard nothing from Ethan Feinsilver, the *News & Record* reporter who had shown up at the first class.

Nobody could miss Rodriquez's presence as he went about his work.

One of the students, Nancy Boyles, a widow and Civil War buff, was standing beside Jack, who was in uniform for the demonstration.

"Maybe we're going to be in the paper," she said, as Rodriquez snapped away.

But Jack saw that Rodriquez was framing many of his photos so that the battle flag loomed large in them.

"If we're in the paper," he said, suddenly somber, "it probably won't be good."

Rhonda Winters, the campus director, stayed later than usual to watch the re-enactors, and she too became concerned about the way Rodriquez was framing his shots. After the demonstration, Jack told Winters that the photographer's close attention to the flag probably didn't bode well for whatever story the *News & Record* was planning. He just hoped it wouldn't end up causing a problem for the college, he said.

• • •

The battle flag was big in the news at this time. Hardly a week passed without some mention of it, usually centered around the years-long fight to have it removed from South Carolina's capitol in Columbia, the only place where the flag still flew over a seat of government (although the state flags of Georgia and Mississippi incorporated the battle flag into their designs). It had been placed there in 1962 in observance of the Civil War's centennial, and critics maintained that it had remained as a symbol of defiance to the civil rights campaigns that began in the '60s.

The battle flag became a national issue in the late 1980s with an attempt by black legislators to have it removed from the dome of Alabama's capitol in Montgomery. (It would be taken down in 1994 after a judge ruled that an obscure state law forbade it.)

In 1991, the NAACP adopted a resolution calling the battle flag "the ugly symbol of idiotic white supremacy racism and denigration." The "tyrannical evil" symbolized by the flag was "an abhorrence to all Americans and decent people of this country, and indeed, the world," the resolution went on, "and is an odious blight upon the universe." All NAACP units were instructed to commit their resources to removing the flag "from all public properties," and many began demanding removal not only of battle flags but of depictions of battle flags, as well as other Confederate symbols, including memorials.

The NAACP resolution put the group in direct conflict with the Sons of Confederate Veterans, which, under its constitution is an "historical, educational, patriotic, non-political, non-sectarian and non-racial organization." The SCV was charged upon its founding in Richmond in 1896 with "the defense of the Confederate soldier's good name, the guardianship of his history, the emulation of his virtues, the perpetuation of those principles he loved...."

"Remember," each SCV member was instructed, "it is your duty to see that the true history of the South is presented to future generations."

With the battle flag under assault, SCV members faced a daunting and largely futile task in their obligation to defend it. The mainstream news media, the federal government, and many other institutions and organizations, including state and local governments, churches, schools and corporations, took up the NAACP's campaign to banish the battle flag as a symbol of racism and slavery.

The SCV could not deny that the flag had been used by racists and extremists, but it had issued its own resolution about that two years prior to the NAACP resolution, condemning "in the strongest terms possible" the use of the flag and other Confederate symbols by the Ku Klux Klan and all other groups and individuals "who espouse political extremism or racial superiority."

The Ku Klux Klan also flew the U.S. flag and the Christian flag, SCV members liked to point out. If association of the battle flag with a racist group made it a symbol of racism, why was that not also true for the U.S. and Christian flags?

That the battle flag was regarded as a symbol of slavery was an historical misperception, the SCV argued. It was not the flag of the Confederate States of America. (There had been three of those, the first the Stars and Bars, which the battle flag was often mistakenly called.) The battle flag was just that: the flag that Confederate troops followed into battle. It did not represent slavery but the service, valor and sacrifice of the men who fought for the South.

Slavery had been legal in all thirteen states that formed the Union, SCV members pointed out. At the time of the American Revolution, New York City had nearly as many slaves as the entire state of Georgia. The slave traders were based in New England. After slavery ended in the North, its textile factories thrived on the cotton grown by Southern slaves. The U.S. flag had flown over slavery for decades. Why shouldn't it be banished?

Such arguments went largely without effect. The thrust of the campaign against the flag and other things Confederate overwhelmed the SCV's efforts and left them fighting brushfires in the face of conflagration.

Even their rare victories were sometimes thwarted. In Maryland, North Carolina, and Virginia, states that allow civic club logos on vehicle tags, they won court battles to have the SCV's battle flag logo on their tags. But one major North Carolina manufacturer, Alcoa, banned from company parking lots the vehicles of employees bearing the SCV emblem. (Topeka, Kansas, barred all vehicles with Confederate emblems from city-owned parking lots.) When the SCV won a court ruling to place its logo on welcome signs in Hickory, N.C., along with the logos of other civic clubs, the city removed all the other logos rather than allow the SCV's.

Faced with the formidable forces aligned against them, the SCV, which in recent years had grown to some 28,000 members, felt as beleaguered and helpless as their forebears who had faced such overwhelming odds on the battlefield. (Ironically, one of the few groups supporting them was the Sons of Union Veterans.)

Many SCV members felt that the NAACP had begun this attack to ensure its own existence. With overt racism subdued, the KKK essentially out of business, and strict enforcement of civil rights laws, hate crime laws, civil lawsuits, and affirmative action making racial discrimination difficult, the NAACP needed a new and visible enemy to give members purpose and to keep contributions flowing, they believed. Southerners who honored their ancestors who fought and died in the Civil War, and who revered the symbols under which they served, were an obvious and easy target.

Many SCV members came to believe, however, that this was more than just an attempt to falsely brand them with the old racism and radicalism of the KKK. It was a campaign to demonize all things Southern, to rewrite history, to strip them of their heritage, and to impose a new and approved form of intolerance and bigotry. Like their ancestors before them, they saw no choice but to fight.

Jack was a staunch defender of the battle flag and other Confederate symbols. He had written letters to newspaper editors and made speeches proclaiming that the flag did not represent slavery, racism or intolerance. He also publicly denounced the Ku Klux Klan and other groups that promoted racism and extremism. But his unwillingness to accept what he saw as intolerance also extended to the NAACP.

Late in 1997, after N.C. NAACP president Melvin Alston of Greensboro, who preferred to be called by his nickname, Skip, denounced the battle flag and the SCV, Jack wrote a letter to the editor of the *High Point Enterprise.*

"Ignorance, prejudice and intolerance are no more becoming to the media or the leader of the NAACP than they are to the Klan or kindred organizations," he wrote. "The media don't bother to do their research before they rail against all who honor the Confederate flag, and often don't even know the difference between the Stars and Bars and the battle flag, which do not even resemble each other."

Alston, he wrote, should talk with a black minister in Roanoke, Va., Charles Green, also an NAACP member.

"As reported in the *Roanoke Times* on April 30, Green visited the local chapter of the SCV where he was greeted warmly..... After attending the meeting, Green decided that the SCV doesn't promote bigotry and racism. 'You perceive things about people and organizations because of what others tell you,' he said. 'I was surprised at how well I was received. It's a terrific group of people. They don't believe in the Ku Klux Klan or militias. They asked me to come back and I plan to go.'"

The SCV and its predecessor, the United Confederate Veterans, always had been "integrated and multicultural," Jack pointed out, going on to tell of honored black Confederate pensioners who had belonged to both organizations in the early part of the century.

"Confederate veterans and their descendants have always been welcome regardless of race, religion or national origin," he wrote.

At the fourth class, during which Jack taught about the fall of most of North Carolina's coast early in the war, he found himself being questioned during the break about pro-South groups. He mentioned two of the most prominent: the League of the South, which had been formed by an Alabama history professor just four years earlier, and the Council of Conservative Citizens.

"Now that one I absolutely want nothing to do with," he said of the latter. "That's taking KKK and making it CCC the best I can tell from the stuff they sent me wanting me to join. I don't know enough about the League of the South to tell whether they're a straight-up group or whether they've got some racist agenda."

Johnnie Branch, one of the two new SCV members in the class, mentioned that someone recently asked him if the SCV promoted secession.

"We don't advocate secession," Jack said. "That doesn't mean that individual members don't. But we're not out to overthrow the government. We're out to honor our ancestors and what they fought for."

"Do the Sons of Confederate Veterans have many African-American members?" asked Dedra Routh, a Randolph County native who had taught second grade in the county schools for ten years until she quit to spend more time with her children.

"There aren't many," Jack said. "There are some."

He told about a black psychiatrist in Dallas, Tx., Emerson Emory, who had been invited to speak at the dedication of a monument to black Civil War soldiers in Arlington National Cemetery until the organizers learned that he intended to talk about Confederate blacks, whereupon he was quickly disinvited. He spoke too of Nelson Winbush, a retired black teacher from Kissimmee, Florida, who traveled widely speaking about his great grandfather who had served in the Army of Tennessee.

"There are black Sons of Confederate Veterans, but they have a hard time. They're very much ostracized by the NAACP."

Jack asked Routh if she read the High Point newspaper.

"Greensboro," she replied.

"You get the liberal side of things," he said. "Ever read Armstrong Williams, a black columnist?"

"I read Thomas Sowell."

Jack was a fan of Sowell, a North Carolina native, a Harvard graduate, a professor at Stanford University, and the author of many books, whose column appeared in the *Courier-Tribune* of Asheboro and the *High Point Enterprise*. "They're soul brothers," he said, adding that both were black conservatives, and neither had problems with the Confederate flag or Confederate heritage.

"If a black man walked in this door and I could find his ancestors, I'd sign him up in a minute," Jack went on. "I'd give him a Confederate flag to carry in the Jamestown Christmas parade when we march there, right beside Skip Alston in the county commissioners' car. Do my heart good."

The Frazier Camp had no African-American members, but Jack noted that a black visitor accompanied a recent speaker to the camp and was welcomed. Camp meetings begin with the pledge of allegiance to the U.S. flag, he explained, followed by salutes to the N.C. flag and battle flag, and the singing of "Dixie." The visitor stood and went through the ritual.

"After the meeting we told him how happy we were to have him and how we appreciated his participating and that he didn't have to participate in the singing of 'Dixie' and saluting the Confederate flag, and if we'd made him feel uncomfortable we were sorry about that. He said he didn't feel uncomfortable, he was Southern, too."

Next week's class, Jack noted, was to be about the service of blacks and native Americans to the Confederacy.

"When was the Trail of Tears?" a student asked, referring to the forced removal of native American tribes from the eastern part of the country.

"In the eighteen thirties," Jack replied. "People who want to associate the Confederate flag with racism and slavery need to look at things like the Trail of Tears that took place under the American flag."

The U.S. government set upon a course of "planned genocide to completely annihilate a race of people, the American Indians," Jack said, warming to a topic that had fascinated him since childhood. Following the Civil War, General William Tecumseh Sherman, who left such a swath of destruction, death and misery through the South, led U.S. troops that attempted to carry out that plan, he pointed out.

"It was plainly stated that the solution to the Indian problem was the elimination of the Indian. Official policy. It's right there in black and white. Kids aren't taught that at school."

Yet nobody was demanding that the U.S. flag be banished because of it, he noted.

"The only culture you can't belong to anymore is Southern," Jack said. "Everything else in this multicultural society is given recognition, and you're encouraged to be proud of your heritage, except if you're Southern. And we're going to remedy that if it's the last thing we ever do."

Seven

The fifth class would be the source of the unbelievable events to come and the tribulation that would follow. Its subject was the contribution of blacks and Cherokee Indians to the war effort in the state, and it was taught by Herman White.

When Jack asked his fellow SCV members for help with the course, White, the camp chaplain, was quick to volunteer. His interest in the war, like Jack's, went back to childhood, but his family connections were much closer.

White, who was sixty-four, had grown up on a farm east of High Point hearing tales of his grandfather's adventures in the war, stories that led him to look forward to one of his greatest childhood pleasures, the arrival of the bookmobile, so he could search out books about the war.

Not until many years later, after long research, would White know the full extent of his grandfather's role. Ed White served under Stonewall Jackson in the 11th N.C. Infantry, and was left for dead on the battlefield at Winchester, Va., in May, 1862. Union forces discovered that he was still alive and took him to a field hospital.

Many years later, Ed White regaled his children with tales of how happy he was to regain consciousness and see the faces of the Yankee doctors who saved him. White later was returned to Confederate forces in a prisoner exchange. He would be captured and exchanged again, then wounded once more before the war ended.

After graduating from Jamestown School in 1952, Herman White married his high school sweetheart and went to work in a hosiery mill in High Point. In September, 1960, he and his wife, Shirley, attended a service at Jamestown Church of God, where both answered the call to salvation, an experience that took his life in a new direction. "The Lord called me to preach on the seventeenth of November, nineteen and sixty," he said. He preached at revivals and served as a guest minister until he got his own small church, Archdale Church of God, in 1967. More than thirty years later, he still was pastor there.

For White, preaching was a calling, not a career. He continued working, and spent many hours studying, taking courses at Lee College in Cleveland, Tn., and at Southwest Bible College in Jessup, La., where he eventually earned a master's degree in ministry. His work, his church, his studies and family responsibilities left little time for history, but the stories about his grandfather, who died before he was born, kept tugging at him, and in the mid-'80s he began making time to explore them. The quest took ten years and nearly mesmerized him.

In 1996, White and his wife attended their high school class reunion. Rahlo Fowler, who graduated two years behind them, was a guest. They got to talking about the Civil War, and White told Fowler about his research on his grandfather. Fowler invited him to a Sons of Confederate Veterans meeting. He went, met Jack, and applied for membership. Jack later helped with his family research.

"He was like a bloodhound," White recalled. "He wouldn't quit until he found what he was looking for. He was always trying to help."

White came to be almost in awe of his new friend.

"I could stand and listen to Jack and be just as fascinated as when I was a little kid listening to stories about my grandfather. If you want to talk about the history of the war, Jack would be the Mickey Mantle or the Mark McGwire of that period, and I couldn't even play in a Class D league. A lot of professors couldn't shine a light to him and that's not reflecting on anybody."

Like Jack, White had strong feelings about the war, but in one way, he acknowledged, he was different.

"I'm more one-sided. He could understand the other fellow. It's harder for me to grasp the other side of that thing."

At the time Jack asked for volunteers, White just had learned that his great, great grandfather on his mother's side had been a slave owner in Randolph County, where slaves were few and opposition to slavery strong, and he was eager to start looking into that aspect of his family. That was why the item on Jack's list of classes about the role of blacks and Cherokees caught his eye. He could combine research for family and class. He offered to take it and Jack accepted. Soon afterward, White visited his great aunt, Pearl Coltrane Craven, who was ninety-one, to find out everything she knew about slaves in the family.

• • •

As he introduced White on the evening of October 15, Jack joked about his preacherly reputation for long-windedness.

"Herman asked me if I thought we'd be able to start on time," he said. "I said, 'That won't be the problem. Stopping on time will be the problem."

White, Jack told the students, likely would provide a closer connection to the war than they would experience again. Few SCV chapters had any true sons of Confederate veterans, he said, but the Frazier Camp was blessed with three. And two were related to White: his father, David, who was ninety-four; and his uncle, Wiley, ninety.

White probably spent more time researching his subject than all the other lecturers combined, Jack said. "He's really gone beyond the call of duty."

Indeed, White submitted the longest bibliography by far, listing twenty-six sources, including books, periodicals, official records, and personal interviews. He had copies for each student, along with his five-page, single-spaced lesson plan, plus pages of book excerpts, records, and articles.

Short and balding, with a bushy, walrus-like mustache, White wore a dark suit, a wide tie and tinted wire-rimmed glasses as he came to the lectern. A man of deep convictions and strong opinions, his instincts inclined more to preaching than teaching, and despite Jack's admonition to stick to facts and ignore politics, White had no hesitancy about injecting his conservative political views and fundamentalist religious beliefs into his lecture.

Inexplicably, he began on such a note, referring offhandedly to a recent item he read about religious views on slavery.

"I'm not going to deal with that issue tonight," he said. "I will say this. For those people that want to tell you that God's word condemns it, I can show you where they know no more what they're talking about than I know how to fly a seven-forty-seven. That doesn't mean we're promoting it. That would be the last thing I'd want to be involved with. But what we're talking about is truth, and people tell so much that is not the truth. They do God that way. They do our ancestors that way. The Bible says know the truth and the truth will set you free. Lot of people don't like the truth. There's an old saying that the truth never hurt anybody. That's an erroneous old saying, because people will kill you for the truth."

With that, White went on to talk for thirty minutes about the two companies of Cherokees from western North Carolina who joined Confederate forces and served throughout the war, seeing combat in Tennessee and Virginia, but mainly fighting skirmishes against Union sympathizers in the state's rugged mountains, a divided area at war with itself.

Suddenly realizing how long he'd been talking, he quickly switched topics.

It was necessary to confront "numerous myths and outright lies" in discussing the role of blacks in the war, he said, reading from the lesson plan. "In dealing with these issues we are not supporting the institution of slavery, but dealing with a factual presentation that was a reality at that time...."

He interrupted to point out that in some of the materials he'd handed out, which included period documents, words appeared "that are not my terms. I want that understood."

His lesson plan was just an outline, and he departed from it to talk about a column by Thomas Sowell in which he wrote that while slavery had existed throughout recorded history, individual freedom was a relatively new concept that came to fruition in this country and that inevitably would have ended slavery with or without war.

"It was on its way out," White said. "There are those that refuse to proclaim the truth about that, but it was on its way out."

Jefferson Davis was one who promoted this idea, but believed that slaves had to be prepared for freedom, lest they end up in worse conditions, White noted. Davis and Robert E. Lee had spoken against slavery, yet both now were "being painted as ogres."

He returned to his outline to read that most historians ignored the state of free blacks in the South prior to the war.

"Many blacks were property owners," he read, "some downright wealthy, and some of these were slave owners as well."

One historian who had done his work, White said, was Loren Schweninger, a professor at the University of North Carolina at Greensboro. His book, *Black Property Owners in the South, 1790-1915*, was the best source for that information, he said, showing it to the students. "It's chock full of facts."

White was easily sidetracked, and this led him to show other books, talking about them and their authors before returning to his next topic: "Race Relations in the South Before and During the War."

After the passage of the Fugitive Slave Act in 1850, outraged abolitionists and Northern newspapers began a campaign to portray Southern slave owners as cruel and brutal, like the character Simon Legree in Harriet Beecher Stowe's novel *Uncle Tom's Cabin*, published to huge success in 1852.

These were part of the "myths and outright lies" White referred to, picturing the relationship between slaves and owners as being "void of any feeling...mean to them, brutal, just plain sadistic."

This defied reason in one respect, White noted, because slaves were major investments and to abuse them was to deprive owners of their worth. No doubt some slave owners were brutal, he said, just as some parents are abusive of their children. But this was not the norm. Most slave owners, he said, "treated the people they owned with respect and kindness."

One indication of this, he said, returning to his lesson plan, was a study by a Louisiana minister of slave narratives in the National Archives. (In the late 1930s, the federal Works Progress Administration paid writers and academics to interview thousands of ex-slaves in seventeen states and set down their memories of slavery.) The Rev. Steve Wilkins had studied the narratives of four Southern states, White said, without naming them, and found that more than seventy per cent of the ex-slaves "had only good experiences to report about their life as a slave in the South."

Although he didn't mention it, White had taken this from the book *The South Was Right* by twin brothers James and Walter Kennedy, both SCV members. First published privately in 1991, the book was greatly expanded and re-issued by Pelican Press in Louisiana three years later. Heavily sourced and foot-noted, it used excerpts from many early works, some now disputed by historians, to make the South's case. Examples of ex-slaves' "good experiences" included accounts of never being whipped, being allowed to earn money, granted time of their own, being allowed to attend church, cared for when they were sick, and having food similar to their masters'.

As further evidence of the relationships between slaves and owners, White turned to his great, great grandfather, Jesse Coltrane. He'd included a photo of him in the material he'd given the students.

"If you know where Coltrane Mill is down here on the Deep River, that's him. It's still down there."

In addition to the grist mill, Coltrane owned a lot of farmland in the area that was now the Cedar Square community. His wife, Abigail, had been a teacher, and each afternoon she gathered the slave children at her kitchen table and gave them the same lessons she had taught her earlier students, White said. At night, she taught the adult slaves to read and write. That was against the law, he pointed out, drawing attention to copies of the law he passed out earlier. That his ancestors ran this risk clearly showed that they cared for the slaves, he maintained.

"They didn't want them to be ignorant. They wanted them to be able to function in society. Well, it sounds like what they were doing was getting them ready to be free, don't it?"

At the end of the war, White said, Jesse Coltrane gave each of his male slaves ten acres of land, and the descendants of those slaves still lived on that land in what appeared to be a prosperous community just a few miles south of the campus.

"Whew, mercy," he said, turning to look at the clock before moving on to his next topic: "Examples of Northern Racism & Contempt for the Warm Relationship of the Races in the South."

Northerners regarded both blacks and whites from the South as "backward and debased," he told the class, returning to his text. He went on to speak about an English abolitionist, James S. Buckingham, who, after a visit to America in 1842, wrote "that the prejudice of color is not nearly so strong in the South as in the North. In the South it is not at all uncommon to see the black slaves of both sexes shake hands with white people when they meet and interchange friendly personal inquiries. But at the North I do not remember to have witnessed this once; and neither in Boston, New York or Philadelphia would white persons generally like to be seen shaking hands and talking familiarly with blacks in the streets."

"You know what that's called when people condemn people when they themselves are guilty?" White asked. "God calls them hypocrites.... Okay, I'm at a place where I can stop."

"Yeah," Jack spoke up. "That's a good stopping place right there."

Following the break, White read an entry from the diary of a Maine soldier as an example of Northern contempt, noting that it contained language that he didn't use: "'Two hundred years of slavery have not elevated the...' Here he substituted "N-word." "'...or his master. The only advancement has been in the way of unnatural selection; the line of demarcation between black and white is not as positive as true virtue demands, but is dimmed by a kind of neutral tint that cannot but be regarded with suspicion.'

"Well, bless his heart," White said mockingly. "He was wonderful, wasn't he?"

The North had expected a massive slave revolt in the South at the beginning of the war, and a grateful reception from blacks for invading Union troops, White said. The British, too, had expected slaves to join them during the Revolutionary War, after offering freedom, but had been surprised. They thought again that slaves might side with them in the War of 1812, but had instead found blacks fighting against them at the Battle of New Orleans.

"The Yankees didn't learn either," White said. "When Northern armies invaded the South offering freedom, of course, this wasn't new to the slaves, they had heard it before."

Some slaves did go over to the North, he said, and some were organized into segregated military units commanded by white officers, about which much had been written, but in comparison to the total population of blacks in the South, "it really was a small percentage."

On the other hand, little had been written about blacks, both free and slave, who stood with the Confederacy, he said, and what had been written often was belittled because many people "refuse to accept the truth."

These people ask, "'Why would they do that?'" White said. "It was their country. That's why they were doing it."

The South simply couldn't have prosecuted the war without blacks, he said, going on to point out that black support had fallen into two categories, military and civilian.

On the civilian front, blacks kept the farms and plantations producing food, cotton and other crops necessary to the war. Blacks kept the railroads running and worked in other industries vital to the war effort. Some maintain that slaves and free blacks did this only because they were forced, White said, but who was there to force them? In most places, only women, children and elderly men were left. Slaves could have slipped away without resistance, but most didn't. Something other than slavery bound them.

In the case of free blacks, self-interest caused many to serve the South, White pointed out. Many owned property and wanted to protect it. He told of a black plantation owner who volunteered for Confederate forces and after being turned down devoted himself to producing food for the troops.

"He wanted to save the way of life he had," White said.

In the category of military support, White said that blacks served as cooks, teamsters, and musicians, and many volunteered in part because they were paid. Slaves also accompanied their owners, or their owners' sons, as servants and bodyguards. They usually wore uniforms, were armed and often fought alongside the troops. There were accounts of such slaves delivering their masters' dead bodies home, then returning to their units to continue the fight, he noted.

White offered three examples from period documents of blacks serving with Confederate forces, which he included in his lesson plan.

The first was from a doctor with the U.S. Army Sanitary Commission who witnessed the occupation of Frederick, Md., by Stonewall

Jackson's army in 1862. He reported that "over 3,000 Negroes must be included in the Confederate troops." They were uniformed, he said, and most were armed—"rifles, muskets, sabres, bowie-knives, dirks, etc."

White again quoted from the Maine private's diary describing a Union marksman shooting a rebel sniper from a tree and discovering him to be black.

The third example was a report by a British observer with Robert E. Lee's army at Gettysburg. Captain Arthur Freemantle described a slave leading a Union prisoner through a Pennsylvania village, a sight, he noted, that "would not have been gratifying to an abolitionist...nor would the sympathizers both in England and in the North feel encouraged if they could hear the language of detestation and contempt with which the numerous Negroes with the Southern armies speak of their liberators."

Among the many items White handed out were pages from the multiple volumes of *North Carolina Troops: 1861-1865* showing many listed as "Negro." Few records existed about the service of most, but one black musician, a fifer, William Revels, who enlisted in Surry County in 1861, was described as having been wounded in the right shoulder in New Bern, in the left leg at Winchester, Va., and in the right thigh at Gettysburg. White also handed out copies of an article from *Smithsonian* magazine, "The unlikely story of blacks who were loyal to Dixie," which told of many blacks, free and slave, who served with Confederate forces.

The last item in White's lesson plan was a subject on which he had touched earlier: free black property owners and slave holders in the South at the time of the war.

Free blacks in Virginia owned property and slaves as early as 1647, White said. The 1790 census showed 150 free black families in Charleston, and forty-nine of those owned a total of 277 slaves. Free blacks spent a lot of money buying family members out of slavery, he said.

"It may have been strictly that to begin with, but that certainly changed."

By late in the eighteenth century, a small group of profit-motivated black slave holders had begun to emerge, he said, but that information didn't appear in school history books.

"Were you ever taught that?" he asked. "I wasn't."

The scheduled time for the class was fast approaching its end, and Jack kept an eye on the clock as White drifted into a rambling story about his grandfather buying a farm from a black man in Patrick County, Va., at the turn of the century. When White worked his way back to the subject, he told of a slave in Martin County who had accumulated an estate of nearly $6,000, a large sum at a time in which many men worked for ten dollars a month. In 1856, White said, a group of white builders in Smithfield complained about constantly being underbid on projects by free blacks.

"Suffice to say, even the economic plight of slaves and free blacks was much different than what the northern abolitionist liberals claimed during the time of slavery, and that the northern liberals and so-called civil rights crusaders of today still claim...." he said. "They continue their lies decade after decade because they're afraid of the truth. These radical, left-ring..." He paused, chuckled and tried again. "...Left-*wing* socialists—and that's what they really are—have an agenda that's full of half-truths and outright lies, the same tired old lies of the nineteenth century abolitionists.

"...If the truth is told, it's a threat to their flow of cash, which they use to live their extravagant lifestyles as they fly around the country to try to tell those that will listen to them about how it is that they are fighting for them to get their rights."

White had only one line left on his lesson plan, of which each student had a copy: "In closing, remember that this in NO WAY CONDONES the institution of slavery...."

"So in closing—because I've got to...." He looked nervously at the clock, then at Jack, "...cause he keeps looking at me...."

"I'm going to hire myself out to your congregation," Jack interrupted, "tell 'em how good a job I do keeping you on time, Herman."

Jack was getting up to close the class. He knew that White's tendency was to continue talking.

"In closing, again, and I don't think there's anyone here that misunderstands," White forged on, "but I want to emphasize. What we're dealing with is not promoting slavery. It's not saying yea nor nay— we're not dealing with the morality of it. There are people that says it's immoral. For it to be immoral as far as I'm concerned it'd have to be contrary to God's word, and it's not. If anybody wants to talk to me about that other than now, I'll be glad to do it, 'cause I know a little about the Book. It was a fact of life in a period of our history. All we're dealing with is the truth of it.

"It's still practiced in parts of the world today. I think Jesse Jackson needs to go over there and work on it. That would get rid him for a while, wouldn't it?" he said with a little laugh. "But seriously, this is not promoting it. It's not saying it's right. It's not saying it's wrong. We're just simply dealing with the truth of it. And again, as the scriptures say, the truth will set folks free."

Jack was distressed about White's insertion of his political and religious views into his lecture. He had been wary about letting White take this subject, but he had been impressed with his enthusiasm, the depth of his research, the hours of work he put into preparation.

He still was upset when he called Rahlo Fowler the next morning, worried about how the students had taken White's views.

Although they never complained to Jack, two students later said that they were put off by some of White's remarks, but they set that aside to consider the factual material he presented.

Eight

No people ever were less prepared for an appeal to arms than North Carolinians at the time the state seceded, Jack said on October 22, as he began the sixth class on the state's role in supplying the Confederacy.

An agricultural state, with little manufacturing, North Carolina chose to arm, outfit and supply its own troops, which eventually would lead to problems with Confederate leaders who distrusted the state because of its Unionist leanings.

The adjoining central counties of Randolph, Guilford, Davidson and Forsyth, all with strong Union sympathies, were home for many Quakers and Moravians who were morally opposed to war, as well as slavery, but many worked in industries to supply Confederate troops in lieu of military service.

Governor Zebulon Vance, elected in 1862, a Unionist before the war, would have a running feud with Jefferson Davis. Jack had the official records of the war on CDs, and he searched them for letters showing the extent of the disputes.

"This probably illustrates that the Confederacy never would have survived if we'd won the war," he said before reading excerpts from the letters.

The original colonies came close to losing the Revolutionary War because of the lack of a strong central government, he said. States' rights were a primary reason for secession, and if the South had won the war, that issue likely would have split the Confederacy, too. North Carolina, with its strong independent nature, no doubt would have insisted on becoming a country of its own.

Jack went on to tell how the state mobilized for war, how dependent it became on the blockade runners who brought supplies into Wilmington, and to describe the state's railroads and their importance.

No railroad directly connected Richmond to Atlanta, but that would be possible if tracks were laid from Greensboro to Danville, Va. Jefferson Davis wanted that line built. Vance opposed it. But construction began, and the line was barely finished in time for the evacuation of Richmond at war's end. Because of it, Jack said, Davis and his cabinet ended up in Greensboro with Vance during negotiations for the final surrender. But more on that would come in the last class.

Jack lugged boxes of books into the classroom on the following Thursday, October 29, for a workshop on tracing Confederate ancestors.

Dedra Routh, one of the ex-teachers in the class, had been looking forward to this night from the beginning. A Civil War buff from childhood, she had requested a trip to Ft. Sumter for her high school graduation present. She knew that her great, great grandfather, Stokes Hopkins, enlisted in Confederate forces in 1861 at age twenty-eight. But she knew little else and wanted more.

Jack used his books to show her that Hopkins fought at Fredricksburg, was captured at Petersburg and taken to the Federal prison at Point Lookout, Md., where he remained until the end of the war. Family members had told her that Hopkins supposedly was wounded at New Hanover Junction, Routh said, but the records didn't show this, and Jack knew of no such battle. He wrote down the information, however, and said he would check into it. Later, he reported back that a skirmish had taken place at New Hanover Junction and no doubt her family lore was factual.

As a Marine in World War II, Nancy Boyles' late husband, Roba, participated in the invasion of Iwo Jima. She agreed to go to Marine reunions with him if he would take her to Civil War battlefields. Ten years earlier they attended the re-enactment of the 125th anniversary of the battle for Gettysburg. Her husband had been told that his grandfather served in the Civil War, but he made no effort to verify it. Nancy knew that his grandfather's name was William Riley Boyles, and with that, and Jack's help, she soon learned that he'd served in Company D of the 53rd N.C. Infantry, was wounded at Gettysburg and died four days later. She wished her husband could have known that when they attended the re-enactment, she said.

After learning about her great, great, great grandfather, Dedra Routh hurried out to the parking lot to call her mother on her car phone. Her mother had told her that four of her great, great, great uncles fought in the war. She returned with the name of one, Moses Chisholm, and

Jack helped her discover that he was at Appomattox when Lee surrendered. Long afterward, Routh still would remember how excited she was. This class, she said, provided inspiration for her to begin a much deeper look into her family history.

"Didn't we have fun?" Jack asked as he and several students were leaving the classroom at break time.

"We had a grand time," Routh agreed.

Bob Zeller was just ten days from ending a twenty-four-year newspaper career when he arrived at the Archdale campus to present his half of this night's class. A native of Washington, D.C., who had grown up in Hyattsville, Md., Zeller was a graduate of the University of Missouri School of Journalism. He had been an investigative reporter in Jackson, Miss., and Long Beach, Ca., before becoming the stock car racing writer for the *News & Record* in Greensboro and two sister papers in Roanoke and Norfolk, Va., all owned by the Landmark Corporation.

Zeller had published three biographies of stock car racing stars, but his real love was elsewhere. He was one of the country's leading private collectors of original Civil War photography. Parts of his collection had been shown in major museums, and some of his photographs had been included in the Smithsonian's traveling exhibit of Matthew Brady's work.

Few people knew that most Civil War photography had been done with three-dimension cameras to be used in stereoscopic viewers. Zeller had become an authority on the subject and lectured widely. A year earlier, he had published *The Civil War in Depth*, the first 3-D pictorial history of the war, and he was finishing a second volume. He was leaving newspaper reporting to concentrate on his books and to follow a dream of one day opening a 3-D Civil War photography museum at Gettysburg.

Zeller had developed a technique for projecting his 3-D photographs onto a screen, and presented a slide show at a Frazier Camp meeting in July. Jack asked him to give it again during the course.

"What you are about to see is unique in the presentation of the visual history of the Civil War," Zeller told the students. "I am proud to be the person to let you in on one of the last secrets of the Civil War—the full visual magic of its photography."

With that, class members were swept into the war. Startling images followed one after another, gruesome battle scenes intermixed with shots of prison-like pens where slaves were kept awaiting sale, fugitive slaves fleeing across the Rappahanock River, black Union soldiers in combat, two of 185,000 who served, more than 38,000 of whom lost their lives. Some of the final scenes showed Richmond in ruins and a haggard President Lincoln in his last formal portrait just three months before his assassination.

Later, several students recalled Zeller's presentation as the most moving and memorable part of their course. As Hope Haywood, also an ex-teacher, drove home to Asheboro that night, the starkly realistic photographs still raw in her mind, she found herself bursting into tears. "It really made me see what a terrible, horrible war it was and how it affected the whole nation," she recalled.

With only three classes left, some of the students were enjoying them so much that they already were dreading their end. Dedra Routh was one. She had dropped another course so she could concentrate on this one. She found herself looking forward to Thursday evenings.

"The whole class was so rich," she said. "It was the richest, broadest curriculum. It was just wonderful. To me, it was like eating candy. You just didn't want to stop." Her husband, Dan, later recalled that she came home excited from every class, eager to tell what she had learned.

Louise Canipe, the eldest member of the class, had grown up in the mountains of North Carolina, had ancestors who fought on both sides during the war, and wanted to learn more about them. She always sat on the front row so she wouldn't miss a word. "From the first night, I felt I was supposed to be there," she said. "I thought, *Oh, this is going to be so interesting,* and it was. I really learned a lot."

As weeks went on, Canipe began telling anybody who would listen that this was the best class she ever attended. "I couldn't say enough for it," she recalled.

"It was fascinating," said Tom Corns, co-owner of a plant that produced private-label detergents for Wal-Mart and other major retailers. Corns had become an avid genealogist as a teen-ager and had traced thirty-five ancestors who served in Confederate forces, as well as others who fought in the American Revolution. "You could look around the room and tell that everybody in there was interested."

Joan King, who had grown up in the mountains of southwestern Virginia, recently had learned that she had ancestors who fought for the Confederacy. She was attending the course with her twenty-one-year-old son, Jeremy, a recent graduate of RCC. She was uncertain about the course in the beginning. "I guess I expected a lot more dry facts, sort of like history in high school. But it really was interesting. I was really impressed."

Nancy Boyles enjoyed the classes so much that she wanted to share them with everybody she knew. After every class, she called her sister, Annie Chappell, to tell her what fascinating things she'd learned. She had a friend who was part Cherokee, and after hearing that two Cherokee companies fought with North Carolina troops, she took the materials from the class to show her friend. "I just thought it was great," she said.

When Hope Haywood registered for the course, she was wary about its co-sponsorship by the Sons of Confederate Veterans. She wasn't interested in material that was blatantly biased. She didn't know anything about the SCV, though, and didn't want to make judgments without giving the course a chance. Early on the first night, as Jack talked about the SCV, the battle flag and the prejudices against it, she thought this probably wasn't for her. But as he got deeper into the preliminaries leading up to the war, her attitude began to change. She decided to return for the second class, and she never stopped coming.

"It really was about the war, about what took place in North Carolina," she said. "I learned so many things I never knew. It was a very good, very informative course, historically accurate, very mentally stimulating and very moving."

Indeed, Haywood, who had a master's degree in education, turned out to be precisely the person to whom Jack hoped to direct this course. She left teaching to spend more time with her children, but she planned to return, and she hoped to teach either fourth grade, where North Carolina social studies were introduced, or eighth grade, where North Carolina history was taught. "I kept thinking this would be such a great course for eighth grade teachers," she said.

All the students were impressed by the effort that had gone into the course. It didn't escape their notice that the volunteers and guest lecturers outnumbered them by more than two to one. Rarely were so many engaged in teaching so few.

One other thing united the class: their admiration and respect for Jack. They were amazed at his ability to answer the most obscure questions, to instantly pull from his brain amazing facts and statistics.

"The man was unbelievable," said Dedra Routh. "Mr. Perdue was so upbeat and so full of energy and wanted us to know everything. I can't think of a professor I ever had who was so enthusiastic, so knowledgeable. It was like he couldn't tell it to us quickly enough."

"I was astounded at his depth of knowledge," said Hope Haywood. "He was just like this big, walking history book. I had professors who didn't know nearly as much as he did about the facts of the war. He brought people into it, made them see it."

"He was so passionate about it," said Louise Canipe. "The first night I knew I was going to learn a lot from this man, and I did."

"Jack was great about these kinds of things," said Tom Corns, "very professional, very knowledgeable. He always backed up his presentation with facts. Whether you agreed with him or not, you found out that he was always accurate."

"Jack was a good teacher, so honorable," said Johnny Branch, a grandfather who delivered furniture for a company in High Point and recently had discovered that he had ancestors who fought for the Confederacy. "He knew his stuff and he was eloquent in speaking about it. That was the most pleasant group of people, and we were all really learning and enjoying it so much."

It was just such feelings that would make it so difficult for the students to accept what was about to happen.

Nine

Jack had heard nothing from Ethan Feinsilver, the *News & Record* reporter, since the first class six weeks earlier, and a month had passed since the newspaper's photographer visited the outdoor encampment. The course soon would be over, and Jack assumed that Feinsilver's editors had passed on a story.

But on October 30, the day after Bob Zeller showed his dramatic slides to the class, Feinsilver called Herman White at home to question what he had taught. If he wanted to know that, he could have attended the class, White remembered telling him. He was not going into all of that over the telephone.

Feinsilver, he said, asked that he fax him a copy of his lesson plan.

"I can't do that. I don't have a fax machine," White recalled telling him.

"He said, 'You sure sound evasive. Why are you being so evasive?'"

That riled White. He didn't like the comment or Feinsilver's attitude, but he didn't want to show anger and instead responded that he wasn't being evasive.

"I told him I would talk to him about it," White said, "but I wanted to be able to look him in the eye when I did."

Soon afterward, White called Jack to tell him about the conversation. He had no doubt, he said, that this guy was going to be trouble.

Rick McCaslin felt as if he had been ambushed at birth by history. Born in Atlanta, he grew up in Ocean Springs, Ms., surrounded by reminders of history and a passel of eccentric relatives (He had both Jewish and Baptist forebears.) who talked endlessly about the Civil War and their ancestors who fought in it. It seemed only natural for him to major in history and political science when he went to Delta State College as a presidential scholar. He got his degree in two and a half years, went on to Louisiana State University for a master's in history, then got a Ph.D. at the University of Texas.

He expanded his dissertation about the mass hangings of Unionists in north Texas, and it became a prize winning book: *Tainted Breeze: The Great Hanging at Gainesville, Texas, 1862*. McCaslin served as associate editor of the Andrew Johnson papers before becoming an associate professor of history at High Point University. A specialist on the Civil War, he contracted with the University of Arkansas Press to produce photographic histories of the war for South Carolina, North Carolina, and Tennessee. The South Carolina volume came first, and the second, *Portraits of Conflict: A Photographic History of North Carolina in the Civil War*, had been published in 1997. McCaslin gave a talk about the book at the Frazier Camp and Jack asked if he would expand it and present it in the course.

After hearing from White, Jack was not surprised that Feinsilver showed up again on November 5, the night of McCaslin's lecture. He thought McCaslin should be aware that a reporter was present and pointed him out.

Feinsilver, who declined to be interviewed for this book, had been at the *News & Record* for not quite ten months. He grew up in Washington, D.C., the only son of a prominent psychiatrist, David B. Feinsilver, an authority on schizophrenia, who was suffering from terminal cancer. Ethan Feinsilver had graduated from the University of Chicago and worked for a smaller newspaper before coming to the *News & Record*.

Few newsroom staff members had gotten to know Feinsilver well, primarily because he was isolated most of the time as the sole reporter in the Randolph County bureau in Asheboro, a town of some 21,000 residents, about twenty-five miles south of Greensboro. Randolph was a rural county, traditionally conservative and Republican. Feinsilver chose to live in Greensboro, a city with five colleges and universities and a population of nearly 224,000.

Some news staffers got the impression that Feinsilver felt himself to be better than his assignment, that he viewed Randolph County as a "redneck backwater," and held in contempt the people he had to write about regularly. In his short time there, his attitude and brash tactics had turned many of those people against him.

73

Sheriff Litchard Hurley quit speaking to Feinsilver when he attempted to interview an undercover female drug agent after being told that revealing her identity could endanger her life.

County Manager Frank Willis also kept his distance. "He was no friend of mine," said Willis, who claimed that Feinsilver only was interested in searching for something controversial and negative to write about county government.

Cathy Hefferin, the public relations officer at Randolph Community College, always tried to get to know new reporters in the county and make them feel welcome. She called Feinsilver on numerous occasions to invite him to different functions, she said, but he never responded, and she finally quit trying.

George Gusler, the executive vice president of the Randolph County Chamber of Commerce also called Feinsilver to welcome him to the county and invited him to drop by for a chat, but Feinsilver never came.

Worth Hatley, the county's affable superintendent of schools, had frequent dealings with Feinsilver and attempted without success to befriend him. Feinsilver constantly tried to pit him against the county commissioners, the school board, or students' parents, Hatley said.

When Feinsilver was researching a story about school funding, he kept pointing out how much commissioners spent on other things and how little they valued education, Hatley noted as an example.

"He wanted to put things like, they do this and they do that, but they don't look after children. I said, 'Ethan, no, it's not that way. We have a good relationship with our commissioners.' But no matter what I said he would just keep on and on trying to drag me into the middle of something. It was always something that would be controversial. I got to the point where I did not trust him. Any time he came to me, I'd be extremely guarded and make a record of everything I said."

Asheboro Mayor Joe Trogdon felt the same way. "I was real careful what I said around him," he said. "I always kept somebody with me when I talked to him."

Feinsilver's troubles extended to his editors as well. He was admonished for being arrogant; for reluctance to be a "team player," a highly valued trait at the *News & Record*; for chronic lateness; for failing to follow story filing and budgeting procedures; and for low story production.

Feinsilver responded in writing, disagreeing that he was arrogant and not interested in teamwork. He acknowledged the actions that prompted the criticism, however. He wasn't satisfied with his own job performance, he said, and couldn't articulate why he was "having trouble doing the kind of exciting work I want to do."

Perhaps he needed a mentor, he suggested, or a support group, which he was attempting to put together.

But now Feinsilver had found the exciting story for which he had been searching, a story that would gain worldwide interest and win praise from his editors and fellow reporters.

A dynamic speaker with a strong sense of narrative, Rick McCaslin, like Bob Zeller the week before, had built his presentation around photographs, but his mainly were portraits of individual soldiers cast from an overhead projector. Through these images he told of the major battles in which North Carolina troops fought.

First at Bethel, farthest to the front at Gettysburg and Chickamauga, last at Appomattox. That had been the motto of North Carolina troops, McCaslin said. He then took the students straight into the war with the urgency and drama of a TV documentary.

As usual, Jack went outside during the class break to smoke his pipe. Herman White and some of the students were there as well. As they were coming back inside, White recalled, Feinsilver appeared and asked if they could talk now. He and Jack agreed and started toward an empty classroom. On the way, Jack got held up by a student, and White and Feinsilver went on to the classroom and sat at a table facing each other.

"He started asking about what I had taught," White remembered, "so I started at the beginning with the Indians, but he interrupted. He said, 'I don't want to hear about that.' I said, 'I thought you wanted to know about the class I taught,' and I started in again on it. He said, 'Let's get past that.' I said, 'Did you not tell me you wanted to know about the class I taught? Then let me tell you about it.'"

That part wasn't controversial, White remembered Feinsilver saying.

"I told him, 'Neither is the other.' He said it was. I said, 'You don't want to know what I actually taught at all. You just want to create some kind of controversy where there isn't one."

By that time, Jack had joined them. As White remembered, Jack said, "If it's controversial, why hasn't somebody complained?"

The class had been advertised in advance, Jack pointed out. News stories had appeared about it. The co-sponsorship by the Sons of Confederate Veterans was plainly stated. Nothing had been hidden. Nobody objected to the class beforehand, and not a single complaint had been made in the eight weeks it had been ongoing. The students seemed to be enjoying it and getting a lot out of it, and if he didn't believe that he should talk to them. "There's no controversy here," Jack said.

What had been taught about blacks fighting for the South was controversial in itself, Feinsilver maintained, as White remembered, because he had spoken with a National Park Service historian at Petersburg, Va., who said it was a myth that blacks had fought for the Confederacy. That was when White realized Feinsilver had a copy of his lesson plan.

White said that it was no myth, and what he taught was backed up with verifiable, factual material included in his lesson plan.

"I told him that if I didn't feel like it was true, I wouldn't teach it, no more than I would preach something that I knew wasn't true."

Feinsilver wanted to know exactly how many blacks had fought, White remembered. Jack said it wasn't possible to know that. Because blacks with Confederate forces weren't in segregated units, as in the North, it would take going through the records of every unit looking for men designated as "Negro" to determine that, and even then there often would be no way of knowing in what capacity they served or whether they fought.

Feinsilver kept demanding a number, White said, and he and Jack kept insisting that they couldn't provide one.

"'He finally said, 'Well, what's the most you've ever heard?'" White recalled. "It was a hypothetical question. I told him thirty-eight thousand right off, because I'd read that recently."

Jack said that 30,000 was the number he'd seen mentioned most frequently, White recalled, but that he'd even run across an estimate of 90,000 made by a black scholar at a Virginia university.

For a while, White said, he and Jack tried to answer Feinsilver's questions and explain the roles free blacks and slaves played during the war and why they did so. But Feinsilver challenged whatever they said.

"It was almost like a dog chasing his tail," White recalled. "No matter what we said, he wasn't going to believe that any blacks had fought for the South."

Feinsilver's attitude was contentious and increasingly acrimonious, White said, and he didn't appreciate it. He was a gesticulator and when he used his index finger to make a point, Feinsilver pushed it away, telling him sharply, "Don't point your finger at me!"

White pointed right back. "It was childish," he said, "but I had to do it. I said, 'This is emphasis. It's not a gun. Don't you push my finger away any more.' If something like that had happened years ago before I got saved, I'd have smacked him. I hunted fights when I was in school."

Feinsilver contended that it was wrong for taxpayers to be footing the bill for this class, White said, and Jack reminded him that it was a self-supporting, community-outreach class. Even so, Feinsilver maintained, the use of the building, the equipment and electricity constituted an improper use of tax money.

Would it be improper if a class co-sponsored by a local NAACP group used the building for a course on African-American history or the civil rights movement? Jack asked. That would be different, White recalled Feinsilver saying, because what they taught would be correct, but what was being taught in this class wasn't.

Jack and White could see no point in continuing the conversation. Feinsilver's intent was clear to both.

"You're going to make some kind of racial thing out of this," White told him.

"You're trying to make us out to be just like the KKK," he remembered Jack saying.

By the time Jack and White got back to the classroom, Rick McCaslin had taken the students through the major battles of 1863 and 1864 and soon would be coming up on Robert E. Lee's surrender at Appomattox.

At Feinsilver's request, three female students remained after class so he could question them. They were the two former teachers, Dedra Routh and Hope Haywood, and Joan King, who attended with her son.

During the break, Feinsilver had spoken to two male students, Hal Surratt, an accountant from Archdale whose great, great, great aunt, Mary Surratt, was hanged for conspiracy in the assassination of Abraham Lincoln, and Johnny Branch, a new member of the SCV.

Branch recalled Feinsilver asking if he thought that Jack was qualified to teach about the Civil War. He responded that Jack was a wonderful teacher who backed up everything with documented facts. Branch balked when Feinsilver asked about slavery. "He seemed to want to lead you into some controversy," Branch said. "I told him he couldn't get anything out of me because there was nothing controversial about it."

Surratt's conversation with Feinsilver was equally brief, perhaps, he thought, because his responses to Feinsilver's questions were not what he wanted to hear. He saw no problem with what had been taught about slavery, he told him, and did not think the class was biased. Surratt remained in the classroom out of curiosity as Feinsilver interviewed the three women.

Feinsilver's first question, they later remembered, was: "Do you disagree with anything you've been taught in this class?"

"I didn't answer," Haywood said, "because I was thinking, What's not to agree with?" She'd just sat through two hours of often moving stories of North Carolina soldiers as they fought through the major battles of the war. "How do you disagree with that?"

"I knew right from that first question that the man was trying to create a controversy," Routh recalled. "It was the way he asked it. I knew he was fishing for something, anything he could find to create what he wanted."

"Every question had to do with slavery," King recalled. "It was the only issue of the Civil War he wanted to talk about. It was like, aren't you upset that you're being taught all these things? Did you believe all this stuff, that blacks actually fought for the South, that slaves loved their masters? Nothing that we tried to say to him seemed to make any impression. We were trying to tell him how much we'd learned about the role of North Carolina in the war. It was like he would briefly listen to what you were saying, then go right back to the same thing. I didn't feel he was there to find out what the class was about. He had some kind of agenda. He certainly didn't want the information I was trying to convey to him. You just got really frustrated."

"He would just badger them," Hal Surratt said of Feinsilver's technique. "He wanted to hear something, and he would just push and push and twist what they said to try to get out of them what he wanted to hear."

"I could tell he had an agenda," Haywood recalled. "It was obvious the way he phrased his questions and the way he kept pushing. Dedra got really upset. I just said to myself, 'His mind is already made up. He really doesn't want to know what's going on in here. It doesn't matter what we say. I don't have time for this. I have a child at home who needs to get to bed.' I just got up and walked out."

Did taking this class make them feel better about being Southern? Rick McCaslin remembered Feinsilver asking.

That was just one of the questions that set Routh off.

"I got really angry," she said. "I was furious. I stood up and told him that I didn't appreciate these questions and the way he was asking them, that he was just trying to make something from nothing. I told him that we were here because we wanted to learn about North Carolina's role in the Civil War and about our ancestors, and that was all that this was about."

She gathered up her things and stormed out.

Soon after finishing his lecture, Rick McCaslin recalled, he introduced himself to Feinsilver and told him that if he had any questions, he'd be happy to answer them.

"He turned his back on me," McCaslin said.

Later, when McCaslin noticed how agitated Feinsilver was making the women, he walked over, offered his card and told Feinsilver that if he wanted to talk about any of this, to give him a call.

"He took it, looked at it, threw it onto the table and said, 'I'm real busy. I don't have time for that,'" McCaslin recalled. "I thought, strike two."

Not to be undone, McCaslin made another approach after the women left in anger. He told Feinsilver that he got over to Greensboro now and then, and if he'd like to get together for a cup of coffee and chat just let him know. His card, he pointed out, was there on the table.

Feinsilver's response, McCaslin said, was: "Didn't you hear me? I said I'm busy."

"I said to myself, 'Well, strike three,'" McCaslin recalled. "A jerk. I dismissed him from my mind. I thought he was just an annoyance."

Louise Canipe was in the classroom when Feinsilver began questioning her classmates, but she didn't hear what was being said because she was talking to others. She left and dawdled, talking, on the way to her car. Just as she was getting to the parking lot, she saw Dedra Routh emerging from the building and waited to ask what happened. Routh was in a fury, Canipe said, and told her about Feinsilver and his questions, including his contention that no blacks had fought for the South.

Canipe recently had attended an annual show for Civil War buffs in Greensboro where she stopped at a booth selling Confederate books and paraphernalia. She told the man in the booth about the class she was taking and how fascinated she had been to learn that Cherokees and blacks had fought for the Confederacy. The man offered her a sheaf of printouts from the Internet about Confederate blacks, much more information than Herman White had provided. She had the material in her pocketbook. She had intended to show it to Jack but hadn't gotten the opportunity. She now returned to the building to show the material to Feinsilver.

"He wouldn't take it," she said. "He wouldn't even look at it. And he wouldn't look at me. He never did look at me the whole time I was talking to him. He just kept saying, 'But did they really fight?'"

She finally gave up and left with the same frustration and anger that she had seen in Dedra Routh.

Ten

When Rhonda Winters, the director of the Archdale campus, arrived at work Friday morning, she found a message from the nighttime administrative assistant, Clara Barracato, saying that a reporter had shown up at the Civil War class the night before and upset several of the students. Winters had no doubt about who that reporter was. As if to confirm it, Louise Canipe soon called, still angry.

Had Feinsilver paid to attend the class? she wanted to know. What right did he have to invade their class, to question what they were being taught, and to upset the students? She was certain that whatever he wrote would not be truthful, and she thought that somebody should let his editors know about it.

Although she hadn't met Feinsilver, Winters was aware of his interviewing techniques. He had called her only days after the *News & Record* photographer had shown up at the third class.

"He said, 'How did you get permission to offer such a controversial course at a community college?'" she remembered. "I said, 'What are you talking about?'"

He was talking about the Civil War class, he said.

"Every question was a leading question," Winters recalled. "He was very antagonistic. He made me angry. I realized that was what he wanted, of course. He wanted me to say something that would make me look bad."

She told him, she said, that what was being taught was documented history from books and other published sources, and there was nothing controversial about it.

"I knew then that if he wrote an article, it was not going to be good," she said.

But weeks had passed and no article appeared. Neither had Feinsilver shown up again. Winters, like Jack, thought that he'd given up on the story and moved on to other things. Now she knew differently, and she called Cathy Hefferin, the college's director of public affairs, to alert her that a troublesome story could be in the works and to tell her what Feinsilver had done the night before.

Later, RCC President Larry Linker remembered that his first knowledge of the Civil War course came on this day. (Continuing education classes rarely drew his attention.) Hefferin told him that students were complaining about being harassed by a *News & Record* reporter.

"We can't have that," Linker told her. "Call his boss and say we love to cooperate but we can't tolerate that kind of thing."

Hefferin said she thought it would be a good idea to advise the editor to take a critical look at any story the reporter wrote before it was published, and Linker agreed.

She called Feinsilver's editor, Lex Alexander, and told him about the reporter's actions and the students' complaints. It seemed obvious to the students that he intended to write his own view of their class, she said, no matter what they told him. Alexander was non-committal, Hefferin recalled, but indicated that he would consider her suggestion to take a critical look at the story.

Rhonda Winters also called Alexander later that day to express her concern about Feinsilver's treatment of the students.

"I told him we didn't appreciate it," she recalled. "He wanted to know how he got them so upset, what exactly was he saying? I said, 'I don't know exactly. I do know he's trying to put words in their mouths.'"

Alexander, she recalled, defended Feinsilver, said he had a right to be there and a right to write about the class.

"Then he got to questioning me," Winters said. "Exactly what *was* this class?"

It was as if he thought the college was trying to hide something, she said. She hung up knowing that the newspaper was unlikely to rein in Feinsilver or to seriously question whatever he was about to write. (Alexander declined to be interviewed for this book.)

Louise Canipe called Winters shortly afterward to tell her that she had spent much of the day writing a letter of complaint to Alexander, and just had mailed it. She also sent him the sheaf of papers she'd tried to show Feinsilver.

Winters told her that she'd talked to Alexander and had learned that he was to be on vacation the following week. The letter wouldn't get there until Monday, and he would be gone. Canipe decided to call Alexander and read the letter to him.

"All the time I was reading it," she later recalled, "I could hear this click, click, click. I said, 'What are you doing? Are you typing?' He said, 'Well, I'm just making some notes.'"

In one paragraph, Canipe wrote: "I have been taking classes all my life and I have never attended a class where someone came in and questioned why we were having the class, what we were teaching, who 'these people are,' etc. I think your reporter is way out of line and he has shown me he is not interested in the truth...but only wanting something controversial to write about."

Canipe didn't get much hope from Alexander. "He wasn't too responsive," she recalled. "He said they were just reporting the news. He didn't pay too much attention to me."

On a copy of the letter that she mailed to Jack, Canipe scribbled that she'd read the letter to Alexander over the phone.

"Seems to be about like Ethan," she wrote.

Later, Canipe said that she had such a sense of foreboding about Feinsilver's intrusion into their class that she couldn't overcome it. "I just knew that something really bad was going to come from it," she said.

A few days after talking with Alexander, she had to go to Asheboro, and on the way back, she stopped at the Archdale Police Department. She spoke to Chief Larry Allen, told him all about Feinsilver and what was going on in their class, and asked if something couldn't be done to stop him.

"He told me the best thing was just not to talk to him," she recalled.

Jack was standing by the overhead projector on Thursday evening, November 12, when he saw Feinsilver ambling into the classroom. He was expecting him.

"I walked over to him and said, 'Ethan, have you been by the office?' He said he hadn't. I said, 'You're here looking for a controversy and we don't have one. You're not a member of this class, and if you want to sit in here, you're going to have to get permission from the office. He said, 'Okay, Okay.' And he got up and left."

Feinsilver did not go to the office, at least not immediately.

Rhonda Winters usually didn't remain on campus during evening classes, but she stayed this night to keep watch for Feinsilver. She did not know him, however, and wouldn't recognize him. The administrative offices were by the entrance of the main building, and as the 6:30 class time neared, Winters saw a man in the hallway who seemed to be lost.

"I went out and asked if I could help him," she recalled. "He said, 'I'm looking for that Civil War class.'"

Her curiosity got the better of her, she later said. "I said, 'Who are you?' He didn't seem to want to tell me at first. He finally said, 'I'm Richie Everette. I'm with the Randolph County NAACP. I'd like to attend that class.' I told him, 'That's fine. I just need to go ask the instructor.'"

That was standard procedure, she recalled telling him. She would do it for any request. They walked together to the classroom, and Everette waited at the door.

"I went in and told Jack, 'There's a guy out here from the NAACP who wants to sit in on the class.' He said, 'That's great. Tell him to come on in.' Then he said, 'No, wait, I'll come out and tell him.'"

Jack introduced himself to Everette and invited him to join the class. Everette asked how long it lasted. Two and a half hours, Jack told him, but there was a break halfway. "He said he'd have to leave at the break," Jack remembered, which Everette later confirmed. "I told him he was welcome for as long as he'd like to stay."

Richie Everette, who was forty-eight, was president of the Randolph NAACP chapter. He had grown up in Asheboro, one of five children of an AME Zion minister. A long-time member of the NAACP, Everette had sought a leadership position partly because he had political ambitions, partly because he was opposed to the NAACP's close relationship with the Democratic Party and hoped to change it from within.

A member of the Reform Party, a supporter of Ross Perot, Everette believed that many blacks were more conservative than the Democratic Party and were ill-served by the NAACP's unwavering devotion to it. He also opposed some NAACP positions. He believed, for example, that school vouchers, which the NAACP and Democrats rejected, were an advantage to black families. He lived in vastly white rural Randolph County, and his seven-year-old daughter, who already was on her way to becoming a master gymnast, was home-schooled. But if vouchers were available he would have chosen a private school for her. He also thought that the NAACP's campaign against the Confederate battle flag and other Confederate symbols was a waste of energy and resources that should be applied to more important problems. "I don't care what kind of flag you fly," he said later. "I'm not going to let a symbol get inside my head."

Everette had become first vice-president of the Randolph County chapter three years earlier, and had risen to the top office a few months later when the newly elected president resigned. He recently had been elected to his own two-year term.

While making calls on Asheboro businesses seeking donations for the local chapter, he stopped at the *News & Record* and met Feinsilver, who told him that he wasn't authorized to make contributions and would have to talk with his bosses. Everette returned a couple of weeks later to learn that the newspaper declined even to offer a complimentary subscription.

While he was there, however, Feinsilver asked what he thought about the Civil War course at RCC. He didn't know about it, he said.

Feinsilver told him the classes were taught by Sons of Confederate Veterans, Everette recalled, showed him a course outline and a lesson plan highlighted throughout. Feinsilver indicated that he had talked with state NAACP officers in Greensboro, and Everette thought he'd better find out what was going on. That had brought him to the Archdale campus on this night, he said, although he was concerned that people might think he was attempting to draw attention to himself. His wife and others, he said, tried to talk him out of going.

From Feinsilver's description, Everette said he thought that the course could be espousing racial hatred. He even thought that he might be turned away.

After Jack welcomed him to the class, Everette took a seat beside Dedra Routh.

Jack didn't think that Everette's appearance was mere coincidence. If Everette really wanted to know what this course was about, surely he would have shown up well before the next-to-last class, he thought. Jack had little doubt that Everette was there because he told Feinsilver that no complaints had been made. Feinsilver either was making certain that one was about to be lodged, Jack thought, or was hoping that Everette would be turned way, or that some confrontation might ensue, giving Feinsilver instant controversy and purpose for his story.

Winters had no doubt why Everette had shown up either. She was back at the administrative offices, talking with Clara Barracato, when a tall young man stopped to ask if there was a campus spot where students regularly gathered. Barracato told him that the only place was the canteen. He thanked her and left.

"Rhonda, that was Ethan," Barracato said after he was out of hearing.

Winters knew that Feinsilver hadn't sought permission to visit a class, as rules required, and she was not going to let him get away with it again. (Not until later would she realize that this had been his way of making it appear that he had done so.) She followed and saw that he didn't go to the canteen but to Jack's class. He already had taken a seat when she got there. The class was underway, however, and she didn't want to disrupt it.

Dedra Routh saw Feinsilver come in. "I noticed him glance at Richie Everette like, "'Okay, What do you think?'" she recalled.

None of the students later doubted that Everette had come at Feinsilver's request. If his visit had been a surprise to Feinsilver, whose only interest in the course was racial, the students thought that he would make an eager attempt to interview him at the break, but he didn't.

Mike Grader moved to High Point from Indiana to become administrator of a medical group. A low-keyed, soft-spoken man, he grew up in Texas and majored in history in college, with European and Far Eastern history his main interests. His master's degree, however, was in health care management.

Grader's forebears were from Mississippi, where his mother was born, and about five years earlier, he had learned that his great, great grandfather, John McCraney, had served in the Civil War. On a family visit to the Shiloh Battlefield in Tennessee, he typed McCraney's name into a computer database, and up popped information that he had fought as a private in the 6th Mississippi Infantry, which suffered sixty per cent casualties there. That piqued Grader's interest.

History was recreation for Grader, and he wanted to be involved in a group that allowed him to continue to learn. He had found that group earlier in the year when he joined the Frazier Camp. "If it was just a bunch of rebel rousing, I wouldn't be there," he said. He was impressed with the camp's monthly programs on the war and its efforts to encourage area students to become interested in history. He also was impressed with Jack.

"Jack was the reason I got as involved as much as I did in the SCV," he remembered. "Jack was one of those people who was so enthusiastic about what he believed in, and so knowledgeable. He led by example. He had a knack for pulling people into involvement without being brassy about it. In a nice way, he would ask what you could do, and whatever it was was good enough."

When the RCC class came up, Jack didn't even have to ask Grader.

"I said, 'Jack, if you need help, I'll do something,'" Grader recalled.

The next thing he knew, he said, he was scheduled to lecture about one of the most controversial generals in the war, William Tecumseh Sherman, who negotiated the final surrender of Confederate troops in North Carolina. Although he knew little about Sherman, Grader had a personal connection to him. His great, great grandfather not only fought against his troops at Shiloh and Vicksburg but had been with the forces that were pushed ahead of Sherman's army during its entire march through the South.

Grader spent weeks reading about Sherman, and brought all of his books to class in a cardboard box, the pages bristling with markers.

Sherman was determined to make South Carolina pay a harsh price because it had been a firebrand state, first to secede, first to fire on federal forces at Ft. Sumter, Grader told the class, and he left Columbia, the state capital, in ashes before moving on to North Carolina, although the source of the fires remained in dispute.

Soon after Grader began his lecture, Richie Everette passed a note to Dedra Routh asking what she thought of the class and what they did in it.

"I whispered to him how much I enjoyed it," she recalled.

Tree tops flashed with fire as Sherman's men entered North Carolina, marching through the turpentine-producing pine forests, a four-mile-high column of smoke blotting out the sun. Someone later described it as walking through a burning cathedral, Grader said, and Sherman himself called it "the damnedest marching I ever saw."

Sherman had expected to be more warmly received in North Carolina because of the state's pro-Union sentiment, and he encountered no resistance until after he seized Fayetteville and divided his troops into two columns to move northward on Goldsboro, a railroad center that harbored supplies his men needed.

As he entered the state, Sherman learned that his old antagonist, General Joseph E. Johnston, commander of the Army of Tennessee, had taken charge of the remaining Confederate troops in North Carolina, which numbered only about half of his own forces. Still, he became more cautious.

Johnston hit Sherman's left flank south of the village of Bentonville in a three-day fight that claimed nearly 5,000 men. It was the war's last great battle, and Grader described it in detail.

Three weeks later, on April 13, the mayor of Raleigh surrendered the state capital to Sherman's men without resistance.

By this time, Jefferson Davis and his cabinet had fled to Greensboro, where Davis was sleeping in a boxcar and dreaming of fighting on, perhaps in guerrilla bands if necessary. But Johnston met Sherman in a farmer's log cabin near Durham's Station to begin discussing surrender terms. Grader described their first meeting before Jack requested a break.

During the break, Richie Everette approached Jack in the hallway and said that he'd like to take the entire course.

"I told him we'd be happy to have him and I'd even let him know if it was offered again," Jack said.

Everette then expressed curiosity about the Sons of Confederate Veterans.

"He asked me, 'How do you get to be a member of this group?'" Jack recalled. "I told him you just have to be a male over the age of twelve with an ancestor who served with Confederate forces. He said, 'Some of us black folks have a hard time finding those.'"

That might not be as difficult as he imagined, Jack recalled telling him. How far back did he know of his ancestry? He knew of one relative going back to the 1800s, Jack remembered him saying.

Jack had a brochure on tracing Confederate ancestors. He went back into the classroom to get it, gave it to Everette and offered to help him find an ancestor who had served with Confederate forces. If they couldn't find one, the SCV also had honorary memberships, he remembered telling Everette, and he'd be happy to grant one.

"He said he'd have to think about that," Jack said. "We shook hands and he left. He and I didn't seem to have any problems."

Everette later agreed that Jack's memory was mostly accurate, although he didn't recall Jack offering an honorary membership. But it was possible, he said, that he did.

And while he had not felt unwelcome or threatened at the class and heard nothing indicating hatred or anything that was racially offensive, he said, he wondered whether the history being presented was authentic, although he didn't have the knowledge to discern that.

"What I told people unofficially," he said later, "was that I felt like the course was what is commonly known as hidden racism."

Rhonda Winters had stationed herself outside the class as break time neared to make certain that Feinsilver didn't slip past her. She eavesdropped as Jack and Everette talked, and recalled that Jack did offer Everette an honorary membership.

After Everette departed, Winters searched out Feinsilver in the classroom.

"I went over to him and said, 'Are you a visitor in this class?' He said he was a journalist with the *News & Record*. I said, 'I don't care what you are. All visitors have to report to the office for security reasons. He said, 'Jack knows I'm here.' I said '*I* didn't know you were here.'"

This was the third time he had come into this class without permission, she recalled telling him, and he would have to pay tuition if he wanted to stay and continue coming. Being a reporter didn't make him different from anybody else.

During the second half of the class, Grader talked in depth about the negotiations between Sherman, Johnston and Confederate Secretary of War John C. Breckinridge, describing how Sherman granted such lenient terms that he later would be relieved of command and threatened with charges of treason.

As the class time neared its end, Grader admitted that he had known little about Sherman when he agreed to teach about him.

"I probably know more about Sherman now than anybody should be allowed to," he said. "I'm almost convinced that if I met Sherman, I'd probably like the guy, and that's quite a concession from me."

He went on to tell of his own great, great grandfather's odyssey ahead of Sherman's army, and how he ended up fighting at Bentonville. It was ironic that he and John McCraney should end up in North Carolina, Grader said, because McCraney's own great grandfather had come to this country from Scotland in 1735, landing at Cape Fear, and settling in southeastern North Carolina, only to have his descendants move south and west. After he moved to the state three years earlier, Grader said, he'd been amazed to learn that McCraney had been mustered out of the Confederate Army only a few miles from his house north of High Point, given a Mexican silver dollar, and left to make his own way back home to Mississippi. He was one of only eight men to survive the war from his original unit of 900. The class chuckled when Grader said that he was pretty sure that McCraney had used up all the family's luck for generations to come.

"Anybody got any Sherman stories?" Grader asked, opening the class to discussion and questions.

A couple did have stories passed down by family. More had questions. Grader had mentioned earlier that Greensboro, a town of only 1,000 at the beginning of the war, was swollen by nearly 100,000 people by the end of April, 1865—Confederate troops waiting to be mustered out, the wounded from Bentonville, occupying Federal forces, and refugees of one sort and another. But that was to be the topic of the final class the following week.

In anticipation of that, Grader recommended a book called *Confederate Guns Were Stacked at Greensboro* by Ethel Stephens Arnett, available at the High Point Library. Jack spoke up to give an assessment of the book. It was long out of print, he said, difficult to find, and valued at about $250 for a copy in fine condition.

"I had one," he said, "and it disappeared. A reporter borrowed it. From the Greensboro *News & Record*. Left town with it and has never come back. I'm not lending Ethan anything."

The class laughed.

"Anybody else got any questions for Mike?"

Nobody did.

"Somebody didn't sign the roll," Jack said, looking it over. "I got one, two, three..."

He counted to ten, then counted again. "No, I've got 'em. Ethan was messing up the count."

This brought more laughter.

All of the students had carefully avoided Feinsilver this evening, not even speaking to him.

"I thought you were going to sign up for this class, Ethan," Jack said. "We don't allow but two visits free."

"She came and told me that," Feinsilver said, referring to Rhonda Winters conversation with him during the break.

"Did you pay your tuition? We need the money for the essay contest."

The class laughed again.

"I told her, 'That's fine, tell me what the charge is and I'll get it to you.' Then she walked out."

"She probably went to make you a bill," Jack said to more laughter.

Feinsilver never paid the tuition. There would be no need for that.

Part III

Civil Wrongs

> *A lie travels around the world while Truth is pulling on her boots.*
> **—Charles Spurgeon**

Eleven

Jack was like an alarm clock, Annie Laura joked. He went off at six every morning and climbed immediately out of bed, ready to face the day. He went straight to the coffee maker, poured his first cup, fixed a cup for her and delivered it with a good-morning kiss.

Then, cup in hand, he and Lady, the gentle, eight-year-old Doberman pinscher who slept at the foot of their bed, walked up the tree-lined driveway to fetch the High Point and Greensboro newspapers. Jack always returned to the basement den and plopped into his blue recliner to read the papers, Lady settling at his feet. Annie Laura, who liked to linger in bed, would come down a little later, take her place on the end of the sofa and pick up whichever newspaper Jack wasn't reading.

Jack followed the same ritual on Sunday, November 15, but this time when he opened the *News & Record*, he saw himself prominently displayed in his Confederate uniform, staring balefully into the distance on the front of the local news section. Above that photo was another, much larger, also in color. The battle flag, stretched full in the wind, dominated a third of it. Tuck Barber stood beside the flag, his back to the camera, and Jay Callaham, another of the re-enactors who helped with the third class, knelt on one knee demonstrating field gear to the students. Above this photo was a headline: *Studying The Confederacy In Randolph County*.

A much bigger headline topped the article that began alongside the photo of Jack: *Course reopens war's old wounds*. Beneath that was a subhead: *A Civil War course with a pro-Confederate slant angers black leaders and is part of larger clash between Southern heritage and civil rights groups*.

The article under Ethan Feinsilver's byline was datelined Archdale. These were the first two paragraphs:

A course at Randolph Community College teaches that most black people were happy under slavery and that tens of thousands of black men fought for the Confederacy because they believed in the Southern cause.

Southern history experts are calling the teaching 'pseudo-history' and pro-Confederate 'propaganda.' Civil rights leaders are calling it offensive, and the state NAACP and state committee of the U.S. Commission on Civil Rights say they may lodge formal complaints against the college after they review the course curriculum.

Later, Annie Laura wouldn't be able to recall exactly what Jack said after reading the article. She remembered his reaction being "more of disgust than anger." At the time, he didn't anticipate all the turmoil that the article soon would set swirling about him. He waited a couple of hours before calling Rahlo Fowler.

"Have you read the Greensboro paper this morning?" he asked his friend.

"No, I don't take it," Fowler said.

"Better go get one," Jack told him. "Ethan has really done a number on us."

Rhonda Winters' husband, Marlon, head of the School of Business at High Point University, brought in the *News & Record* at their rural home in the Jackson Creek community of Randolph County west of Asheboro. He handed the local section to his wife without comment.

"As soon as I saw it," she recalled, "I just thought, *Oh no.*"

But as she read it, anger took hold. By the time she had finished, she hardly could contain herself. "I was livid I was so angry," she said. "I knew we were in for it. I knew that Monday was going to be bad."

Dedra Routh knew that Feinsilver's story was coming. He had called to her home near Gray's Chapel, east of Asheboro, Friday night wanting to ask more questions, and she refused to answer. He told her his story would be published Sunday. "And you're not going to like what you read," she recalled him saying.

Dan Routh went out to pick up the paper from his driveway Sunday morning. He began reading the article as he walked back to the house. "Is this what they were teaching?" he asked his wife, handing her the paper.

She didn't even get through the first paragraph before she shouted, "No!"

"It was unreal," she recalled of reading the article that morning, "total disbelief. The more I read, the angrier I got. I was just incredibly angry."

Near the end, she came upon a quote attributed to herself. "I didn't say that!" she told her husband. "It's lies! It's all just lies! How can a newspaper do that?"

In his reporting, Feinsilver employed an old and cheap journalistic trick: seize upon a sensational tidbit, call people who are certain to disagree with it, or be enraged by it, and get their reactions—an easy formula for controversy.

The information in his opening paragraph was unattributed. The reader had no hint of who had taught this, when or how, and videotapes of the classes show that it never happened.

Moreover, the false information appeared to be deliberately provocative. Many African-Americans deeply resent the notion that slaves in the South were happy, an image that endured, in some part, due to popular books and movies such as *Gone with the Wind*.

The remainder of the article was replete with factual errors. Among them were the name of the course, the number of classes, the number of students. The last name of Tony Horwitz was misspelled throughout. Horwitz was author of *Confederates in the Attic*, a popular book about obsessive interest in the Civil War in the South that had come out earlier that year.

In the third paragraph, Feinsilver said that the college stood behind the class and quoted Cathy Hefferin, the public relations director, calling the course's content "factual historical material." Hefferin had spoken to Feinsilver only once, on October 5, four days after the third class and ten days before the class on the role of blacks and native Americans in the war, and he didn't ask about content, she said, of which she knew nothing.

In the fourth paragraph, Feinsilver wrote that teachers and students said they were "removing a taint of racism that in the last 30 years has made teaching about the Confederacy one-sided and simplistic." Lecturers and students who spoke to Feinsilver say they told him no such thing.

In the fifth paragraph, Feinsilver wrote that unnamed "academics and observers of Southern culture" saw "the dispute as typical of the clashes sweeping through the South as civil rights and Confederate heritage groups square off over the memory of the Civil War." The class, however, had been in dispute with no one but Feinsilver, and had clashed with no one but Feinsilver. It would become part of a bigger picture only because Feinsilver and the *News & Record* made it so with this article.

Feinsilver wrote that the course was taught by High Point-area SCV members. Only three of Jack's guest lecturers—Rahlo Leonard, Herman White, and Mike Grader—were SCV members. Darla Barber, Bob White, Bob Zeller, and Rick McCaslin were not.

Among the things students had learned, Feinsilver wrote, was "how Union General William Tecumseh Sherman let his troops plunder North Carolina homes, and how none of the Union generals was half the leader that Confederate General Robert E. Lee was."

The videotape shows that Mike Grader, who taught the class on Sherman, made no mention of Sherman's troops plundering North Carolina homes. Tapes also show that neither Jack nor any lecturer made the claim that none of the Union generals was half the leader that Lee was, nor does that appear in any of the materials used in the course.

Feinsilver wrote that the organizers of the course got into "highly sensitive" territory in their attempt to "restore pride to their Confederate ancestors," as they described their intent.

The organizers were Rhonda Winters, who proposed the course, and Jack, who prepared the curriculum and lined up the guest lecturers. In his introduction, Jack wrote, "I am proud of my Southern heritage....I hope by working together we can instill that same pride in Southern students and a sense of understanding in other students." But Jack and Winters said that they never stated that the intent of the course was to restore pride in Confederate ancestors. The only intent, said Winters, was to teach North Carolina's role in the war.

Feinsilver claimed that the course taught that the war "was not fought over slavery but over the right of Southerners to self-determination."

Tapes show that wasn't so. Jack taught that the war had many causes leading back many years; that slavery played a bigger part in some areas of the South than in others; that North Carolina did not secede because of slavery; that most North Carolinians thought themselves to be fighting in defense of their homes and their right to government of their choice, not in defense of slavery; and that, contrary to current popular view, the North did not begin the war on a moral crusade to end slavery, but to preserve the Union.

Feinsilver wrote that the instructors "extrapolate from a 1930s series of interviews with ex-slaves that 70 percent of slaves were satisfied with their lives in captivity."

The videotapes show that no instructor extrapolated anything from the slave narratives. Only a single brief mention of the narratives was made. That was by Herman White, who cited a study by a Louisiana minister of the narratives from four states of the seventeen in which interviews were conducted. The study concluded that more than seventy percent of the ex-slaves in those states had "only good experiences" to report about their lives under slavery. White mentioned the study as an indication that slaves were not widely brutalized by their owners, as Northern abolitionists maintained, and extrapolated nothing from it about slaves being satisfied in captivity.

White included a paragraph about the study in his lesson plan, and it was that on which Feinsilver, who didn't attend the class, based his claims that students had been taught that "most black people were happy under slavery" and that "70 percent of slaves were satisfied with their lives in captivity." The paragraph, however, included no such conclusions.

Feinsilver went on to write that instructors "use diary accounts from Northern officers, among other sources, to teach that as many as 38,000 black people fought in the Confederate Army."

Only one lecturer, White, dealt with blacks serving in Confederate forces, and the videotape shows that he claimed no numbers and used three period sources, all included in his lesson plan, to show that blacks fought for the South. None was a diary account from a Northern officer.

The only time he mentioned a number, White said, was when Feinsilver interviewed him and Jack on the night of Rick McCaslin's class. They kept telling Feinsilver that there was no way of knowing how many blacks had served with Confederate forces, and he asked what was the largest number they had heard. Their responses were the source for Feinsilver claiming the course taught that "tens of thousands of black men fought for the Confederacy because they believed in the Southern cause."

Feinsilver wrote that among the experts contending that the course's teachings were invalid was one whom instructors claimed to be in support of their views, historian Loren Schweninger. But the videotapes show that the only mention of Schweninger was by White, who recommended his book on black property owners as the best on the subject and made no claim that he supported any view presented in the class.

Later, Schweninger said that he couldn't remember for certain, but he seemed to recall that Feinsilver told him the class was teaching that most blacks were happy under slavery and that tens of thousands had fought for the South because they believed in its cause, and he was asked for his response to that. If that was being taught, he told him, it wasn't valid.

Feinsilver went on to quote University of North Carolina at Chapel Hill professor William Barney, whom he described as "the author of numerous books about the Civil War." Actually, Barney's specialty was the antebellum South, and he had written two books about secession, another about the period of 1848-1877, and a fourth examining how the South held out for so long against the more powerful North.

"It's not that the North was all right and the South was all wrong," Barney was quoted. "But it's the height of absurdity to say that slavery was not the central issue."

Feinsilver wrote that Barney compared this to neo-Nazis teaching that the Holocaust never happened.

Later, Barney said by e-mail that he no longer could recall specifics of what Feinsilver told him, "but I certainly didn't have the sense then or now that I was misled in any fundamental way."

The tapes show that neither Jack, nor any lecturer, taught that slavery was not the central issue. In addition to teaching that slavery as an issue varied in importance in different Southern states and was especially strong in the deep South, Jack also taught that the question of whether slavery would be allowed in new states and territories was a major issue leading to the war, as was the failure of northern states to enforce the fugitive slave act and Article IV, section 2, of the U.S. Constitution.

Feinsilver wrote that author Tony Horwitz called the course's teachings "historical fiction."

In an e-mail from Australia, where he was living at the time, Horwitz, a former reporter for the *Wall Street Journal* and Pulitzer Prize winner, said that he only dimly recalled his conversation with Feinsilver, but that "the class he was writing about did sound as though it was a slavery apologist sort of thing."

"I do think it's historical fiction to suggest that slaves were happy and that slavery had nothing to do with the war—a still common Southern viewpoint," he said. "However, I also am not happy with the northern stereotype, that anyone who cherishes their rebel heritage is necessarily a closet klansman."

Yet, Horwitz, like others Feinsilver called, had no way of knowing what had been taught. For Feinsilver to use him to proclaim the teachings "historical fiction" was fiction as well.

Feinsilver also wrote that Horwitz said that some Confederate groups were using the language of civil rights to turn "political correctness on its head."

He went on to quote Jack: "African Americans celebrate Kwanzaa (which Feinsilver misspelled 'Kwaanza'), Native Americans hold powwows. Everybody can celebrate their culture but we can't."

What Jack actually said in his introduction was: "Much is made of the fact that we are a multicultural society. African Americans celebrate Kwanzaa, Native Americans hold powwows, and various other ethnic groups hold festivals celebrating their heritage. Why then are Southerners singled out with scorn for promoting their heritage?"

Many of the students had ancestors who fought for the South, Feinsilver wrote, and not only were they discovering a lot to be proud about but they were resentful that some of what they were learning "is almost forbidden in public discourse."

But the five students who talked to Feinsilver said they didn't tell him anything about being resentful, or that what they were learning was "almost forbidden in public discourse," nor did they say that they were finding a lot of which to be proud.

Feinsilver then quoted Dedra Routh: "Just because we're celebrating our Southern ancestors doesn't mean we're trying to condone slavery."

She said nothing about celebrating her ancestors, Routh said, and deeply resented the false quote because she thought it made her and other class members somehow seem to be secretly rejoicing in slavery.

Feinsilver reported that Johnny Branch said he was finding it fascinating "just to learn our side of the story."

"Like other students," Feinsilver wrote, "he believes what Perdue is teaching."

This implies that Branch, as well as the other students, believed that most blacks were happy in slavery, and that tens of thousands fought for the Confederacy because they believed in its cause, which, Branch said, was something he never heard in class, as did all the other students.

The errors, distortions, and fabrications in Feinsilver's article weren't limited to what he wrote. Errors of omission also were committed.

As public reaction soon would prove, the article gave the impression that this course was part of the college's regular curriculum, paid for with state funds, forced onto innocent young students.

Cathy Hefferin, RCC's public relations director, was especially resentful about that. In her single telephone conversation with Feinsilver, she said, he asked how the college could justify using tax money to pay Jack to teach what he was teaching.

She explained that adult continuing education courses fell into two categories. The college used state funds to pay instructors for career enhancement courses, such as computer science, but instructors in hobby and personal interest courses were paid by student fees. Yet, Feinsilver didn't include this, and she thought he did it deliberately for the effect he achieved.

He also excluded other information that would have given readers a fairer view.

He failed to note that the lecturers included an area university history professor, a retired college instructor and administrator, as well as a reporter from the *News & Record*.

And while Feinsilver quoted professors claiming Jack's teachings to be invalid and comparing them to the teachings of neo-Nazis claiming that the Holocaust never happened, he provided no information about Jack's background as historian, his long service on historical and genealogical boards, his preservation efforts, his research or writings, or his widely known reputation for honesty and integrity, leaving him to appear as just a neo-Confederate ideologue championing false history and espousing Southern pride. Neither did Feinsilver report that for many years, *News & Record* reporters had used Jack as a source for local and regional history, and that the newspaper never before had found reason to question his accuracy or truthfulness.

Feinsilver also quoted state NAACP president Skip Alston (Feinsilver called him chairman.) and Randolph County NAACP president Richie Everette in opposition to the class without mentioning that the NAACP had an agenda against the Sons of Confederate Veterans and that Everette, after hearing about the class from Feinsilver, had attended one of the class sessions, where he had been politely received, and, as Everette later told reporter Norman Hines of Asheboro's *Courier-Tribune*, found nothing offensive about what he saw and heard there.

Twelve

Jack's sister, Betsy Neese, an elementary school counselor who lived in Greensboro, not far from their childhood home, didn't read the newspaper Sunday morning. She was unaware of the article on her brother's course until a neighbor called after church and mentioned that she'd seen Jack's picture in the paper.

Betsy read the article and knew instinctively that it was false.

"I knew he hadn't taught that," she said. "Jack wouldn't do that."

She knew what a thorough researcher he was, what a stickler for accuracy, how honest he always had been. She knew, too, that this had to be troubling him deeply. His integrity, his word, his honor, his good name were extremely important to him and had been since childhood. She recognized that this article called those traits into question and realized that it no doubt would provoke an angry public reaction.

Betsy also knew that Jack wouldn't let anybody know how deeply distressing this was. "He would hold all that inside," she said, "and always did as a child."

Betsy had planned to visit Jack and Annie Laura this afternoon. She left a camera at their house earlier and told them she'd be coming to get it. But now she thought she'd better call first.

"Will it be safe for me to come over?" she asked her brother teasingly.

"Lady will keep everybody at bay," he said.

As Betsy expected, Jack had little to say about the article or how it was affecting him, but she could tell that it was bothering him. He did say that he didn't intend to respond, that an attempt to defend the course would indicate that it needed to be defended, and it didn't. Besides, he said, anything he said likely would be distorted, misreported, or blown out of proportion, only making matters worse.

•   •   •

Larry Linker had spent three days at a Chamber of Commerce conference at North Myrtle Beach. He drove home Sunday afternoon with no hint of what was about to befall him and the college of which he had been president for the past ten years.

At sixty-four, Linker was an outsized man in both stature and personality. He stood six-feet-six and had a genial, back-slapping, country-boy manner that served him well. He loved his job and was proud of his accomplishments.

Linker had indeed been a country boy, growing up in Cabarrus County, near the textile-manufacturing town of Concord, where his father owned a small farm. As a teen-ager, he had only two goals: to get out of high school and to buy himself a 1940 Ford coupe. As soon as he accomplished the first, he got a job as a spooler at Cannon Mills in Concord that paid a dollar an hour, enough to allow him to get that '40 Ford.

He was eighteen when at the mill he met the person he later would consider to be his guidance counselor, a wizened little man in a felt hat and overalls, who one day asked, "Boy, do you want to be doing this when you're my age?"

Linker soon enrolled at N.C. State College in Raleigh. Four years later, he became an agricultural vocation teacher in Ashe County, in the mountains of northwestern North Carolina. He continued his studies at nearby Appalachian State Teachers College winning his master's degree and becoming a school principal, before earning his Ed.D.

In 1963, the legislature authorized the creation of a technical junior college system, and Linker learned of a job opportunity at Randolph Industrial Education Center, which had opened in Asheboro in the fall of 1962 with seventy-five students, eight instructors and three staff members. Linker became the school's technology coordinator in July, 1963. Over the next thirty-five years, he wore many administrative titles as the school grew from a single building into a twenty-seven-acre campus with a branch in Archdale, nearly 2,000 curriculum students, more than 8,000 continuing education students, and a nationally known photography program that attracted students from all over the country. Linker had been named the institution's second president upon the retirement of M.K. Branson in 1988, the year the school became a community college.

"This school is my life," Linker was prone to say. He thought of the staff, faculty, and students as family, and devoted long hours to seeing that the college continued to grow and improve.

Tired when he arrived home from the conference, Linker didn't bother to read that day's newspapers. He drove to campus early the next morning with no hint that people all over the nation, and even in other countries, were reading and hearing that the college he loved was teaching its students that most of the South's slaves had been happy, because the Associated Press had transmitted Feinsilver's story throughout the world.

Linker, who often arrived on campus before his staff, had no idea that anything was out of the ordinary until he found his telephone answering machine overwhelmed with messages. The first had been left at 9:15 Sunday morning. It was from a woman who didn't give her name. "We were the most deplorable thing that ever happened," he said, describing it later. "We ought to be plowed under and planted in cotton."

The stream of angry and vitriolic messages quickly sent him in search of Sunday's *News & Record*.

Cathy Hefferin lived in Liberty in the northeastern part of Randolph County, about twenty miles from the Asheboro campus. A native of West Virginia, and a graduate of West Virginia University's School of Journalism, she had been a reporter at newspapers in her home state and North Carolina before becoming Randolph Community College's director of public affairs. She hadn't read Sunday's *News & Record* either, and didn't know what awaited when she arrived at work Monday morning.

As she entered the administration building at eight, she encountered Linker outside his office, Feinsilver's story in hand.

"Have you seen this?" he asked.

She took it to her office to read. The first paragraph convinced her that the college was facing an imminent public relations disaster, and she told that to Linker.

Both were angry that Feinsilver called nobody in the college administration to get a response to his claims. They were incredulous that the newspaper's editors allowed such provocative and inflammatory statements to appear without allowing them to confirm or refute them, especially after the call Hefferin made to Lex Alexander ten days earlier.

Linker saw through Feinsilver's technique of seizing on a sensational item and getting the responses he wanted, and he had serious doubts about the article's accuracy. So did Hefferin, especially after reading Feinsilver's false claim that she had defended the course as providing "factual historical material" when he hadn't even spoken to her about it. She also was disturbed that Feinsilver made the class appear to be part of the college's regular curriculum, after she made clear the difference between community service and curriculum courses.

But accurate or not, the article had appeared. And people believed it to be true. The ringing phones and Linker's answering machine were proof of that. Their immediate problem was to deal with that reality. And they had to act quickly.

"Can you write a statement?" Linker asked.

"I'll draft something," she said.

She returned to her office and wrote it hurriedly.

> Randolph Community College supports an open educational atmosphere where varying views may be presented that are not necessarily the views of the College.
>
> The course entitled "North Carolina History: Our Part in the War for Southern Independence" is a noncredit continuing education class that is a self-supporting community service class, which means it is completely supported by the fees charged, not by state tax dollars. It is not a required history course for any program at the College.
>
> Another example of a community service class that is offered at RCC is the "Creating Racial Unity" class that has been offered at the Asheboro Campus for several years, which strives to create genuine understanding and unity between races by offering a forum for open discussion.

Linker approved the statement, and they agreed that until they could learn more about what actually had been taught, it would be their only response. Linker said he would instruct other staff members to forward all news media calls to Hefferin's office.

Linker prided himself on answering his own phone, and while Hefferin was in his office, he took a call from a radio station and read the statement.

Later, Hefferin would think the statement had been too brief and inadequate and wish she had included more in it.

•　•　•

This day would come to seem almost surreal to Linker, Hefferin, and other staff members, and the whole week would turn out to be that way. Linker quickly learned that he couldn't answer his own telephone unless he wanted to spend his day dealing with angry callers, reporters and radio talk show hosts. He had taken several calls, including a congratulatory one from a South Carolina woman who said she had been planning to send her son to the Citadel in Charleston but after reading about the enlightened teaching at RCC she was now thinking of enrolling him there.

The phones rang so incessantly that Linker had to assign four people to handle them.

While Linker set about alerting key members of the college's board of trustees and officials at the community colleges system in Raleigh about what was happening, Hefferin began returning callback messages. Many were from radio talk shows from cities across the country, whose hosts had seized on the "happy slaves" story as their topic of the day. Most wanted to put Jack or Linker on the air. Hefferin could offer only the college's statement. She and her assistant, Joyce Wolford, faxed it as fast as they could put it through the machine.

At mid-morning, Feinsilver called wanting to know who had given final approval for the course. Hefferin was wary and took notes. She was sure somebody had, she told him, but didn't know who and would try to find out. Feinsilver also wanted to know which major media outlets had been calling, and Hefferin named some of the bigger ones. She also told him that she didn't say what he attributed to her.

"He said, 'Well maybe I got you mixed up with Rhonda,'" she recalled.

Before this day was out, Hefferin would talk to many more reporters and to producers of all the major network TV morning shows, plus many cable network shows. Most of the TV producers wanted to pit the instructors in debate with NAACP officials or other civil rights leaders. The BBC telephoned, as did ABC's "Nightline." These calls only added to the surreal nature of the developing events. Could Ted Koppel actually find nothing more important to be concerned about than what eleven willing adults were learning in a community service Civil War class in Randolph County?

The Asheboro campus was not the only place feeling the effects of Feinsilver's article Monday. Rhonda Winters headed to work still angry about the story, preparing for the inevitable calls from bosses seeking explanations. She arrived to learn that the Associated Press had spread the story worldwide, making the situation even worse than she imagined. Phones were ringing without letup.

"That first day was just really, really bad," she recalled. "We couldn't do anything for answering the phones. Some of the calls were just really ugly, telling us what low-down, awful, horrible people we were."

Never before had she faced anything like this. "Really, I think, we were in shock, not knowing how to respond or what to do."

Reporters, radio talk show hosts and TV producers were calling as well. Winters' administrative assistant, Carol Nunn, took the brunt of the calls. Feinsilver was among the callers, too. He wanted to speak to Winters, but Nunn said that she wasn't available.

"I probably wouldn't have said anything nice to him," Winters said. "And I didn't want to give him anything else that he could print."

Later she couldn't clearly recall much of this day, except for how frantic and miserable it was. She remembered talking to Jack, who was adamant that nobody had taught that slaves were happy. She remembered a conference call late in the morning with Linker in which she emphasized Feinsilver's treatment of the students and expressed her belief that his story had no relationship to the reality of the course. And she remembered her relief when the day finally drew to a close, although she was certain that the troubles Feinsilver had brought upon them were just beginning.

Jack began the day unaware that the Associated Press had spread his name throughout the world, but he quickly realized what had happened when calls began coming from around the country. He screened them with his answering machine.

A TV crew showed up at his door, and after politely telling them that he had nothing to say, he quit responding to the bell.

He spoke several times during the day with Rahlo Fowler, telling him he had no intention of playing into the media's hands and offering himself for sacrifice. He would answer no questions, grant no interviews. His plan was to wait until all the hullabaloo died down, then prepare a reasoned and detailed written response to all the falsehoods and inaccuracies in Feinsilver's article. Fowler agreed with that strategy.

Jack also related his plan to Herman White, who disagreed with it, believing that Feinsilver's lies should be answered immediately. Jack told him that he was free to do as he saw fit, and White's respect for

Jack caused him to hold back, too.

Jack did take a call from Larry Linker, the first time he had spoken with him. Linker wanted to know if he or any other lecturer had taught that slaves were happy, and Jack assured him that never happened.

Dedra Routh had been so upset about Feinsilver's article that her husband, Dan, called the *News & Record* Sunday afternoon to complain. He asked to speak with a high ranking editor and was told that none was present. On Monday morning, Routh called again. This time he got Ed Williams, the city editor.

Routh recalled telling him that Feinsilver's story was false, that his wife was in the course, that she had attended every class, had not heard what Feinsilver claimed, and had been misquoted by him.

Williams, said Routh, told him that the newspaper stood behind its story. "He just brushed me off," he said.

The *News & Record* was in a state of anxious and uncertain transition when Feinsilver's article appeared. Executive editor Pat Yack had resigned two months earlier, after being at the paper for less than five years, and many reporters and editors were worried about who the new editor might be.

Publisher Van King, who once had been a reporter, columnist and editor at the paper, had lured Yack away from the Eugene, Oregon, *Register-Guard*, but it was believed that he would hire from within this time. The two top candidates were thought to be metro editor Tom Corrigan, a newsroom survivor quick to test corporate winds and tack in new directions, and city editor Ed Williams, who had been promoted twice by Yack.

Neither prospect was pleasing to many in the newsroom. Some were especially fearful that Williams might get the job. Once one of the newspaper's better reporters and writers, Williams had become dreaded and despised as editor. Blunt and quick to belittle, he was considered a "control freak" and had alienated and enraged even the finer and more experienced reporters. A delegation of reporters went to King to express their concerns.

At the time Feinsilver's article appeared, Corrigan and Williams, both of whom declined to be interviewed for this book, were in a situation in which they needed to win King's favor while making certain that no newsroom disasters occurred before he made his decision. They didn't need a crisis that might call into question their editorial judgment and management skills.

Both were aware that King was impressed with Feinsilver's story. As people involved with the class were reading it in disbelief and anger Sunday morning, King read it, and, as he later stated publicly, told his wife, Jean, "This is going to be a big national story."

Dedra Routh felt that the newspaper had portrayed students and lecturers as racists. She was particularly concerned about what this might do to Jack. She called him Monday night. He picked up when he heard her voice.

She expressed her indignation about the article and told him she'd had a call from ABC News on her answering machine, although her number was unlisted. (Dan Routh called ABC demanding to know how they got his number; he was certain that Feinsilver gave it to them.) Jack apologized, saying he was sorry that she and other students were being bothered.

"I told him I was just so afraid this was going to hurt him," Routh recalled. "He said, 'No, it's not going to hurt me. Don't worry.'"

The *News & Record* was in a self-congratulatory mood Monday, some newsroom staffers later recalled. (Newsroom sources used in this book cannot be identified for fear of retribution.) Rarely did the paper have a story that moved on the national and international news services, or that got picked up by the *New York Times*, the *Washington Post, USA Today*, and most other major newspapers.

Feinsilver worked in the Greensboro newsroom on Monday instead of in his basement office in Asheboro. He basked in the congratulations of fellow reporters, editors and word that the publisher was especially pleased about his story, as he gathered information for a second-day assault on RCC and the course.

Thirteen

The *News & Record* promoted the RCC course to page one Tuesday morning and gave it an incendiary headline: *A firestorm of national media attention engulfs Randolph Community College as civil rights groups protest a course's claims about slavery.*

Feinsilver began this story with the attention his previous article received, saying now that the course taught that slaves were "mostly happy."

On Sunday, most blacks were happy in slavery. Now all were "mostly happy."

Feinsilver went on to report that unnamed "mainstream historians" claimed that no evidence existed to support the course's teachings and that the Anti-Defamation League supported an investigation by the U.S. Commission on Civil Rights.

When questioned about historical accuracy, college officials stood behind the course, he wrote.

But Feinsilver had spoken to only two officials, Rhonda Winters and Cathy Hefferin, and that was well before the class on blacks in the Confederacy. Both said he didn't mention anything about slavery or ask about accuracy. His published claims caught them by surprise.

Hefferin started reading this day's article in her car at a convenience store in Liberty, where she picked up the newspaper on her way to work. She was already angry by the time she reached this point. She soon would be fuming.

The college's statement, Hefferin now read, "appeared to downplay the course's significance."

Her attempt to dispel the perception that this was a curriculum course foisted onto innocent young students had been turned against her.

Like Feinsilver's earlier story, this one leaped from point to point with no apparent reason or sense of cohesion. He reported that the executive director of the state NAACP, George Allison, planned to meet later in the week with state community college system president Martin Lancaster (Feinsilver called him director.) to ask for data to back up the course's claims about slavery and black Confederate soldiers. This would be news to Lancaster, who at this time was on his way home from China and had not communicated with Allison.

Feinsilver named several of the major newspapers and TV networks that carried his story before recapping the errors, fabrications and distortions that appeared in his original report.

Mainstream historians, he wrote, without naming them, "dispute claims that black people were loyal to the Confederacy and happy in slavery." The happiness of slaves kept escalating. Now all, not most, were completely happy, not mostly happy, as they had been in the first paragraph.

The article jumped back to Hefferin's statement, saying that RCC "supports an open education (The statement said educational.) atmosphere where varying views may be presented that are not necessarily the views of this college."

Left unanswered, Feinsilver wrote, were questions about whether varying views were "equally legitimate" that had been raised by "academics at other Southern colleges."

Yet he cited none of those academics, and the two he quoted after the statement was issued didn't raise such questions.

Hefferin now read that she had said she didn't know if anyone at the college reviewed the curriculum before the course was offered. She hadn't said that, she knew, and she later verified it in her notes. She'd told Feinsilver that she was sure somebody had reviewed it, but she didn't know who and would have to find out.

Feinsilver now turned to two professors at the University of North Carolina at Chapel Hill, sociologist and author John Shelton Reed and historian Harry Watson, co-editors of the journal *Southern Cultures*, whom he quoted about identity politics and grievances.

Watson, Feinsilver wrote, saw the national media attention about the course "as pure shock 'that anybody is defending slavery in this day and age.'"

Watson later said that he made this statement based on information provided by Feinsilver. Yet, no lecturer defended slavery.

Feinsilver next quoted Dwight Pitcaithley, chief historian for the National Park Service. The course's goal of "uplifting of Confederate pride," he said, "is not just evoking Civil War images of *Gone With the Wind*. It's evoking 1950s images of water cannons and dogs.'"

Pitcaithley had no memory of speaking to Feinsilver or any other reporter about the course, although he recalled following the story in the press. After reading Feinsilver's articles later, he responded, "I still have no recollection of talking to a reporter about this or of making the statements attributed to me." It was possible he had talked to Feinsilver, he said, but the statement attributed to him "does not sound like something I would have said. My guess is that the reporter, while researching the subject, got me confused with someone else."

Whatever the case, Jack and his guest lecturers were being compared to Birmingham commissioner of public safety Eugene "Bull" Connor assaulting civil rights demonstrators, although no claim had been made, other than Feinsilver's, that the course's purpose was to uplift Confederate pride and neither the college, Jack, nor any of the lecturers or students saw it in that light. It also should be noted that the use of fire hoses and dogs against civil rights demonstrators came in the 1960s, not the '50s.

Feinsilver now revealed that Randolph County NAACP president Richie Everette attended the previous week's class and told Jack that he wanted to sign up for the entire course.

"I envision the SCV as their heritage being hate toward blacks and hate toward—quote—Yankees," Everette was quoted. "But if it's not, we need to sit down and they need to convince us this is not what they're saying."

No mention was made, though, that Everette had experienced no hatred and heard none expressed during the class.

Yet, without evidence, Feinsilver allowed Everette to portray the instructors as members of a hate group, although the SCV never promoted hatred, and Jack not only had publicly denounced hate groups and extremists in the past but also during the course.

When Hefferin talked with Linker about this morning's story both agreed that they should require Feinsilver to submit future questions in writing so they would have proof of their answers.

Hefferin told this to Feinsilver when he called later in the morning. "He seemed upset that we were requiring that, wanted to know why," she recalled. "I said, 'Because everything we've said so far has been misquoted.'"

Feinsilver soon faxed several questions to Linker: Who gave final approval to the course? Did all student fees go to the instructors? Had Linker looked into the course's content? What did he think of the claims about slavery and black Confederates? Had he talked to the instructors this week? Would the course be offered again?

Linker realized that newspaper stories that received great attention were more likely to win journalism prizes, and those that produced results had even better chances. He felt he knew the purpose of Feinsilver's first question, as well as his earlier question to Hefferin about the same thing. The newspaper thought it had established that the college had committed a great wrong and now it wanted somebody to pay for it with his or her job.

"They wanted me to give them somebody," he said later. "They wanted a scapegoat. I wasn't going to do that."

At 2:15 that afternoon, Hefferin faxed Linker's response to Feinsilver. He was preparing a comprehensive news statement, Linker said, and would try to cover his questions in it.

This day was no less hectic or frantic for college officials than the previous one. The normal activities of the administrative offices had ground to a halt as the staff attempted to deal with the crisis. Phones still rang relentlessly. Reporters, radio and TV producers continued to call, as did people with angry complaints or congratulations about the course, although calls commending the course were beginning to outnumber the negative.

Yet Linker knew that the crisis was not diminishing. It was growing, and it only could get worse. The last class was to be Thursday, and reporters were calling wanting to attend, requesting that cameras be allowed in the classroom. Would CNN go live with the last days of the Civil War in Greensboro and Randolph County as presented by Jack Perdue? Would Ted Koppel show up?

But before that, another matter had to be addressed. A call came from the office of Wyatt Kirk, chairman of the Department of Human Services and Development at A&T State University in Greensboro, a traditionally black institution that counted Jesse Jackson among its alumni, along with the students who organized the first Woolworth's sit-in. Kirk also was director of the state advisory committee of the U.S. Commission on Civil Rights.

This commission, an agency of the executive branch of the federal government with subpoena powers, was established in 1957 and charged with investigating complaints that citizens were being denied their right to vote or to equal protection under law. Each state had an advisory committee of thirteen unpaid members, which conducted hearings on matters forwarded to it by the national commission, as well as recommending issues for the national group to consider. The state committees were overseen by regional offices, North Carolina's in Atlanta.

What had attracted the committee to this course? Wyatt Kirk remembered that Feinsilver called and asked if he was aware of the Civil

War class at RCC and what it was teaching. He said that he wasn't. Feinsilver told him about blacks being happy as slaves and tens of thousands fighting for the Confederacy because they believed in its cause.

"How is the college letting this happen?" Kirk responded, and Feinsilver quoted that in his original article, in which he reported that the committee would be holding hearings on the class at its upcoming quarterly meeting in Greensboro.

But as Kirk recalled his first conversation with the reporter, Feinsilver asked if the committee planned to do anything about the course, and Kirk told him that nothing could be done unless somebody filed a complaint alleging a civil rights violation.

He heard no more, Kirk said, until Friday, November 13, two days before Feinsilver's first article appeared, the day after Richie Everette, the Randolph County NAACP president, attended the class. Then Everette called saying he wanted to file a complaint because the course was being sponsored by a group to which he was not allowed to belong. Soon afterward, Feinsilver called back to ask if the course would be on the agenda for the committee's next meeting and Kirk told him that it would.

Everette, who later changed his name to Rashidi Zalika to honor his African heritage, said that he did not remember calling Kirk, although it was possible that he did. He thought that the state NAACP office had made the complaint. If he did it, he said, it was on the instructions of the state office.

The hearing on the course was set to begin at one p.m. Wednesday at A&T, less than a day away when Wyatt's office called requesting that the college send a representative.

Linker asked Marcia Daniel, the vice president for educational programs, to attend. Daniel, who had grown up in Denton in nearby Davidson County, had worked for the community college system for more than twenty years but had been at RCC for only sixteen months. It was she who gave final approval to the course.

Later that day, Daniel called Richie Everette to see if he planned to attend the hearing. He did. No sense in taking two cars, Daniel told him. Would he like to ride with her? He accepted and they agreed to meet at the campus at noon.

Fourteen

When Jack led Lady up the driveway to fetch the newspapers Wednesday morning, he found that Feinsilver melodramatically portrayed him on the front page as a fugitive in hiding.

The article began:

> The world is at Jack Perdue's doorstep, waiting to
> hear his side of the story on his controversial Civil War class
> at Randolph Community College.
> But Perdue is not answering the bell.

Producers for "Nightline" and "The Today Show" had joined CBS News "in the hunt for Perdue," Feinsilver wrote.

He went on to report that NAACP officials stood ready to debate the course on the air but TV producers wouldn't allow it without Perdue.

Feinsilver quoted Patrick Griffin III, the commander-in-chief of Sons of Confederate Veterans, whom he called "Rick." Griffin liked to use controversies to tell the country his point of view, Feinsilver wrote, but he wouldn't criticize Jack "for keeping quiet."

Griffin, a contractor from Darnestown, Md., hadn't read about the course in the news. He didn't know about it until he started getting e-mails on Monday from SCV members around the country.

Griffin, who had become commander-in-chief in August for a two-year term, called Rahlo Fowler to find out what was going on. Fowler was state heritage officer, the person charged with investigating and attempting to remedy what were called "heritage violations"—a student sent home from school for wearing a battle flag pin on her dress; the city of Hickory refusing to allow the SCV insignia alongside those of other civic groups on the city's welcome signs. Fowler never had dealt with anything of this magnitude, involving the national and international media, a state college system, the U.S. Commission on Civil Rights, and broad issues of free speech and academic freedom. He welcomed Griffin's counsel and suggested that he call Jack.

Griffin and Jack talked at length about the course and how best to deal with the situation.

While Feinsilver's story this day again recapped the false information from his earlier articles, it also contained one subtle but significant change. No mention was made of slaves being happy. Now they were satisfied.

Only one new false claim appeared in this report. The college's statement two days earlier "did not address questions of historical accuracy or decisions about the relative value of different views," Feinsilver wrote, going on to say that attempts at clarifying these matters were unsuccessful. He had included no question, however, about "the relative value of different views" in those he faxed to Linker on Tuesday.

The *News & Record* also published its first letters to the editor about the course on this day. One, from S.A. Smith of Asheboro, asked:

> *How do I, as an educated and caring parent, ratio-*
> *nalize raising my child in a county where this kind of racist*
> *propaganda is not only tolerated but actually underwritten*
> *by the educational system and presented as a credit-earning*
> *course? How do I continue to send my child into a school*
> *system where the teacher who might be his teacher in the*
> *future actually considers this obscenity to be an appropriate*
> *choice for a continuing education course?*

Now the *News & Record* was allowing its readers to assail students in the course as racist.

When Jack got back to his recliner, he found the course mentioned in the *High Point Enterprise* for the first time. But not in a news report. The *Enterprise*, which competed for readership with the *News & Record*, hadn't carried the original AP story, nor had it generated any news reports of its own. But when Jack turned to the editorial page, he spot-. ted this headline over the lead editorial: *Local Civil War Course Teaches Dubious History*.

The editorial was based completely on Feinsilver's stories with no attempt by the author to seek information from other sources. It called the course "a Confederate heritage study," which it was not, said it was based on "hearsay" history, an assertion based on hearsay facts, and claimed it was creating "more tension than understanding," although the *News & Record* actually had created whatever tension existed, not the course.

"Under the guise of heritage studies," the editorial intoned, "instructors...are attempting to rewrite the history of this dark period of America's past."

Jack didn't miss the irony in that. Using false and misleading information and no other evidence, the editorial writer was accusing *him* of rewriting history.

This charge and Feinsilver's portrayal of him as a fugitive in hiding would cause Jack to rethink his decision to keep quiet until the ruckus died down.

Later on this morning, Jack got a call from Liz Bryant, his distant cousin in Virginia who helped with the family research. She hadn't known about the controversy until somebody told her that Jack's name had appeared in the *Roanoke Times* on Monday. After reading the article, she realized how upsetting it must be for him.

She and Jack always joked with each other, and she tried that when she called.

"I said, 'I want to speak to my celebrity cousin,'" she remembered. "He said, 'I'm not a celebrity.' He didn't even sound like Jack. He said, 'Liz, they're trying to crucify me.' I said, 'Tell me about it.' He said, 'It's too long a story to tell.'"

He did talk a little about it, though, and Bryant encouraged him to get a lawyer. He was thinking about that, he said.

It was his mood that concerned Bryant most.

"He told me, 'Liz, from all they're writing and saying about me, I'm afraid that one day you're going to say, 'I don't even know anybody named Jack Perdue.' I said, 'Jack, there is absolutely nothing that anybody could say about you that would ever make me say that.'"

Marcia Daniel and Richie Everette chatted about music and their jobs (Everette worked at the Goodyear Plant north of Asheboro.) as they rode together to the advisory board meeting of the civil rights commission in Greensboro. They spoke only briefly about the course, she telling him that she hoped he understood that no underlying motives were involved, that no racism had been intended, and that all the documentation she had seen supported that the class was taught from an historical standpoint.

Everette told her that he knew the college wouldn't knowingly allow racism or hatred to be taught.

The hearing was in a teaching auditorium in Hodgin Hall. The *News & Record* had published a "Want to Go?" box on page one with Feinsilver's story this morning, and about twenty-five people turned out, most of them black, some of them students, an unusually large turnout for the committee's regular meetings. Only seven of the thirteen committee members were present, six of them seated behind tables at the front of the auditorium. TV cameras lined one wall. Reporters, notebooks and pens in hands, were scattered through the audience.

Daniel expected to be only an observer, and her feeling was that Everette thought the same. But when they arrived, Kirk greeted them and asked their names.

"Oh, we've been waiting for you," he said, and led them to seats near the front. One person was already speaking, and when he finished, Kirk asked Daniel to introduce herself, state her position at the college and face the board's questions.

She was completely unprepared, and later only could remember thinking, *What has Larry Linker gotten me into?*

All of the board members clearly had read Feinsilver's articles and accepted them as factual. No questions were about civil rights violations, only the content of the course, the college's intent in offering it, the procedures for approving and screening it. The committee seemed confused about the difference between curriculum and community service courses, Daniel recalled, and she spent a lot of time trying to explain that. Many questions concerned the use of public money, despite Daniel's explanation that the course was supported by student fees.

The guidelines used for approving this course were the same, Daniel said, as those for other community outreach courses, such as the one on racial unity, a free class that the college had offered for years, and another taught by a local authority on angels, one of the most popular ever held at RCC. As for consideration of content in determining whether a class would be offered, she was no more qualified to speak to the history of the Civil War in North Carolina, she noted, than she was to confirm the existence of angels.

"Are we going to enter the theological debate are angels among us?" she asked. "I haven't met many this week."

Committee members asked Everette about racial relations in Randolph County, and he said that there were no serious problems. In speaking about the course, he told the board that he had attended part of one class, had been well received, had heard nothing offensive. His opposition to the course was that it was co-sponsored by Sons of Confederate Veterans, a group which he maintained was hostile to blacks, although he offered no evidence of that. "I think they should have to prove beyond the shadow of a doubt that they are not a hate group," he said.

The meeting was opened to anybody who wanted to speak, and many did. Joseph DiBona, a professor of education at Duke University for more than thirty years, had been on the committee for ten years and had served four years as chairman. He was struck by how angry and rancorous the speakers were, far more so than at any other committee meeting he could recall. DiBona believed that college classrooms should be open to all viewpoints, even the outrageous. "Some people think that's dangerous," he said later. "I don't share that view." But after seeing the speakers' anger and the passion with which his fellow committee members opposed this course, he would vote to send the matter to the national commission.

Among those who rose to speak were Greensboro's three most outspoken black leaders: Skip Alston, the state president of the NAACP and a Guilford County commissioner; Earl Jones, Alston's mentor and close friend, a member of the Greensboro City Council for twelve years, a broker of the city's solid, well-organized black vote (African-Americans made up thirty-seven percent of Greensboro's population.), who wielded great power in local politics (Jones would lose re-election in 2001 after being unable to account for funds in the federally-funded anti-poverty program he headed.); and Ervin Brisbon, a community activist often described in the press as a "firebrand," a volatile man with a reputation for disrupting public meetings and shouting down speakers. All three were notorious for branding as racist any group or individual who opposed them or found their disfavor. However, Brisbon, who had proclaimed that integration was a tool of white supremacist culture and the NAACP a spy group to control the black community, often was at odds with Alston and Jones. He was on this matter as well.

In 1989, Brisbon had campaigned unsuccessfully to have Greensboro's Civil War historic markers removed, claiming they were racist. He and a group of A&T students, with a TV crew in tow, disrupted an SCV meeting at Greensboro College, where a *High Point*

Enterprise writer was about to speak on an article he'd written about the war. Brisbon and his group left quickly after they were welcomed to join the proceedings and the TV crew departed.

On this day, however, Brisbon complained that the committee was wasting its time on the course and letting the media determine its agenda instead of focusing on serious civil rights matters, such as the death of a young black man, Daryl Howerton, who, nude, mumbling and lunging at passersby with a knife on a public street, had been shot by two Latino Greensboro police officers. "I don't care what that cracker teaches," Brisbon said of Jack.

Alston and Jones more than made up for Brisbon's lack of concern about the course in their attacks on the SCV and the college, and as usual Jones was the more vociferous of the two.

"Only through coercion or duress would a slave speak favorably about slavery," he proclaimed.

"It's a shame that an organization even exists that celebrates the carnage, rape and murder of the black people," he said of the SCV.

RCC was reflective of "white denial in America," Jones went on, and was trying to downplay this course because it was about race.

"If a course was taught at Randolph Community College entitled 'Why Women Enjoy Being Raped,' perhaps you could understand why this issue is so important," he lectured Daniel. "It's the same thing."

The whole point of the course, he claimed, was to allow whites to say that "slavery is not as bad as we thought, so we don't owe reparations, we don't need affirmative action." (Only this part of his comments would be reported by the *News & Record*.)

Later, Daniel recalled her frustration as she sat through this. She had lived her life with prejudice to none. She always reached out to people of other races, other backgrounds. She focused on black literature in college, got her master's degree in education at A&T. She worked to get blacks and students of other races into college and to encourage them to make it through.

"I just kept thinking what an unlikely soul I was to be stuck in the middle of that," she remembered.

At the end, Wyatt Kirk urged the committee to recommend a full commission forum on the course.

"If people are angry about this and upset about this, then it has to be addressed. We have to talk about the truth and what that means. Otherwise we are part of the propaganda."

The vote was six to one in favor of his suggestion.

• • •

All of RCC's previous encounters with news media had been positive and amicable—stories about the construction of a new building, the beginning of a new program, the launching of a fund-raising drive, the sponsorship of a community event. Neither Larry Linker nor Cathy Hefferin ever had faced adversarial or hostile reporters until Feinsilver came along. Neither ever had been confronted by an angry public response. By Wednesday, both were showing the strain from the previous two days, yet both knew that the situation only could grow worse.

Linker had begun to think that outside help, more experienced at dealing with such matters, was needed, and he broached that to Hefferin on Wednesday.

"Yes," she told him, "I would welcome help."

The person to whom Linker turned was Rick Amme, a local celebrity.

Amme, who had grown up a Navy brat, had become a popular reporter at WFMY-TV, Channel 2, in Greensboro in the 1970s. He later worked in Norfolk and St. Louis for four years, before returning to North Carolina to become news anchor at WXII, Channel 12, in Winston-Salem, for eleven years. In 1994, he started his own consulting firm. He called himself a crisis manager. If you were the head of a company or any other institution suddenly caught in a media onslaught and didn't know how to handle it, Amme was the person to call. His job, as he saw it, was to shield the organizations that hired him and to mend the damage to their reputations. He had some basic rules: act fast, get it over with, do the right thing, don't make it worse.

Linker had been impressed by a column Amme wrote for a regional business publication. And after talking with another college president who had employed him, he called to tell Amme about the situation in which he and RCC now found themselves. Amme asked that he fax him some of the news reports. Hefferin not only assembled news stories from area papers but did an Internet search of national coverage and faxed a stack of material to Amme later that day.

Amme was accustomed to clients who waited until they were so deep in the mire that they couldn't see their way out before they sought help, and this case seemed to be no different.

Early TV news was reporting Wednesday evening that the U.S. Commission on Civil Rights would be coming to hold a hearing on the course; Linker had received a call from Skip Alston that day and scheduled a meeting with him and other NAACP representatives for Thursday morning; and the final class was to be held Thursday evening. Yet no decisions had been made about dealing with any of it. National networks might even show up for the class, Amme discovered.

"When I heard that and saw how nasty the news coverage was, I called back that very night," he remembered. "I said, 'You've got to stop this now; you're bleeding.'"

Even as Amme talked to Linker Wednesday night, other events were developing.

Bob Buckley was one of many reporters who called Jack on Tuesday. He realized from the newspaper stories that Jack wasn't talking and probably wouldn't. But his pitch was different.

He had seen the deficiencies in Feinsilver's stories from the beginning. He considered the reporting to be "very sloppy" at best and doubted it was accurate.

A graduate of the University of Missouri School of Journalism, Buckley, who grew up in Chicago, had worked at TV stations in eastern North Carolina, Spokane, and Las Vegas before coming to WGHP, Channel 8, in High Point four years earlier. In the message he left for Jack, he expressed his doubts about Feinsilver's articles, adding that he would give a fair and honest hearing to anything Jack wanted to say.

When Buckley got to work early Wednesday afternoon, he was surprised to find a return call.

Jack conferred several times Wednesday with Rahlo Fowler and Patrick Griffin before returning Buckley's call. Annie Laura later said that Jack admired Buckley's reporting, thought him to be honest, and believed that he could be trusted to report truthfully what he had to say.

That was this: the claim in Feinsilver's stories that provoked all the volatile reaction was false; nobody taught that slaves were happy, and Feinsilver hadn't attended the class in which the role of blacks in the war was discussed, thus had no idea of what actually was taught.

Buckley tried to convince Jack to go on camera, but he demurred. The last class was scheduled for the following night and he didn't want to risk jeopardizing it. He also was working on a complete answer to Feinsilver's charges and would address all at one time, he said. Meanwhile, he would fax Buckley a statement, and Rahlo Fowler would come to the station for an on-camera interview.

Buckley arranged for the studio interview with Fowler, then called Loren Schweninger, the history professor at UNCG who had been quoted by Feinsilver that the course's teachings weren't valid. Schweninger agreed to an interview at his home in the early evening.

Buckley knew he had a hot story, and it was tentatively scheduled as the lead for the late news at 10:30.

It was after dark when Buckley and his photographer finished the interview with Schweninger and made the fifteen-minute drive back to High Point. Buckley then called the *News & Record* and asked to speak to Feinsilver. He didn't expect to get him, but Feinsilver answered.

"I started asking him about the story," Buckley remembered. "I said, 'Now you said this, where did you get that?' He began to panic. He said, 'Are you interviewing me?' I said, 'I'm asking where you got this.' He said, 'I can't be interviewed.' I said, 'What do you mean you can't be interviewed?' He said, 'I can't talk about this.' I said, 'Well, who can?' He said, 'You'll have to talk to my boss.'" (Feinsilver later said he was instructed not to talk to anybody about the course or his articles about it.)

Feinsilver told him that he would have his editor call, Buckley remembered. Buckley didn't know whether he'd get a callback or not, but he figured if he did, it would be right before his deadline. He knew that the newspaper's editors were aware of TV deadlines and that they were likely to call then so they could say what they had to say and get off without being questioned at length.

As Buckley remembered, that was what happened. Metro editor Tom Corrigan called just as he was getting ready to go on air. Buckley asked how Feinsilver got this story.

"He said he used normal reporting techniques," Buckley recalled. "I said, 'He wasn't in that class, was he?' He wouldn't answer."

Corrigan only would say that Feinsilver "took extensive notes and interviews outside the classroom."

"He kept saying, 'We stand behind our story,'" Buckley said. "He must've said that three or four times, and I believe at one point he said, 'We stand behind our reporter,' as well."

Minutes later, Buckley was on the air live, publicly raising questions for the first time about the accuracy of the *News & Record's* articles.

"We spoke with Jack Perdue at length today, though he said he couldn't talk to us on camera, he did send us this statement which he says explains how this went from being a class to being a controversy.

"And Perdue puts the blame squarely on the back of the author of an article in the Greensboro *News & Record*.

"Perdue says Ethan Feinsilver reported that Perdue's class teaches that most black people were happy under slavery and that the vast majority of black people were satisfied with their lives as slaves.

"No such statement was made in the course, writes Perdue, and he says Feinsilver wasn't even at the class on the nights he claims those statements were made.

"As for all the sudden attention..."

Rahlo Fowler appeared on screen saying, "I was amazed and shocked also."

"Rahlo Fowler is the heritage director of the Sons of Confederate Veterans who says his group abhors slavery as much as anyone."

"That institution was horrible, it wasn't or is not condoned by us," Fowler said.

"A few minutes ago," Buckley went on, "I spoke with Tom Corrigan, the metro editor at the *News & Record* who said he believes the story is accurate. He says Ethan Feinsilver got his information outside of class, from interviews with the instructors."

Only this morning the *News & Record* had portrayed Jack as hiding out, unwilling to talk, but now that he had spoken, the newspaper chose not to report it. Neither did any other news agency, no doubt unwilling to give attention to a competitor's scoop.

Fifteen

Although the state advisory committee only approved a resolution asking the U.S. Commission on Civil Rights to consider holding a hearing on the RCC course, which first had to be approved by the regional office in Atlanta, Feinsilver reported on the *News & Record*'s front page Thursday that the full commission definitely would conduct a hearing "within the next three weeks, possibly at the college."

When Larry Linker read this, he recalled thinking that if that was the commission's intention, it would be nice to have the courtesy of a call informing him, but he had heard from nobody, nor would he in weeks to come.

Feinsilver's claimed source for this information was Mary Frances Berry, chairperson of the commission, a lawyer and professor of American social thought and history at the University of Pennsylvania, with a reputation for leftist views and autocratic rule over the commission. Feinsilver wrote that while Berry declared the course's teachings inaccurate, the commission would not challenge the college's right to offer it.

"I think colleges have a right to behave in a stupid manner if they want to," Feinsilver quoted Berry. (Berry did not respond to requests for an interview for this book or to written questions submitted to her, and the accuracy of her quotes cannot be verified.)

The commission, Feinsilver said, would contrast the course's teachings with prevailing scholarship "to remove any credibility they might have gained through their connection with a state academic institution."

The course should be investigated, Feinsilver further quoted Berry, because its teachings could contribute to "a climate that may lead people to violate someone's civil rights."

The commission had power to subpoena witnesses, Feinsilver reported, but Berry didn't think that would be necessary.

"I expect Mr. Perdue and everybody we invite to cooperate."

Later, Jack said that he relished the prospect of appearing before the commission, but that he would insist on being subpoenaed. He liked the image of a U.S. citizen hauled before a federal board of inquisition for the crime of teaching history.

Feinsilver's proclivity for inaccuracy continued as he described the events of the advisory committee meeting the day before. He misspelled both of Marcia Daniel's names. He wrote that RCC had invoked "academic freedom" to defend the course's teachings, although nobody at the college had used that term or attempted any defense of the course's content, which the administration had not yet had time to investigate. Feinsilver wrote that Jack had not responded to scores of interview requests from national news organizations, but failed to mention that he had granted an interview to High Point TV reporter Bob Buckley in which he denied that anybody had taught that slaves were happy or satisfied and pointed out that Feinsilver hadn't attended the class in which he claimed that happened.

In its vote to request a full hearing on the course, the advisory committee "decided it would be better to bring different versions of history together and decide which is correct," Feinsilver wrote.

He quoted chairman Wyatt Kirk: "We're going to put to rest distortions and misperceptions."

Jack was not the only person involved with the course who wondered how the commission could conduct a fair hearing when its chairperson, with no knowledge of the course, already had determined that it was inaccurate and had declared the college "stupid" for offering it.

Later, when Jack could look back less passionately at the events of this week, he would marvel at the reactions and priorities of the news media. During this and coming weeks, he, the SCV, RCC, his lecturers, and even his students, repeatedly would be the targets of invective and name calling from newspaper columnists and editorial writers from all over the nation for teaching something that hadn't been taught. But not one columnist, editorial writer, or scholar would express any concern that an agency of the federal government was planning to determine a "correct" version of Civil War history. Nor would any columnist or editorial writer express any concern that a person or educational institution could become the object of investigation by a quasi-judicial federal agency for nothing more than speech that somebody might judge to contribute to "a climate that may lead people to violate someone's civil rights."

• • •

For the second day, Feinsilver's story made no mention of happy slaves, only the satisfied. Surely, after Bob Buckley's call Wednesday night, editors had asked Feinsilver whether he had attended the class in which he claimed students had been taught that slaves were happy, and they must have questioned him about that provocative allegation as well.

Later, Johnny Branch, one of the students in the course, wouldn't remember exactly which day he received a call at home from Feinsilver, but he knew it was in the week following the first article. He was reluctant to talk with him.

"I didn't like the guy," he said. "I felt he had stirred up this hornets nest by picking out one little thing in the course, not even attempting to report what all the class was about.

"This time he asked me about slaves being happy. He said, 'Don't you think they were teaching in that class that slaves were happy, and do you think that slaves were actually happy?'"

Branch said that wasn't so. He thought that Feinsilver was looking for confirmation for his false claim. He had his course materials at hand and read to him what White actually said about the survey of the slave narratives conducted in four Southern states.

"He said, 'Well, Johnny, you've got to realize, these white people were very uncomfortable talking to slaves and the slaves were lying to them,'" Branch remembered. (Not all of the writers conducting the slave interviews were white, incidentally. In Virginia, they were black.)

Clearly, after Buckley's call, if not earlier, Feinsilver acknowledged to editors that he hadn't attended the class in question, and either at that time, or shortly afterward, he also admitted that "happy" was *his* description, not a word that he knew to have been used by instructors in reference to slaves.

That single provocative word attached to slaves was the reason his story gained international attention and created such an angry reaction. But now that he had admitted that "happy" actually was his interpretation of what was taught, even though he hadn't heard the lecture, the newspaper's editors chose not to reveal that to readers. Neither did they notify the Associated Press or any of the many newspapers and other news outlets that had spread the "happy slaves" story so widely.

Instead, Feinsilver was instructed to stop using "happy" and use the instructors' terms.

In a written response, Feinsilver said that he understood the reason for the directive and already had ceased using "happy" because he saw that "some people could take my word out of context and make it harder to defend."

Still, he insisted that the word was a "fair and accurate paraphrase."

The instructors' "main point," he said, was that blacks in the South were happy being slaves, got along with their owners, didn't want to be freed, and fought for the Confederacy because they loved it.

"If you loved your company, didn't want to leave, had good relations with your boss and told an interviewer you had 'only good experiences' there, I would say you were happy at that job," he wrote.

Jack's and Herman White's denials were "back-pedaling" and "predictable," he said, and he wished they would stand behind their teachings "and have the historical debate they're always complaining no one will let them have."

Feinsilver was expressing concern about having his word taken out of context after basing the precept for his story on a single paragraph from a lesson plan that he took out of a context he could not have known from a lecture he never heard.

Instead of using "happy," he switched to "satisfied," and later to "content," although no instructor had used those words to describe blacks in slavery either.

Jack was more upset this morning about what he read in the *High Point Enterprise* than about Feinsilver's newest report. The *Enterprise* published its first news story about the class, a short item on Wednesday's hearing buried at the bottom of an inside page. In it, Jack read Earl Jones' description of the SCV as a group that "celebrates the carnage, rape and murder of the black people," a charge to which the *Enterprise* offered no countering information.

But even more disturbing was a column at the top of the editorial page by Leonard Pitts, a nationally syndicated African-American columnist for the *Miami Herald*, under the headline, *Sons of old sins tell new lies*.

Pitts wrote that all decent people should be outraged by the RCC course's "offensive thesis: that the overwhelming majority of blacks were happy in slavery."

"You look at the people pushing a fraudulent, morally bankrupt version of those horrific days and you wonder about them. Are they evil? Are they stupid? Or are they, like the slaveholders of old, merely embracing a delusion they must believe in order to continue believing in themselves?"

Pitts called the course's teachings "idiocy," and declared, "the

South's cause was slavery, pure and simple."

"The sons of the Confederacy prostitute truth for the benefit of disgraced forebears and a discredited system," he wrote. "They would desecrate sacred soil, stealing from dead slaves whatever little dignity remains."

Pitts did not use Jack's name, but Jack was all too aware that his name already had been widely published and broadcast as the course's instructor, and that he was well known in High Point and nearby communities and many readers of the *Enterprise* would know that it was he whom Pitts was claiming to be without honor, morally bankrupt, a liar promoting fraudulent history, desecrating sacred soil, stealing dignity from dead slaves. They would know that it was he about whom Pitts, without any knowledge of him or of what he actually had taught, was questioning if he were evil.

Later, Martin Lancaster, president of the North Carolina Community College System, couldn't recall whether he was in Beijing, Shanghai, or Hong Kong when he read in the *International Herald Tribune* that a North Carolina community college was teaching that most blacks in the South had been happy in slavery. Lancaster, a four-term former Democratic congressman and assistant secretary of the Army in the Clinton administration, was on a trade mission to China with Democratic Governor Jim Hunt. Later that day, he talked by telephone with Steve Scott, the college system's chief operating officer, who filled him in on the situation and told him that Larry Linker was keeping him informed of developments. Both recognized that this was a matter in which they could not involve themselves. Community service courses were controlled by each college individually. This was a problem for Linker and his board of trustees to resolve.

Lancaster arrived home on Tuesday, November 17. On the following day, he received a call from Democratic state senator Eleanor Kinnaird requesting a meeting to talk about the course. The meeting was set for eight-thirty Thursday morning, and Lancaster's schedule showed that it was to be with Kinnaird and a representative of the NAACP.

Conservative Randolph County was represented in the state legislature by two of the state's most liberal senators, Kinnaird of Carrboro and Howard Lee of Durham. This was because much of Randolph and three other small-population conservative counties were lumped in the sixteenth senatorial district with populous Orange County, where the state's seat of liberalism, Chapel Hill, home of the university, was to be found. Kinnaird, a former mayor of Carrboro, adjoining Chapel Hill, worked as a lawyer for North Carolina Prisoner Legal Services.

In a brief interview, Kinnaird said that she called Lancaster a day after reading about the RCC course. She did so, she said, because she knew from her own reading about the Civil War that the course was "presenting things that were not factual."

"Certainly the thrust was to emphasize something that was not factual."

Material presented in such a class "should be the result of research by historians," she maintained, and that was not the case with this class, which, she said, was "not appropriate for a community college."

She called George Allison, the state director of the NAACP, to talk about the course, she said, before requesting the appointment with Lancaster. While Allison was not a constituent, she said, she knew his sister, who was. She acknowledged that she did not call officials at RCC, or any of the students or instructors who were her constituents to learn their views. Asked why she hadn't, and how she knew what had been taught without talking with them, Kinnaird claimed that the questions were becoming adversarial and stopped the interview.

After talking with Allison, Kinnaird called the University of North Carolina and asked for the name of an authority on the history of North Carolina and the Civil War. She was given that of Harry Watson.

Watson, who grew up in Greensboro, was a professor of history, whose specialties were the antebellum South, Jacksonian America, and North Carolina history. He had published at least one book in each of those fields. He also was director of the Center for the Study of the American South, and co-editor of the journal *Southern Cultures*, known for his liberal views. Feinsilver had called him on Monday, February, 16, the day the AP version of his story appeared in the *News & Observer* of Raleigh and other area newspapers, and later quoted him about the media attention being "pure shock 'that anybody is defending slavery in this day and age.'"

Kinnaird asked him to accompany her as a supporting authority to her meeting with Lancaster, Watson said, and he agreed. He did not think her purpose was to stop the course.

"Senator Kinnaird wanted to make sure that classes in the community college system were being taught responsibly and accurately. She was asking for some sort of a professional backup if the curriculum of a course was not recognized as what historians regard as accurate."

Lancaster wouldn't speak to Kinnaird's and Watson's intentions.

"Certainly the tenor of their visit was that they did not like the course."

He told them, he said, that personal interest community service courses were strictly a local matter, determined by popular demand and not involving state funds. The state system didn't have the staff or resources to control such courses, and even if it did, he thought it wouldn't be appropriate. Local communities, who knew what they wanted and needed, should have those choices. He had complete faith in Larry Linker to handle this situation.

Watson recalled Lancaster saying that he thought the course had been blown out of proportion in the press and that questions had been raised about the accuracy of the reports.

"He didn't get specific about chapter and verse," Watson said.

Kinnaird's only comment about the meeting was that Lancaster had given them "a polite hearing."

Later, Watson said that he had misgivings about his presence at the meeting and about politicians involving themselves in what can and can't be taught on state campuses.

"There are a lot of pitfalls on that path, to be very understated about it," he said. "The next person to be targeted might be me or one of my colleagues."

Watson knew that North Carolina had undergone one unpleasant and tumultuous experience with legislators trying to control speech on campuses.

In 1963, late in the term of liberal Democratic governor Terry Sanford, who later became a presidential candidate, U.S. Senator, and president of Duke University, the legislature, over Sanford's objections, enacted a law forbidding certain people from speaking at state-supported colleges and universities. Communists, those who pleaded the fifth amendment when asked about participation in communist causes and groups, and those advocating the overthrow of the government were not allowed to have their views heard. Known as the "speaker ban law," it raised great outcries on campuses and in the press, provoked demonstrations, threatened accreditation, and brought national derision to the state before it finally was declared unconstitutional by a federal court in 1968.

Despite this knowledge and his misgivings about his role in the meeting with Lancaster, however, this would not be the last time Watson would involve himself in the RCC course.

Soon after Lancaster ended his meeting with Kinnaird and Watson, another meeting was about to begin at RCC's Archdale campus, this one between college and NAACP representatives. Larry Linker and Cathy Hefferin arrived about half an hour before the meeting, followed soon afterward by Marcia Daniel. Rhonda Winters, the campus director, greeted them in the lobby, where they stood talking about the unbelievable events of the week.

In the past three days, Winters had heard from several students in the course who were upset and angry about the *News & Record's* stories. They wanted to know what was going to happen. Would the last class be held? She could tell them little. To this point, the class was still scheduled, and earlier this morning, Winters had called every student to warn that they likely would be besieged by reporters and TV cameras if they chose to attend. Demonstrators might even be present. She reached all but two or three, and for those she left messages. All with whom she spoke, she discovered, were adamant about attending. They felt that their course had been totally misrepresented, and they would not be intimidated by reporters, or anybody else. Winters also talked with Jack, who said he was prepared to give his lecture no matter what developed.

Winters told this to Linker as they awaited the arrival of the NAACP representatives. She made her own feelings known, as well: she agreed with the students.

"Please don't cancel this class," she remembered telling Linker. "If you do, it will make us look guilty, and we haven't done anything wrong."

Skip Alston, Earl Jones and Richie Everette were the NAACP representatives who showed up, and Linker, Daniel and Hefferin accompanied them to an empty classroom to talk.

"It was a very friendly meeting," Hefferin recalled. "They basically wanted to know what we knew about the class. They didn't put any pressure on us. They just wanted information."

"They were concerned about what had been written about the class," Linker remembered, "and they were rightfully concerned if some of the things that had been printed were in fact what we were doing."

He wanted them to understand that he and his staff were trying to determine the facts, he said, but indications were that some of the allegations were not true, and he would keep them informed of what they learned.

Everette recalled that he was basically a spectator at the meeting, deferring to Alston and Jones. The case they presented, he said, was that the public saw this as a course that was exciting and dividing people, and whether or not the articles were true, perception was reality.

Linker went on to talk about all of the stress of dealing with the news media, and Alston and Jones responded sympathetically, Hefferin recalled.

But about halfway through the meeting, bright lights flashed on in the hallway outside the classroom and a TV camera appeared at the window of the door. Bill Sherck of Channel 8, the first reporter to arrive, later said that his station received a call from the NAACP office in Greensboro tipping them off to the meeting. Another TV crew arrived shortly afterward. The cameras could not be avoided as the group left the classroom.

Linker stood before them to say that it had been a good meeting, as did Alston.

Later, Linker respected how savvy the NAACP had been at manipulating the news, even though he resented the false impression that these bits of TV footage created.

Rick Amme had seen the look many times before. A man who liked analogies to war, he compared it to shell shock. "I spend most of my time working with people who have a media gun to their heads. It's absolutely devastating to them. They can't sleep. They can't eat. They're exhausted. It's hard for them to think clearly. It's absolutely awful."

He saw that harried and drained look in Larry Linker when he arrived at the Asheboro campus for his first meeting with college officials Thursday morning. The group that gathered around the big table in the board room with Amme included Linker, Hefferin, and Daniel, along with the executive committee of the board of trustees—chairman Jerry Tillman, a former school principal and assistant superintendent of Randolph County schools, and businessmen Jack Lail and Jim Campbell. Alan Pugh, whose law firm represented the college, also sat in. Pugh had been counsel to former Republican governor Jim Martin, as well as counsel to the speaker of the N.C. House of Representatives, Harold Brubaker of Asheboro, and secretary of the N.C. Department of Crime Control and Public Safety.

Linker was upset and angry about the *News & Record*'s treatment of the college, and Amme was not surprised at the way he began this discussion. Many clients did the same.

Experience taught Amme that the biggest mistake leaders make in these situations is that they become defensive and dither, allowing damage to build, especially if they feel they have been wronged by the press.

"The first thing they want to do is attack the reporter. They want to yell and scream and say, 'Look at all the blood.'" They want to take on the reporter and the news agency, attempt to right the wrong, he said. "It's a battle you're not going to win. Even if a reporter is wrong, they're still going to kill you."

To Amme, the perception created by the press was the reality that had to be confronted, right or wrong.

"From the way it was being reported, this looked like a bogus course teaching bogus information under the auspices of this college, and it was doing nothing to correct it. So my thinking was let's fix it."

He believed in quick, decisive action. Stop the bleeding; cut the oxygen to the media's fires; get out of the heat and the spotlight; buy time to think and plan rationally. Crisis management, he liked to say, acknowledging that it was not original with him, was nothing more than "common sense at lightning speed."

"I came in firing," he recalled.

His recommendation: suspend the class and announce an investigation.

But he found reluctance to that approach.

Amme's impression was that nobody in the room believed Feinsilver's reporting was accurate, or the *News & Record's* treatment of the college fair, but all agreed that the school was in deep trouble because of it, its reputation on the line.

Linker wanted to let the class continue, and a long debate ensued over what that would entail. The press would insist on being present, and nobody could predict what kind of circus that might create. Keeping the press out wasn't an alternative. That would fuel the fire, giving the impression that reports about the class were true and the college had something to hide. To allow reporters and photographers into the classroom would disrupt the class and possibly intimidate the students. Could the press be restricted to a separate room with a video hookup to the classroom? Might demonstrators, pro and con, show up? Would law enforcement need to be present? How would other classes be affected? What about the safety of students and their right of privacy?

Wanda Brown, Linker's administrative assistant, brought in sandwiches as the discussion passed beyond lunchtime.

Continuing the class, Amme argued, would be defacto support of the public perception of it.

"By default you endorse this."

Although the trustees took part in the discussion, and Alan Pugh weighed in with his experiences dealing with the press, the trustees put no pressure on Linker, making clear that the decision would be his, and they would support it, Tillman said later.

"We struggled for a long time with that decision," Hefferin recalled.

As the debate wore on, Amme felt the inevitable consensus building.

"I think Larry was somewhat inclined to tough it out," he said, "but others were more oriented toward fixing this and stopping the bad publicity. And Larry was trying to find a way to protect his faculty. He was caught between what was pragmatic and hanging tough and insisting there was nothing wrong with the course."

At the end, Linker reluctantly concluded that the college's best interests required him to take Amme's advice.

With the decision made, details had to be attended. Rhonda Winters had to be called so she could notify students, and Linker decided to do that himself. A press conference was scheduled for four p.m. A statement had to be written, media outlets informed so reporters and TV crews could get to the campus in time. Linker wanted his faculty to know what was coming before the news became public, and he set a staff meeting for three.

After the meeting broke up at one-thirty, Amme and Hefferin remained in the board room, working on the statement that would be handed out at the press conference. Amme wrote on his laptop computer, he and Hefferin going back and forth to Linker's office to get his input as Linker prepared for the staff meeting.

The statement that Linker finally approved was this:

> *After careful consideration, I have decided that it is in the best interest of the students, faculty and staff of Randolph Community College...and indeed the fine people of Randolph County...to cancel the final class of our civil war course originally scheduled for this evening.*
>
> *We would never intentionally set up any class that is offensive to anyone in our community...and obviously this class has done that. Therefore we are going to step back and take a close look at it...and at our process of approving courses.*
>
> *Let me stress that we have not confirmed whether this course contains the kind of content that is alleged...but*

there is a perception that it does...and that perception is damaging our fine reputation.

My main concern at this point is protecting Randolph Community College...which has been serving the community for 36 years. The news coverage of the civil war course in question has unfairly maligned us...and we will not allow that to continue.

Although we remain committed to the ideals of academic freedom...that freedom should not allow any course that hurts the very people we are trying to serve. While we do not know whether this course does that...there is enough question about it that we cannot allow it to continue without a second look.

Later, Hefferin would wonder how they made it through all the stress of this day.

"That whole day of my life was hell," Linker remembered.

But the most difficult time for Linker came at three when he had to face the faculty.

"That was one of the hardest things I ever had to do. That was a very somber meeting. I'd worked with a lot of these people for years and years, and I had to tell them, 'Folks, I want you to know what I've got to do. We're going to buckle on this one tonight.' I got pretty choked up."

Linker was clearly distraught and exhausted, and some in the audience were concerned about him. They were aware that he nearly had died from a heart attack in 1980.

"They knew I was hurting, and they felt for me," Linker said. "They knew the situation I was in. Tears rolled down their cheeks, a lot of them."

The emotional nature of the meeting made what happened at the end all the more surprising. A faculty member rose to announce that he had prepared a statement in opposition to the Civil War course to be presented to the board of trustees. He invited others to sign it. Chuck Egerton was an instructor in the school's photography program. Linker hadn't expected anything like this and didn't understand why Egerton would choose such a vulnerable moment to take this action.

"I honestly didn't know what he was doing," Linker said, "but Chuck is Chuck."

Egerton received a B.F.A. from the Maryland Institute College of Art in 1978, and came to RCC in 1983 to study commercial photography. After earning his A.A.S. in 1985, he worked as a corporate photographer before returning to RCC in 1990 to become an instructor in the photography program. He would be the college's 1998 nominee for the annual Excellence in Teaching Award presented by the state community college system.

Egerton was a devout follower of the Baha'i faith, a clergyless religion founded by a nineteenth-century Persian nobleman who would become known as Baha'u'llah. Baha'is believed in a global society, with all humanity a single people, but Egerton had become known in Randolph County as a man with strong views about a subject that separated many people: race.

Earlier in the fall, an outcry of racism had arisen from a few in Asheboro's black community because the town's daily newspaper, the *Courier-Tribune*, owned by the Donrey Media Group, didn't immediately publish a photo of the African-American student who had been chosen Asheboro High School's homecoming queen. Homecoming queen photos were not considered priority news. They always appeared in the Lifestyles section and were worked in whenever space allowed. In this case, the queen was named on Friday night and her photo appeared the following Wednesday. (The paper had no Saturday edition and the earliest it could have appeared was in Sunday's edition, for which the Lifestyles section was prepared in advance of the homecoming festivities.) The white homecoming queen at another county high school had to wait two weeks to see her photo published. Yet, Egerton didn't accept the editor's explanation that the delay had nothing to do with race, only with limited news space.

"Unfortunately, it's always race," he wrote in a letter to the editor.

"The *Courier-Tribune* is a white newspaper, its perspective is a white perspective, its allegiance is to whiteness. Everyone else is 'tolerated' and 'allowed,' on occasion, to give their point of view.

"I wouldn't say it's a grand conspiracy in an organized sense; it's really about white society's collective bias in favor of all that is white, it's about our unspoken white privilege and the cumulative historic effect of our unconscious racism...."

Race always had to be a consideration, he argued. To ignore it favored the majority.

"A colorblind society," he wrote, "is an ignorant and crass society...."

Failing to publish the photo promptly, wrote Egerton, was to "ignore the joy, pride and accomplishments of a people who have so long suffered such slow healing wounds from their fellow white citizens."

Egerton and other members of the Baha'i faith had established the Asheboro Support Group for the Healing of Racism in 1991, the same year that he began a community service course called Creating Racial Unity at RCC. Held annually, it was scheduled for spring, 1999.

This was the description of the course in the RCC catalog:

> *A horrible racial murder in Texas, repealing affirmative action, Latina immigration, and racial/ethnic tension have all combined to increase the fear and division of our diverse society. Calling for 'one America,' the President of the United States has initiated a nationwide dialogue on race. Creating Racial Unity offers an honest discussion on the issue of race in a safe environment. Once participants are rooted in the pivotal fact of the oneness and nobility of all humankind, they learn how the disease of prejudice thrives, in all its forms, and how it can be overcome. The course offers the essential tools and experiences needed to create genuine understanding and unity in personal, business, educational and church relationships. Creating Racial Unity is facilitated by an interracial team.*

What the course description failed to mention was that the interracial team that "facilitated" it, Egerton, who is white, and Gloria Whack, who is black, were both members of the Randolph County chapter of the NAACP, Egerton its second vice president. Whack had grown up in Brooklyn and managed a low-income housing facility in Asheboro. The course description also failed to advise prospective students that this course was built around a plan devised by the Baha'i faith and that it not only included Baha'i teachings but controversial positions espoused by the NAACP as well.

Materials used in this course emphasized "institutionalized racism," "unaware (or unconscious) racism," "cultural racism," and "internalized racism."

Power added to prejudice equalled "institutionalized racism," which was defined as "when the institutions of society are in the hands of one group (whites) and operate on the basis of mis-information."

"Cultural racism" was described as ignoring, devaluing and misrepresenting the history and culture of "targeted groups," resulting in a lack of self-knowledge, pride and self-esteem in those groups.

"Unaware racism" was assigned to whites who thought themselves to be free of racism. "Through unaware racism," the materials state, "people of good will hang onto and perpetuate ideas that are false and damaging." Examples of "unaware racism" included offering help when not wanted or needed, using expressions of too easy familiarity, calling people "minorities" when "they are the majority on earth," lumping people under terms such as Oriental or Hispanic, and not appreciating physical features that are different from white.

Those who questioned "unaware racism" were described as being in "denial."

Whites were portrayed as perpetrators of these and other more blatant forms of racism on blacks and other "people of color." This resulted in "internalized racism," described as "when victims of racism believe the lies, the stereotypes, the misinformation and turn it inward, feeling inferior, placing limitations on themselves and taking out the anger, hurt and frustration on themselves and members of their own group. This form of racism is a root cause of the increased drop-out rates, black on black crime, the increased use of drugs and the growing anger, frustration and hopelessness of people of color in America."

These were common themes of the NAACP, but theories open to disputation. A person who lost a job, a promotion, a college acceptance because of affirmative action, a program requiring preferential treatment by race and gender, obviously could have a totally different view of "institutionalized racism" than a course instructor who accepted "white society's collective bias in favor of all that is white," "white privilege," and "unconscious racism" by whites. Affirmative action, a primary platform of the NAACP, was considered by many to be racially divisive and contrary to equality under law, yet the description of the racial unity course described the repeal of affirmative action as "increasing fear and racial division."

Other materials used in the course included an excerpt from the book *Two Nations, Black and White, Separate, Hostile, Unequal* by Andrew Hacker, which claimed that white people created the term "nigger" to justify slavery. Hacker quoted a line from black writer James Baldwin's novel *The Fire Next Time* that "white people 'need the nigger' because it is the 'nigger' within that they cannot tolerate," then went on to postulate that "whatever it is that whites feel that 'nigger' signifies about blacks—lust and laziness, stupidity or squalor—in fact exists within themselves," that "needless to say, white people—paragons of civilization—cannot allow that 'niggerness' is part of their being."

Class materials also delved into international politics and economics, pointing out that industrialized nations constituted twenty percent of the world's population but were responsible for seventy percent of energy consumption, that "global inequities in the distribution of wealth must be dealt with," that "if eighty percent of our species are poor, we cannot hope to live in a world of peace," and that "the achievement of unity is a social process that stems from the recognition, understanding and internalization of the reality of oneness."

Would it be legitimate journalism for a reporter to use these materials to write that a course taught by NAACP members at Randolph Community College teaches that all whites are racists and cannot deal with their "niggerness," that whites are responsible for black-on-black crime and drug use by people of color, and that the only hope for humanity is a one-world economic system under which all resources are equally distributed and all people accept the teachings of Baha'u'llah?

Would that have been any different than the reporting about the Civil War course to which NAACP leaders now were objecting, and to which they had filed a complaint with the U.S. Commission on Civil Rights?

Should the *News & Record* have told its readers that while NAACP leaders were denouncing the Civil War course and claiming that it was a misuse of public funds to offer it on a community college campus that NAACP members had for seven years been teaching a course at RCC totally supported by state funds that promoted NAACP positions on race without informing prospective students of NAACP connections?

The *News & Record* never did so, nor did any other news organization.

Larry Linker called Rhonda Winters before the faculty meeting to tell her that he was cancelling the class.

"I told him I regretted we were going to do that," Winters recalled. "I was very disappointed."

She would call all the students and let them know the decision before the press conference, she told Linker. She also would call Jack.

Jack seemed to have expected the decision. She was sorry, she told him. She wished it were otherwise. She felt responsible for getting him involved. He knew that she had nothing to do with the decision, he said.

The reactions Winters got from students ranged from disappointment to disgust and anger, she remembered.

Some had seen the noon TV news reports of the meeting that morning between college officials and NAACP leaders, had heard what a good meeting it had been, and concluded that Linker had buckled to NAACP demands, a perception that would become widespread as word of the cancellation got out.

The students thought that the college's obligation was to them, not to those objecting to their course. They felt that the *News & Record* and the NAACP had no right to dictate what they were allowed to learn.

TV cameras lined the sidewalk at the entrance to RCC's administration building when Larry Linker emerged at four to face reporters. Looking haggard and forlorn, he stepped to the bank of microphones and read the statement that Cathy Hefferin and Rick Amme had written.

Afterward, he offered to take questions.

Only a few were asked, one about why Jack Perdue wasn't present.

"I don't know if he was invited," Linker responded.

Hefferin thought this had gone well so far, and she didn't want to risk anything going wrong.

"Nobody was asking much," she recalled, "and I felt it was time to call it quits."

She stepped forward and said, "Thank you for coming."

Hefferin hadn't met Feinsilver, and as she passed out copies of the statement, she asked a reporter she knew to point him out.

Some students watched the press conference, and a few reporters quizzed them.

"Everyone around the country must think we're a bunch of rednecks who want to go around hanging people or something," Chad Cranford said.

Sean Walker thought the whole thing had been blown out of proportion by the press.

"I believe that whoever did the initial story took the context and turned it into something," he said. "You get different reporting from everywhere, but for all we know the reporter made it up. I'd hate to think that."

Rhonda Winters planned to stay late at the Archdale campus this evening. She figured that reporters would show up, even though the class had been cancelled. She thought it possible that demonstrators from both sides, not getting the word, might even appear.

She was shocked to see Jack walking toward the entrance late in the afternoon.

"I went out and said, 'Jack, what are you doing here? You know reporters are liable to start showing up here any minute.'"

He knew that, he said, but he wanted her to have a copy of the response he'd written to the inaccuracies in Feinsilver's articles.

They chatted for a few minutes, and Winters later remembered Jack saying, "However this turns out, I just want to do the final class. The students deserve that, and I owe it to them."

Winters told him again how sorry she was that events had taken these turns.

"He put his arm around me," she recalled. "He said, 'Everything's going to be okay. We're going to get through this. It's going to work out.'

"I said, 'Jack, I hope you're right.'"

Reporters, including Feinsilver, did show up at class time. Winters figured that they wanted to make sure that the college wasn't sneaking to hold the class anyway. TV crews videotaped the darkened classroom, the closed door.

Sixteen

The *News & Record* fired its biggest salvo yet against the course on Friday.

In addition to Feinsilver's front-page report that Linker had cancelled the final class after meeting with NAACP officials, the paper published a lengthy lead editorial and two columns, one by editorial page columnist Rosemary Roberts, the other by feature columnist Lorraine Ahearn.

In his account, Feinsilver offered yet another interpretation of what had been taught, this time saying "that the majority of black people loved the Confederacy and were content being slaves." He previously said that tens of thousands of blacks fought for the Confederacy because they believed in its cause, not that the majority of black people loved the Confederacy, and that slaves were happy and satisfied, not contented.

Cancelling the class wouldn't stop the civil rights commission hearing to "iron out the historical facts," Feinsilver reported, quoting Wyatt Kirk, the state advisory committee chairman.

Feinsilver claimed that Larry Linker "pleaded exhaustion" after reading his statement "and refused to answer more than a few questions," another misrepresentation of what happened.

The editorial, headlined, *Civil War is risky in amateur hands*, began with this paragraph:

> *It gets harder and harder to have a quiet community conversation. One day someone voices a few honest questions about a course being taught at Randolph Community College in Archdale. Next thing you know, national newspapers and network TV are beating it to death, and national advocacy groups are jumping to conclusions.*

Upon reading this, Jack later said, he only could wonder if the editorial writer had been reading the *News & Record. Someone voices a few honest questions?* No one other than Feinsilver had raised any questions, honest or otherwise, about the course. The *News & Record* presented a provocative, sensational, false account to the world, was itself leading the daily beating of the course—this day's issue was further proof of that—and now was aloofly standing back and hypocritically proclaiming how hard it was to have a quiet community conversation.

On Wednesday, after Jack told Herman White that he planned to end his public silence, White had written a stinging letter to the *News & Record* denying Feinsilver's account of what he had taught. That letter arrived Thursday, and although it had not yet appeared in print, the editorial took note of his denial.

"...We'll take him at his word," the editorial said, then quickly made clear otherwise.

White "puts great store in some National Archives documents purporting to be an opinion survey of ex-slaves and their descendants," the editorial said.

Not only was the writer displaying a lack of knowledge about the slave narratives, he, or she, was misrepresenting what White said in his letter and did in class. The slave narratives were not an opinion survey of ex-slaves and had nothing to do with their descendants. White cited a survey of the narratives from four Southern states to determine the kinds of experiences ex-slaves reported.

The editorial went on to raise questions that underscored the writer's obvious ignorance about the narratives.

"Was this an informal, man-on-the-street sort of survey? Might there have been some wishful thinking involved?"

The point of the editorial was near the end: "when it comes to history, which all sorts of people want to rewrite, a community college gives amateurs free reign at its peril."

No mention was made that the newspaper's own Civil War columnist, Ned Harrison, was an amateur historian who soon was to teach a Civil War course at Guilford Technical Community College without apparent peril to students or *News & Record* readers—or interference from the newspaper's reporters.

"...In these parts, the Civil War is still a minefield and a media circus waiting to happen," the editorial concluded, without recognizing that in this media circus, the *News & Record* was the ringmaster.

Editorial columnist Roberts concluded that the course's instructors had been supping at "the trough" of Ulrich B. Phillips, a Yale educated historian from Georgia who wrote *Life and Labor in the Old South*, published in 1929, although neither Phillips nor his book were mentioned in class. Phillips claimed that slaves had a good life, Roberts wrote, and "portrayed slavery as a kind of social security system with shackles attached."

"...Teachers who spout off that slaves had a relatively good life," Roberts concluded, "should hear the words of a former slave spoken after emancipation: 'Tisn't he who has stood and looked on who can tell you what slavery is, 'tis he who has endured it.'"

The column that raised hackles anew in Randolph County, especially at RCC, was Ahearn's.

Presented as a memo to faculty about new course offerings from Buck Meatyard, chancellor and head football coach at South Lizard Lick Community College, the satirical column used Southern stereotypes to ridicule RCC and the Civil War class. One proposed course was "Exploring the Real South," which included classes on "Wal-Mart as sociological phenomenon; the art of the chain saw; food sculpture in elbow macaroni and cheese grits; and flea market etiquette."

The final course offering was "Tourism, Marketing and Academics."

"By appealing to regional stereotypes and a sad but desperate need for pride, learn strategies for gaining your small rural community college national exposure."

To many at RCC, the *News & Record* had created this controversy with spurious reporting, was putting the college through an unprecedented ordeal, and now not only was using bigoted stereotypes to deride the college as a stupid, racist institution but was implying that it had deliberately sought the nightmarish experience the newspaper was inflicting on it.

Ken Hamblin was the first nationwide radio talk show host to score an interview with a participant in the RCC course when Herman White agreed to go on his American View Network show on Friday.

The wordy White told about his role in the course and the article by Feinsilver that caused all the sensation, as Hamblin kept hurrying him along. What had Feinsilver written that brought the world down on White and the college? Hamblin wanted to know.

"He said that I said that all slaves were happy," White said.

"Did you say that?"

"No sir. No sir. In the first place, he wasn't at the lecture."

"He embellished," Hamblin said.

"No," White said, "he lied."

"Let me try again, Herman. He mislead."

"Well, okay."

"No, Herman, a lie's a lie."

Hamblin brought up that White had ancestors "who were in fact North Carolina slave owners." White acknowledged that was true and told about his great, great grandpa Jesse Coltrane and his great, great grandmother, Abigail, who had taught slaves to read.

They could have been run out of the county for doing that, couldn't they? Hamblin suggested. Probably so, White agreed, noting that it was against the law.

"I'm not totally ill informed for a colored guy," Hamblin said. "You did know I was colored, didn't you?"

White chuckled and said that he had listened to his show. Hamblin, a conservative, who grew up in the Bedford Stuyvesant section of Brooklyn, the son of West Indian immigrants, called himself the Black Avenger.

Hamblin noted that he had been trying to get Feinsilver to come on his show, but he hadn't responded. Could White send him a copy of the *News & Record's* article?

"They keep doing news articles every day. I don't have enough money to send all those articles," White said to Hamblin's amusement.

"You are aware, sir, that African Americans are very much in denial and in shock that black Africans worked with European traders to capture and merchandise black slaves," Hamblin said. "You certainly must have anticipated what was going to fall on you."

"I anticipated that it could if somebody like Feinsilver came along and wanted to start a little fire and then throw a bucket of gas on it to try to make a name for himself. I never heard of the little dude."

"Was 'little dude' what you really meant to say?"

"I'm being nice," White said.

"I know you are."

"I'm going to pray for him and hope the Lord will forgive him for lying because he can't go to heaven that way."

"Herman White, are you holding up okay under the pressure?"

"Certainly my beautiful bride of forty-five years, she wishes it would go away...."

"You ought to be out bass fishing," Hamblin said.

"I'd rather read history," White replied.

•   •   •

White's letter to the editor appeared Saturday morning. He denied teaching that blacks were happy under slavery, calling the claim "absurd" and "ludicrous." He charged Feinsilver with "fabricating a story to try to incite hatred between blacks and whites." He gave a capsulized version of his and Jack's interview with Feinsilver and recounted what he said about the survey of the slave narratives and why he had included it. (A line was excised in which White wrote that when he and Jack told Feinsilver that he was trying to create a controversy where none existed, Feinsilver responded, "Controversy is what sells newspapers.")

"This kind of reckless and dishonest 'reporting' is a perfect example of why the media of every kind is not trustworthy," White wrote. "In the past, such cowards as the KKK did their despicable deeds under cover of sheets and hoods. There are cowards today who incite anger and hatred and try to cover themselves with claims of freedom of the press. I suppose if one is unknown we will always have to contend with some who will try to become known at someone else's expense."

At two p.m. Saturday, thirty-eight members and supporters of the League of the South—a group from which had sprung the Southern Party, which was fielding candidates for local elections in some states—assembled with signs and battle flags outside the main building on the Archdale campus of RCC for a press conference.

When members of the group called earlier in the week to announce their intentions, Rhonda Winters informed Marcia Daniel and Cathy Hefferin and sought advice on handling the matter. Word came back that the group couldn't be kept off the campus, so long as they weren't disorderly, but that the college didn't have to provide facilities. Winters told the coordinators, Randy and Donna Jamison, that they were welcome to hold the conference outside but requested that they restrict it to thirty minutes, and they agreed.

Winters also called Jack to find out if he knew anything about the group. He didn't, he said, and was upset that they were exploiting the course for their own benefit. He was worried that this might give a radical taint to the course and make it more difficult for the college to allow it to continue, which he still hoped would happen.

"Let me make some calls and see if I can stop it," Jack told Winters, but his calls were without effect.

Two TV news crews and a few newspaper reporters (although nobody from the *News & Record*) showed up to hear the group chant Southern cheers and condemn the NAACP and the U.S. Commission on Civil Rights for their "bullying tactics."

The primary speaker, Larry Walker, refuted Feinsilver's articles and cited instances of blacks, native Americans and Hispanics serving the Confederacy. He also announced the formation of a new area chapter of the League of the South.

Two TV stations carried reports of the press conference, but newspapers ignored it.

"We played it as a civil rights issue," Mike Tuggle later reported on the group's Internet site, "and the press was very receptive."

One pleasant experience from this week of ordeal for Jack came during the weekend: a call from Emerson Emory, a seventy-three-year-old African American psychiatrist from Dallas. Emory, whose white great-grandfather had fought with the 17th Texas Cavalry, was a member of the SCV and later would become commander of one of two Dallas camps. Emory made national news in July when a monument to black troops of the Civil War was dedicated at Arlington National Cemetery.

He had been invited to read a poem and lay a wreath at the ceremony until the organizers discovered that he planned to honor blacks who served the Confederacy. Walter Hill, chief historian of the African American Civil War Memorial Freedom Foundation, rescinded the invitation, writing to Emory that "the heritage and history of the Confederacy...(was) a barrier to this cause and the freedom of American slaves and free people of color."

Emory wrote back that he thought the monument was about blacks in the war, not slavery, and his only intention was to see that all were honored, not to support slavery, an institution he abhorred. In a later conversation, Emory said, Hill adamantly insisted that no blacks had fought for the South, although Emory had documentary evidence of many who served with Texas units. (Many Hispanics also served with Texas units.)

"It's ridiculous that just because you're on the other side, you can't honor them," he told a reporter. "It's just one soldier trying to honor another. It had nothing to do with slavery."

Emory attended the ceremony anyway as a spectator and returned to the cemetery in the night to place his wreath in memory of the black soldiers whose service went unrecognized. Later, when he appeared on a national radio call-in show, he was not surprised to hear from African Americans who supported his stand.

"Many Southern blacks remained loyal to the states in which they lived," Emory said. "Some persons today do not understand such loyalty but such has been our nature over the years, regardless of the conditions under which we lived."

Some of his black friends couldn't understand why he did what he did, Emory later acknowledged. "I think it's one of those things that they don't want to hear anything about," he said.

Emory read about the course and called Jack when he heard that the civil rights commission planned a hearing on it. They had a long chat. Emory was not only charming, Jack discovered, but had a great sense of humor.

Emory told Jack that he would fly to Greensboro for the hearing, accompany him to it, and testify on his behalf. Jack said that he would welcome not only his support but his company.

Seventeen

The weekend brought a respite from news stories, but on Monday morning Jack found himself the subject of the lead editorial in the *Winston-Salem Journal* under the headline, *Amplifying Foolishness*.

This was the second time the *Journal* had editorialized about the course in three days. On Saturday, the paper said that to suggest that slavery "wasn't really that bad is too similar to suggesting that the Holocaust never happened."

This day's offering noted that the outrage about the course and the media attention "provided a far greater opportunity for Perdue and his supporters to spread their views than they ever could have orchestrated on their own."

"With the course's cancellation, Perdue becomes an academic martyr and a hero to those who share his views. Why give a crank a megaphone?"

This would be the single editorial to which Jack, who had seen no sign of anybody attempting to turn him into an academic martyr, could not resist responding.

In a letter e-mailed to the *Journal*, he called the editorial itself "a bunch of foolishness."

> *It is full of misinformation and accusations based on false information. If you are going to criticize a course, an organization and an individual, you should have some first hand knowledge. How do you come to the judgment that I am a "crank" when you have never met me or even spoken to me? Who are you to besmirch my reputation built up over decades of service in civic, historical, professional and governmental organizations in the Triad? How do you pretend to know what was taught in a class that you did not attend*

and the reporter who wrote the article from which you apparently got your information did not attend?....

Your paper should do the gentlemanly thing and publish a retraction and an apology to the Sons of Confederate Veterans, Randolph Community College and to me personally for your mean spirited and potentially libelous editorial.

His response was not published. Nine days after the editorial appeared, Jack got a letter from John D. Gates, the editorial page editor.

Because the last paragraph of your recent letter asks for a retraction and an apology and suggests that the editorial about which you write is "potentially libelous," we are viewing the letter as a legal document, rather than a letter to the editor, and are referring it to our attorneys for a legal response.

You are welcome, of course, to send us a letter to the editor that disagrees with the editorial in question and spells out why you disagree, but in asking for a retraction, you take the issue beyond the letters-to-the-editor realm and make the issue a legal question. For example, your letter would be perfectly acceptable as a letter to the editor without its final paragraph.

That was not acceptable to Jack, who believed that this was a personal attack, not an issue to be debated, and that a retraction and apology were in order. The *Journal*'s portrayal of him as a crank thus stood without response. Jack never heard from the *Journal*'s lawyers.

Skip Alston, the state NAACP president, was a guest on Ken Hamblin's show on Monday. Hamblin told him that he'd spoken with Herman White on Friday and White said he didn't teach that slaves were happy.

"Please help me to understand where the misunderstanding has come about."

"I did not attend the course," Alston said. "We did have a reporter who did attend the course, and one of my chapter presidents did attend one phase of the course. Based on their analysis of it, what they heard in the class and also the course outline, it really disturbed me, some of the topics...that blacks were happy and supported the Confederacy."

Hamblin mentioned the titles of several scholarly books that document blacks serving the Confederacy including *Black Confederates and Afro-Yankees in Civil War Virginia*, by Ervin L. Jordan Jr., an African-American scholar at the University of Virginia. Jordan took up the work of James Brewer, a black professor of history at UNC, whose prize-winning book, *The Confederate Negro*, was published by Duke University Press in 1970, four years before Brewer's death.

"Are you suggesting that as we become more comfortable with ourselves as a nation—I hope that's where we're going—that an opposing view to the conventional history that's being taught cannot be taught in an institution of higher learning?" Hamblin asked.

"I'm saying that the truth needs to be taught," Alston replied.

"Can you tell me what the truth is?"

"The truth is, number one, that blacks were not happy with slavery, and blacks did not support the institution of slavery."

But it was documented fact that free blacks owned slaves and black Africans were involved in the slave trade, Hamblin pointed out.

"When they say blacks were happy and content with slavery—he teaches this in his course—then that bothers me because anyone with half a brain would know that blacks were not happy with being enslaved," Alston said. "Then you look at blacks who participated in the slave trade, basically they done so based on coercion and being in captivity themselves."

"I think, sir, that you're selling conventional wisdom designed to make me as a black American feel comfortable with some lumpy parts of history."

There was no indication of coercion to black African tribal chiefs who sold other Africans into slavery, no coercion to free blacks to own slaves, Hamblin pointed out.

"I'm not holding myself out to be a history professor or a history buff or anything like that," Alston responded. "The bottom line on this course here is that we had gotten information that the course was basically teaching whites that was in the class in support of the Confederacy that blacks supported the Confederacy, that they fought very patriotically for the Confederacy."

Clearly some did do that, Hamblin said.

But only because they were coerced, Alston insisted.

On Friday, Alston had been quoted in news stories that the NAACP would not press for a civil rights commission hearing after cancellation of the class. "We should let sleeping dogs lie. It looks like they're taking care of the problem."

Why had the NAACP decided that? Hamblin asked.

"We sat down and talked with the president of the college," Alston began.

"Who kicked the course out?" Hamblin asked. "Was that a prerequisite?"

The president of the college stopped the course, Alston said. "He chose not to even allow it to go one more day. After he examined the facts, after he looked at the course outline, and after he talked with several people on his staff and several people in the community, he came to the conclusion that the course was not teaching the truth and the true facts, and he came to the conclusion that it was misleading as relates to African Americans and their participation in the Confederacy."

Here Hamblin interjected, "He is so firmly grounded in the fact that he made the right decision that he has declined to talk with us...to return any phone calls."

"I don't think he wants to further the cause of polarizing the college any more."

"I think when you take away the voice of any person teaching a course in a community college, I think when you deny them that First Amendment right, black or white, Northern or Southern, gray or blue...." Hamblin said.

"It's not a First Amendment right," Alston put in. "You got a right to freedom of speech, but you don't have the right to yell fire in a crowded theater."

Hamblin brought up Louis Farrakhan, Stokely Carmichael and others.

"They teach that white people are devils, inherently racist, incapable of being trustworthy. Would you support denying them the right to preach and teach their brand of hatred?"

"I would not support the teaching of hate against any race of people within a public facility that's funded by tax dollars."

The problem with the class in question, Alston said, was that it was being taught at a community college.

"To have that type of material taught in a public facility, that's not appropriate. If he wants to teach anything he wants to teach in the basement of his house, or something like that...that's one thing, but not a public facility."

Alston essentially was making the same argument that right-wing legislators had made years earlier to justify the speaker ban law.

• • •

Feinsilver called the Archdale campus Monday morning saying he needed to speak to Rhonda Winters about making a correction in his original article. He was told that all media calls had to be directed to Cathy Hefferin. Later Hefferin called Winters to tell her that she had received a call from Lex Alexander, Feinsilver's editor, saying that Feinsilver needed to talk with them because he thought he had gotten them confused in his notes and wanted to make a correction.

Winters was adamant that she didn't want to talk with Feinsilver. He was bad news, she said; he had an agenda; he could not be trusted. Reporters didn't have to do face-to-face interviews to make corrections, she maintained. This was subterfuge to give him a chance to grill her on other things. "He wants to know about the approval process," she said. "That's what this is about."

Feinsilver and his editors were in search of a trophy, a college official's head to hang on the newsroom wall, she believed, and she didn't want it to be hers.

Hefferin called back later to say that Linker thought they should do this. Angry and exasperated, Winters called Linker.

"I said, 'Dr. Linker, are you directing me to do this?' He wouldn't say, 'Yes, you have to do this.' He just kept saying, 'We have to be team players. He just wants to make the correction.'"

Against her instincts, Winters agreed to the meeting, but she faxed her objections to Linker so they would be in writing.

When Hefferin called Alexander to tell him that the meeting would take place, she asked that he be present as well. He declined. She said the meeting would take place only if the newspaper agreed that it could be taped, and he said that would be fine, she remembered. It was set for nine Tuesday morning.

Feinsilver reported in Tuesday's *News & Record* that the U.S. Commission on Civil Rights was changing plans for its hearing on the RCC course and that it now also would include the police shooting of Daryl Howerton. Although Feinsilver originally had reported that the hearing would be held within ten days, probably at the RCC campus, he now wrote that it "likely will be held in February" and that no site had been chosen.

"The commission's focus will be more expansive," Feinsilver quoted Robert Knight of the commission's Atlanta office. "How much more expansive? That has yet to be decided."

Feinsilver described Knight as saying that the commission didn't know enough about what was taught in the course.

"A lot of this is allegation. Who would rush out until you find out all the facts?"

The *Atlanta Journal-Constitution* also reported the delay in the hearing but quoted Knight as saying "it might be a stretch to find a rights violation" involving the course.

Cathy Hefferin had a tape recorder when she arrived at Rhonda Winters' office Tuesday morning. Winters also had one on her desk. At ten minutes of nine, Feinsilver called to report that he was running a little late.

Nine o'clock passed, then nine-fifteen, and still he hadn't arrived. "I'll give him five more minutes," Winters said.

At nine-twenty, she announced that the meeting was cancelled. Feinsilver arrived ten minutes later, after Hefferin left. Winters remained in her office as Carol Nunn told Feinsilver that the meeting was off and would have to be rescheduled. Nunn told Winters that Feinsilver was very upset.

Later, Lex Alexander, who was aware of Feinsilver's chronic lateness, called to say that Feinsilver had been late because he'd had a flat tire. Winters didn't believe it. Why didn't he say that when he called to say he was running behind?

The meeting was never rescheduled, but the newspaper did prepare a correction:

> *A quote was attributed to the wrong Randolph Community College official in a story Nov. 15. The characterization of a Civil War course as "factual historical material" was made by Rhonda Winters, director of the college's Archdale campus.*
>
> *In the same story, Tony Horwitz's last name was misspelled.*

The "correction" itself was incorrect. Feinsilver used the quote to make it appear that college officials supported teaching that most blacks were happy in slavery and that tens of thousands had fought for the Confederacy because they believed in its cause, not as a characterization of the course itself. But he never asked college officials to respond to those claims, of which they were unaware until they were published. Winters told Feinsilver that the course was based on published factual material when he called to ask why she allowed the course, well before the class on the role of blacks in the Confederacy.

The inaccuracy of the "correction" turned out to be of no consequence, because the *News & Record* never published it, apparently in retaliation for the cancelled meeting with Feinsilver.

Afterward, newsroom sources wouldn't remember the exact day that Feinsilver underwent an interrogation by city editor Ed Williams that lasted for hours, but later evidence indicated that it was the same day that Feinsilver failed to appear on time for the interview with Winters and Hefferin. Several in the newsroom recalled that Feinsilver looked harried and distraught, and that Lex Alexander was periodically in and out of the meeting.

Feinsilver was put on probation, his job on the line, his colleagues soon would learn. He was required to regularly call back sources to verify that their quotes were correct.

Yet, the *News & Record* continued to maintain that his reporting on the course was accurate and fair.

Eighteen

The bulk of the nationwide news coverage of the course was based on the original article the Associated Press picked up from the *News & Record* and its follow-up stories, but the AP also sent out stories from the *Atlanta Journal-Constitution*, which had a reporter based in Greensboro. Nonetheless, all of the coverage replicated Feinsilver's falsifications and misperceptions, and in some cases added to them.

USA Today turned a course about the Civil War in North Carolina into a course about slavery. The "North Carolina Now" news show on the state's public TV network called it a slavery course as well, as did the *Detroit News.* The *New York Times* called it a "satisfied slaves course" in a headline.

Reactions by columnists and editorialists not only denounced the college, the instructors, students and Sons of Confederate Veterans but enhanced and exaggerated the misrepresentations of the news reports to the point that their commentaries bore no resemblance to the reality in the classroom.

The *Chattanooga Times* called the course "a full-throated glorification of the Confederate South and all that it was...a cruel absurdity masquerading as 'history.'"

"They are 'teaching' that the buying and selling and ownership of human beings just wasn't as bad as people have said," the editorial claimed, going on to accuse the college of abandoning standards of "honesty and responsibility."

The *Fayetteville* (N.C.) *Observer* accused the college of advocating "a sugar-coated version of slavery."

"Only when the adherents of the 'slavery-wasn't-so-bad' school of thought advise their own sons and daughters to skip college and go into the innocent, happy state of forced servitude can anyone accept that they believe what they say," the paper said.

The *Philadelphia Tribune* called the class the "height of absurdity," and claimed that it was justifying "revisionism" by saying that political correctness shouldn't be allowed to rewrite history. "Sometimes people say or do things that make you wonder whether they have totally lost their minds."

"The course laid it on thick about the special bond between slaves and their 'benevolent protectors,'" wrote columnist Tony Norman in the *Pittsburg Post-Gazette*. "The fact that a few misguided Negroes fought for the Confederacy in exchange for their freedom is trumpeted as proof that things weren't as bad as Alex Haley would have had us believe. Needless to say, pressure from VERY ANGRY BLACK FOLKS put an end to this nonsense faster than anyone could say, 'Frankly my dear, I don't give a damn.'"

"When will we understand that it was not wise for black people to reveal their true feelings to white folk because white folk didn't want to hear the truth?" asked Merlene Davis, columnist for the *Herald-Leader* in Lexington, Ky. "When will we realize there is no such thing as a good master, that owning people is not good for master or slave?"

"Anyone who calls the South's seditious attempt to disunite the United States a war for independence is well on the road to misrepresentation," wrote John Head, a columnist for the *Atlanta Journal-Constitution*. "Such prattle, like the course itself, represents an attempt to absolve the South of its worse (sic) sin and to glorify the darkest years of its history."

Chicago Sun-Times columnist Mary A. Mitchell wrote that the NAACP was battling to stop the college "from claiming they have historical evidence that most slaves were happy in captivity" and that the teachers were "peddling stories about slaves who were so happy that they rushed out to shoot the only people who could have helped them escape to freedom." That reasoning, she said, was absurd.

"No word yet on whether the college will offer a course taught by Sons of Nazis who deny the Holocaust ever happened," said an editorial in the *San Antonio Express News*.

Syndicated columnist Hal Crowther wrote that he considered the campaign against the Confederate battle flag "an obnoxious excess of political correctness," but referred to the course instructors as "a pack of Neanderthals" and said the class had "resurrected the notorious Happy Slave Dance."

David Greenberg, Richard Hofstadter fellow in American history at Columbia University, used the course to introduce a column in *Slate*, MicroSoft's on-line magazine, about differing views of slavery by historians. "What was the true character of bondage in the American

South? On that question, historians have never agreed. Positions have shifted with the prevailing political and cultural winds, and the issue remains alive.... Not so long ago, the Randolph Community College view of slaves as happy in their bondage—smiling, singing 'Sambos'—was the dominant view, even among experts."

Jack had planned all along to wait until the news coverage waned, then hold a press conference to refute Feinsilver's charges and answer all questions at once. After conferring with Rahlo Fowler, and with the state and national SCV commanders, he decided to hold it on Wednesday, November 25, the day before Thanksgiving, ten days after Feinsilver's first article.

Fowler called several hotels trying to rent a meeting room, he said, only to be turned down. One agreed but called back later to cancel, saying that the hotel couldn't risk the potential negative publicity. In the end, he called Rhonda Winters, who told him it could be held on campus.

The hierarchy of the SCV in North Carolina turned out. Larry Beeson, the state commander, from the small town of King in Stokes County; Bryan Carawan, the lieutenant commander from nearby Thomasville; Charles Hawks, the chief of staff, from Raleigh; and Fowler, the state heritage officer, stood behind the podium with Jack.

Beeson, a reticent, white-haired, grandfatherly figure, retired from Lucent Technologies, told the reporters about the history and purpose of the SCV, before taking up the matter at hand.

"There are those in our society who have taken upon themselves the job of finding everything that in any form or fashion is in some way considered offensive to some portion of the public, and then attempting to use it as a means of dividing the community," he said.

"We therefore strongly denounce the unethical practice of reporting Mr. Feinsilver has displayed. Facts should never be distorted to create controversy. We cannot change the things that happened during the eighteen-sixties, nor should we try. Events have occurred in the past that no one likes....

"We cannot judge the people of one hundred and forty years ago by today's standards. Things that were acceptable then are not acceptable now, and the War Between the States should not be judged by one reporter's misguided view on any particular aspect of that terrible conflict."

Beeson invited those "who take exception with our position to meet in open forum and discuss these issues so that the public can be properly informed of the entire content of this class and not just one aspect of it."

Jack was wearing sunglasses and a patterned tie, red, white, and blue, with his blue suit. "Most of you have been trying to chase me down for two weeks," he said, after Beeson introduced him, "and here I am."

Earlier, the reporters had been handed a two-page statement written by Jack containing twelve points refuting Feinsilver's articles. They also were given the course outline and Jack's introduction. The statement, Jack said, summarized events leading to "the false and misleading articles published all over the world" and had been drafted after viewing hours of videotapes of the classes.

"This was a class on North Carolina's role in the War for Southern Independence which was well received by the students, and there have been many requests to the college to hold the course again. We look forward to presenting it on an annual basis. It was not a course on slavery as has been misrepresented in the press. We neither approve of nor condone slavery. No such implication was ever made in class and there will be no discussion of that topic at this press conference."

The question session was conducted by William Johnson, an insurance agent from Bear Creek in Chatham County, the SCV's state public affairs officer, who'd never been involved in a press conference. All but two of the questions would be directed to Jack.

Vernon Fraley, a reporter for Channel 2 in Greensboro, began by asking when the next course would be held.

Jack said he still planned to present it each fall.

"Whether or not it will be connected to this institution is something the school will have to decide...."

"You must have known going into this that it was a touchy subject," a female TV reporter said.

"No, we didn't," Jack replied, going on to note that Steve Huffman, the *High Point Enterprise* reporter, who was present, had written about the course before it began, laying out what would be taught and how Jack viewed the war. Advertisements stated that the Frazier Camp was co-sponsoring the course.

"Not one person, organization, the press, or anybody else questioned this course, the fact that it was going to be presented, or what it was going to cover."

"Well, did you at any point consider consulting the civil rights groups?" the reporter asked.

"No, we put out publicity that was free to anybody. Civil rights groups could have called. They could have taken the course. It was open to anybody. We don't feel like we had to consult with somebody to put on a course that adults are interested in coming to take."

"Is it your contention that this whole thing is blown out of proportion or a product of the reporter you have named here?" Fraley asked.

Jack called attention to the last paragraph of his statement, and read a portion of it: "'In summary, it appears that the whole world-wide media has been duped by an over zealous young reporter.'

"I think that is just exactly what happened," he said. "None of these statements he alleges were made in class, and he did not attend the class in which he alleges they were made."

"One of the allegations is that you said seventy percent of the slaves were happy," a female reporter asked. "You say that's incorrect. What did you say?"

"I didn't say anything. I did not teach that particular segment of the course. I reviewed the tapes. That statement was not made. The statement that they were nappy was not made. The statement that they were satisfied was not made."

"Any idea of the source of these alleged comments..." another reporter asked.

"One of your cohorts can probably respond to this better than I can," Jack said, referring to Bob Buckley of Channel 8, who was present, and to whom he had given an interview six days earlier. An editor at the *News & Record*, he said, had told Buckley that the reporter claimed he got his information from talking to instructors outside of class.

"That's not what the article said," he pointed out. "The article said that's what we taught in class and that is not what was taught in class."

"You mentioned you reviewed videotapes. Do you have them available? Can we see them today?"

"They are in the hands of my attorney, and, no sir, they're not available."

Chris Burritt of the *Atlanta Journal-Constitution* asked if Herman White was present.

"No, Mr. White is not here, and I have no idea what Mr. White may have said out of class. All I can do is tell you that these statements were not made in class. We were accused of teaching this. We did not teach this."

Actually, White was only about 100 feet away in the parking lot, talking with two Randolph County sheriff's deputies who had been sent to the campus to ensure order, although Jack may not have been aware of that. Jack had decided that White shouldn't be at the press conference because of his strong religious and political views and the unpredictability of what he might say. He knew that reporters would zero in on White and his views likely would become the sole focus of news reports, undercutting the message Jack wanted to get out.

White didn't know about the press conference until the day before when he learned about it while being interviewed at the *Courier-Tribune* in Asheboro.

Earlier, as Jack and Rhalo Fowler were standing on the sidewalk waiting for the other SCV officers to arrive, White, who believed that a press conference should have been held much earlier, drove up, rolled down his car window, and said, "I guess y'all wonder why I'm here. I thought I'd come by and see what was happening."

"They never said a word," White recalled.

"Could you just simply tell us what in class you did say about black feelings about slavery and black participation in the Confederate war effort?" Chris Burritt asked Jack.

"No, I would not attempt to do that from memory. I went through that tape to see if the alleged statements were made and they were not made.... As I said in the opening remarks, we're going to deal with what the facts are, and the facts are that those statements were not made."

Would he change anything about the course? another reporter asked.

"Hindsight is twenty-twenty," Jack said, "but I don't think we would change much."

He held up a page from the *News & Record* published six days earlier on the same day he had been portrayed on the front page as hiding out from the worldwide media. This page featured Civil War columnist Ned Harrison, who had written about a plan by the North Carolina Tourism Council to promote Civil War history in the state.

"I told the reporter the first night he came when he asked why we were teaching this course, that too much of what is taught dealing with the war all takes place in Virginia, and it's like North Carolina didn't participate," Jack said, "and the North Carolina Tourism Council is quoted in here as saying they want to present the broad picture, and the, quote, broad picture, unquote, includes everyday life during the war, the position and effect of the war on the black community, the impact of the war on women, how the western half of the state clearly preferred to stay in the Union, and the many land battles and naval engagements that were fought in our state in the final days of the war.

"If you'll take that course outline I gave you, it looks like they took our course outline and decided that's what needs to be presented in North Carolina. So, no, I don't think we would change much. We were on the mark with the topics we were dealing with."

"Jack, how do you feel today about Mr. Feinsilver and the *News & Record*?" Bob Buckley asked.

"I have no comments on that beyond what's in the material I gave you."

Feinsilver was not at the press conference. Another reporter, Paul Muschick, had been assigned. Later, when other reporters asked Muschick why Feinsilver wasn't there, he said that he was on Thanksgiving holiday.

Asked whether the college had consulted him before cancelling the final class, Jack said he was told that it was being done for the safety of the students, and he wasn't surprised because of the media circus that likely would have surrounded it.

The students, he said, were his primary interest. "My biggest concern is that their experience turned out to be a bad one when it should not have."

A female reporter asked if Jack had any idea how the class came to be represented as it was in the *News & Record*. "Was something misconstrued? Was something made up?"

"The young man asked the first night why we were teaching such a controversial course," Jack said. "I don't think he ever found anything controversial...and I think he created a controversy. That's my personal opinion."

Another reporter asked Beeson if the SCV was preparing for the U.S. Commission on Civil Rights hearing, and he said that the group intended to cooperate.

"We have nothing to hide," he said. "We are honest, tax-paying citizens of this country who happen to have a Southern heritage and we believe that it's a heritage that needs to be preserved. We realize...that we live in a multi-cultural society today, but we only ask to be able to have our heritage as other groups do."

I'll take one more question," said William Johnson. He paused. "Seeing no hands raised, I'd like to thank all of you for coming out today. We trust that you'll report this accurately, since inaccurate reporting is what brought us all here together to start with."

Reporters who called the *News & Record* after the press conference all got the same response. The newspaper would not answer questions about its coverage of the course. "The *News & Record* stands by the accuracy of its report in this matter," city editor Ed Williams told all inquirers, including the newspaper's own reporter.

All of the *News & Record*'s previous articles about the course had appeared on the front page, with the exception of the first, which had been prominently displayed on the local front. The article about the press conference, however, was restricted to a small space at the bottom of the local front, continued on an inside page. It was by far the briefest of the newspaper's articles about the course, and it ignored the lengthy list of refutations to Feinsilver's claims that Jack had prepared and passed out at the press conference.

Instead, Muschick wrote that Jack claimed to have videotapes proving that the course "did not include material suggesting that slaves were satisfied with their lives.

"When asked to share those videotapes with the media, Perdue said: 'They're in the hands of my attorney and they are not available.'"

Only one of Jack's disclaimers was included: that nobody had taught that slaves were satisfied.

'We were accused of teaching this," he was quoted. "We did not teach this.'"

Jack also adamantly denied that anybody had taught that slaves were happy, the charge that brought all the trouble to the course, but the word "happy" didn't appear in this report. *News & Record* editors had banished it from all articles about the course, whether pertinent or not.

Jack expressed immense frustration after reading this article. It was now patently clear to him that the *News & Record* had no interest in the facts. For more than a week, the paper had relentlessly portrayed him as not being forthcoming, yet when he did present his side, it not only disregarded almost everything he said but made him appear to be evasive for not handing over the videotapes to reporters.

If *News & Record* readers ever were to learn the truth about the course he'd taught, Jack realized, they would have to get it from some source other than the newspaper's reporters and editors.

Nineteen

The *News & Record* was not finished with the course. It asked Harry Watson to write an article about the "right history" of the Civil War in North Carolina, as the newspaper would label it. Watson was the UNC history professor who accompanied Senator Eleanor Kinnaird on her visit to community college system president Martin Lancaster to protest the course.

His article appeared on the front of the opinion section on Sunday, November 29, two weeks after Feinsilver's first article.

An editor's note claimed that the course taught that slaves "were so satisfied with their bondage that thousands spurned the Emancipation Proclamation and fought for the Confederacy." The instructor, Jack Perdue, the note continued, "defended his approach by declaring that 'we cannot allow political correctness to rewrite history or wipe out our heritage,' although black leaders have called his assertions offensive and untrue."

The note's claim of what had been taught was untrue, and the quote from Jack was taken from another context entirely to further falsely report that he defended teachings that hadn't been taught.

Watson wrote that "no serious professional historian" claims that slaves were contented and that no credible evidence existed that significant numbers of blacks fought for the Confederacy.

In all the controversy about the RCC course, he went on, "a more profound irony" was being overlooked. "If published accounts are true, Randolph County's neo-Confederates are not even teaching the genuine heritage of the county's white people, let alone blacks."

The "genuine 'heritage' of Randolph and Guilford counties was profoundly hostile" to the Confederacy, Watson wrote. Confederate leaders thought North Carolina to be a "hotbed of desertion and disaffection," so unreliable that Jefferson Davis didn't want to put its citizens in high office.

"Why aren't we hearing about this heritage?" he asked. "Who is rewriting whom?"

All of what Watson mentioned had been taught in the course, however, plus much of the rest of what he went on to write about in this piece, and more beyond that about wartime activities in Randolph and Guilford Counties. (And even more was scheduled for the last class, which was cancelled because of the uproar.) One reason Watson wasn't hearing about this heritage was because the *News & Record* wasn't accurately or fully reporting what had been taught. Another was that Watson apparently made no attempt to find out for himself.

Jack had learned to expect the *News & Record* to have little or no concern for facts, he said. But he couldn't understand why a "serious, professional historian" would write an article without attempting to learn what actually occurred.

After the *News & Record* failed to report Jack's response to the articles that he believed to have maligned and defamed not only himself, but his guest lecturers, his students, the Sons of Confederate Veterans, and the college, he brought up the idea of taking out ads in the *News & Record* and the *High Point Enterprise* to make the truth known locally at least. The Frazier camp didn't have the money to pay for that, but Jack took the idea to Patrick Griffin, the national commander.

The ad filled much of the lower half of page A-4 in the *News & Record* on Tuesday, December 1, at a cost to the SCV of about $2,500. A smaller version, costing $718, appeared in the *High Point Enterprise* on the same morning.

SLAVERY IS WRONG...AND SO IS FABRICATED JOURNALISM

Recent news articles written by Ethan Feinsilver, a reporter for the Greensboro (NC) News & Record, *give false and misleading statements and accusations about a course on North Carolina's War for Southern Independence at the Archdale Campus of Randolph Community College.*

Why, Mr. Feinsilver, would you (without bothering to attend the class in question) report to your readers that this adult education class "teaches that most black people were happy under slavery..."

WHEN NO SUCH STATEMENT WAS EVER MADE IN THE CLASS?

Why, Mr. Feinsilver, would you (again without attending the class session) write falsely that "the course teaches that the 'vast majority' of black people were satisfied with their lives as slaves..."

WHEN SO SUCH STATEMENT WAS EVER MADE IN CLASS?

You garnered considerable personal attention, Mr. Feinsilver, when your "story" of a southern community college holding classes "defending slavery in this day and age" quickly made front page headlines across the nation.

BUT YOU KNEW FROM READING THE COURSE INTRODUCTION THAT THE INSTRUCTORS HAD ALREADY CONDEMNED SLAVERY TO THEIR STUDENTS. AND HAD YOU TRULY BEEN INTERESTED IN THE TOTAL CONTENT OF THE COURSE, YOU WOULD HAVE KNOWN THAT THE ENTIRE CLASS WAS VIDEO TAPED FOR FUTURE INSTRUCTION... A TAPE THAT NOW REFUTES YOUR OUTRAGEOUS ALLEGATIONS. SO THE REAL QUESTION, MR. FEINSILVER, IS WHY HAVE YOU ENGAGED IN RACE-BAITING? ENTER THE NAACP

Which blindly accepted Feinsilver's fabrications to advance their own agenda of intolerance of Southern and Confederate heritage. They quickly condemned this class and threatened Randolph Community College with formal complaints from the U.S. Commission on Civil Rights.

Mr. Feinsilver's irresponsible—and potentially libelous—reporting, followed by the NAACP's scurrilous threats and divisive, prejudicial rhetoric have defamed a number of guest instructors, including an associate professor of history from an area university, a retired professor from a neighboring four-year college, and an author and writer from Mr. Feinsilver's own paper, none of whom would have participated in a course such as Mr. Feinsilver described.

It is customary among gentlemen, Mr. Feinsilver, to right such misdeeds as yours with a formal retraction and a public apology...in this case not only to the instructors and students involved, but to the citizens of North Carolina. After all, who do you think they will believe...your "story"...or the college's video tapes?

The ad misrepresented one point. The video tapes, which on some nights were shot from two different cameras, were not the college's. They were the property of Jack and Rahlo Fowler, and, as events would turn out, nobody at the college ever would see them.

The ad provoked a lot of talk in the *News & Record*'s newsroom, and management's response brought even more. The metro editor, Tom Corrigan, was at a company retreat in rural Guilford County that morning, but shortly after noon, his administrative assistant, Julie Conklin, sent an e-mail message that went to the entire news staff:

> *Tom called at noon...none of you were around...he said 'not to respond to any news media' on the ad that was in today's paper. If it is just subscribers we can just say that the people who put the ad in the paper were not even mentioned in Ethan's article and that we would not be putting any other stories in tomorrow's paper....*

Conklin thought that she was sending that message only to editors, as Corrigan directed. Two minutes later, she e-mailed a correction.

After learning about the e-mail mix-up, Corrigan sent his own message to the news staff the following day:

> *FYI FOR THOSE OF YOU WHO HAD QUESTIONS ABOUT THE AD IN TUESDAY'S PAPER THAT ATTACKED ETHAN: 1. We're standing behind Ethan and the story. 2. Because we believe in free speech and because we sell ads, people can buy ads to criticize us. 3. We are not responding in force because we don't need to; because we're not the issue even though some people are trying to make us the issue; and because we're not going to lower ourselves to their level. I hope that I've made our support of Ethan clear. If you have any questions, send them to me.*

Four minutes afterward, a news staffer responded with a message sent to the entire newsroom:

> *I'd like to announce the creation of a fund to buy*

ethan a confederate musket to protect himself. Or at least a sword. Yes, definitely a sword. Contributions of dollars or confederate script are welcome.

On the day that Jack and the SCV officers held their press conference, Larry Linker sent a memo to students in the Civil War course about his cancellation of the last class.

"I hope you understand that this was a difficult decision," he wrote, "but it was the right thing to do under the circumstances."

He invited the students to meet with him and the college's attorney to discuss the content of the course at 6:30 p.m. Thursday, December 3, in the classroom where they normally met.

Jack also was invited to attend and to bring his guest lecturers.

Some students were distrustful about this meeting, particularly because the college's attorney, Alan Pugh, came with Linker. Some thought the meeting a sham, mere protocol, that Linker was going through the motions to make it appear that he was undertaking an investigation, but that his decision was predetermined. They felt betrayed by his cancellation of their final class, and they had little faith that he had any genuine concern for them. They believed that he was under intense pressure from the NAACP and the press, and they had seen that leaders of institutions who found themselves in that situation inevitably yielded to it, no matter the truth, no matter right or wrong.

"They were just trying to get out of a sticky situation," said Dwight Steeds, a former banker who had taken the course because of his strong interest in military history.

Pugh's presence, some students thought, was dictated by the college's concern that they, or the instructors, might be considering lawsuits.

Despite these misgivings, all the students but Nancy Boyles, who was out of town, attended. Tom Corns hadn't been sure he could make it. He drove to the campus straight from the airport after hurrying back from a business trip, arriving just as the meeting was about to begin.

All but three guest lecturers—Bob White, Rick McCaslin, and Bob Zeller—were present, as were several of the volunteers who assisted with the camp re-enactment and the class about life on the homefront. Jack deliberately excluded McCaslin, the High Point University professor, and Zeller, the *News & Record* reporter, because he was afraid their association with the course might hurt them with their employers. (Zeller had left the newspaper to start a new career.)

Linker wanted to speak first with students, then with instructors.

He began his presentation to the students by recapping events since Feinsilver's first article, along with all the problems it had brought to him and the college—the relentless phone calls, the TV crews who showed up at his house. Dedra Routh grew more frustrated as he talked.

"This was not what I wanted to hear," she recalled.

Routh had called Linker the day after he cancelled the final class to let him know that she was disappointed and sorry he hadn't consulted with the students before making his decision. He told her he was planning to meet with them soon.

Now she wondered why she had bothered to come.

"It was just a waste of time," she said. "I knew he'd already made up his mind. He was scared. It didn't matter what we said, or what we thought."

Three of the students had written letters to the editor of the *News & Record* denying Feinsilver's claims (Others had written letters to other publications as well.), and the paper had published edited versions of two on this morning.

One was from Hope Haywood, who also called Linker to tell him her feelings about the cancellation of the last class. "I do not know where the reporter got the information that has been reported," Haywood wrote, "but it was not taught in class."

The other letter was from Joan King, who attended the class with her son. "We were given handouts stating that slaves 'were denigrated, corroded by degradation and psychologically disabled by oppression,'" she wrote. "We were exposed to a variety of material that Feinsilver chose not to present."

The third letter was from Louise Canipe, who had written to Feinsilver's editor well before his first article to warn that whatever he wrote wouldn't be fair. Neither of her letters was published.

Linker had read the letters that appeared this morning and from talking with Routh, Haywood and Rhonda Winters had a good idea of the students' feelings before he arrived. Before he left, the students would let him know that they were united. They hadn't been taught that most slaves were happy, or that tens of thousands fought for the Confederacy because they believed in the Southern cause.

"Everybody had heard the same thing," as Johnny Branch later put it. "It just didn't happen the way Feinsilver wrote it."

Linker brought questionnaires for the students and passed them out.

> 1. *Did you hear, or were taught that "most black people were happy under slavery?"*
> 2. *Were you taught that "tens of thousands of black men fought for the Confederacy because they believed in the Southern cause?"*
> 3. *Did the instructor ever defend slavery or the institution of slavery?*
> 4. *Do you feel that you were given a factually researched, well-documented view of this period of history?*
> 5. *Were you ever told that you were not to discuss the course with others? The* News & Record *said that students "resent that some of what you were learning in this class was almost forbidden in public discourse." Did you express this sentiment?*
> 6. *Were you interviewed by the reporter? If yes, was it used in any article? If yes, were you quoted accurately? If no, please explain.*
> 7. *What was your intent in taking this class?*

A space also was provided for comments.

Tom Corns copied the questions so he could pass them on to Jack before the instructors gathered with Linker and Pugh.

The students remained united on their questionnaires as well, their answers unanimous. To questions one, two, three, and five they answered no, to four yes. Answers to six and seven varied according to their experiences.

Linker told the students that he was just beginning his investigation, that he didn't know how it might turn out, but if he had to permanently cancel the course, the students would get their money back.

That was when Hope Haywood spoke up.

"I was just so ill about it all," she said. "I had been to every class. I had gotten so much out of this course. I said, 'Dr. Linker, do you mean to tell me that I've driven up to this campus from Asheboro all these weeks. I've had to get sitters; my husband has had to get his own meals. And you're just going to give me my money back? I don't think that's right."

What about the test she and Routh were supposed to take at the last class so they could have the hours of study applied to their continuing teacher accreditation?

"He said, 'Well, we'll just have to see what we can do about that.'" Haywood recalled. "I said, 'This has been a very good class, and I don't think it should be cancelled.'"

Even Rhonda Winters, who sat in on this meeting and who knew how most of the students felt, was surprised that they weren't more forthcoming. Louise Canipe later wished they had spoken out more stridently. On the following day she wrote to Linker to thank him for the meeting.

"We are the only ones that know what happened in this class, but I feel the class was hesitant in speaking out as much as they could have. If we do not repeat this class...then Ethan will have had his way.... I know you have to make your own decision, but I do hope you will not let Ethan accomplish what he started out to do—destroy. We can not continue to let these events happen and have a few people tell everyone what they can not study...."

"Two weeks of my life in essence have been lost," Linker said soon after beginning his session with instructors. He went on to tell them, as he had their students, about the ordeal he and the college had been through because of news coverage of their course.

"I got a call from the *Wall Street Journal* the day after the markets hit an all-time world high," he said, "and you'd think if they had anything to write about that day, it wouldn't be us."

It amazed him that the media accepted Feinsilver's story as "the gospel truth," he went on, pointing out that neither the AP nor any newspaper called to ask him about its validity before publishing it.

The impact of the media and all that it brought down on the college was not only unbelievable, he noted, but on-going.

"It'll be next summer before I'll be able to read all the e-mail. E-mail is a good way to send hate mail today."

Interestingly, he said, he had received very few responses from African-Americans. The most vitriolic had come from white males condemning the course. He'd heard nothing from the NAACP until three days after the first article appeared, he said, going on to tell about his meeting with Skip Alston, Earl Jones and Richie Everette, which he called "very cordial."

"It was not argumentative. By time that I was able to share with them that I thought we had an over-zealous, irresponsible reporter that was trying to create problems. I was never pressured by their group to do anything."

To this day, he said, he still had heard nothing from the U.S. Commission on Civil Rights.

"If they're coming to investigate me on my campus you'd think that I ought to hear from them."

He told about his meeting with board members and how they decided that it was in the best interest of the college to cancel the last class until an investigation could be completed. He talked about his emotional meeting with his staff and the press conference that followed.

"By Thursday," he said, "I'd had six hours sleep total since Monday. I was a little on the ragged side. Ethan said I pleaded exhaustion."

The media still was hounding him, he said, calling daily wanting to know what his investigation was finding.

It was not his intention to get into historical debate, he told the instructors.

"I've got to try to ascertain quite simply the truth to the allegations that were related in that first article."

Earlier this evening, Jack had given Linker his twelve-point response to Feinsilver's articles, as well as his introduction to the course and other documents. Linker said that he also had read the accounts of the SCV's press conference, plus Herman White's letter to the *News & Record*, as well as an article in the Asheboro *Courier-Tribune* about White and his denial. He had some idea of the group's position, he pointed out, but he had to make an inquiry of his own.

Jack spoke up to assure him that he had been in every minute of every class except for the second half of Rick McCaslin's, when he and White were being interviewed by Feinsilver, and that nobody in any class while he was present had taught what Feinsilver claimed.

"Those things were not said. People have gone off half-cocked on false information."

Just last Sunday, Jack pointed out, the *News & Record* published an article by a UNC professor chastising the class for not teaching the real history of Randolph and Guilford counties during the war.

"We spent a whole hour talking about the Unionist sentiment in Guilford and Randolph counties, and the Quakers seeking alternative service so that they didn't have to fight for the Confederacy. All this that he said we should have been teaching, we *were* teaching, and nobody knows that because they weren't here."

The truth about the class, Jack said, was in his twelve-point response to Feinsilver's articles.

Linker asked about the "tens of thousands" of blacks who supposedly fought for the Confederacy.

"There were no numbers used in class," White told him, and he and Jack went on to explain how that claim came about.

"Was anything said that was demeaning to any minority....?" Linker wanted to know.

"Nothing," Jack said adamantly. "Had there been, anybody who had said it would have been out of the class, whether they had been a student or instructor."

He made it clear to his guest lecturers, he said, that they were not to interject personal opinion, that they had to have documentation for whatever they taught, preferably from the period of the war.

"Was there any intent in teaching this class to foster white supremacy?" Linker asked.

"Absolutely not!" Jack responded, as an uproar erupted in the room.

"That's garbage," said White.

"I had to ask the question," Linker said, as the room quieted down.

As an SCV camp commander, Jack said, he regularly got calls from all types of people asking about joining, some from "the white supremacist element."

"I just tell them, 'You've got the wrong organization.' We don't hold those views. We don't accept members with those views, and we daggone sure don't teach them!"

Feinsilver, however, seemed to think that was the case, he pointed out.

"He was trying to make it sound like we was fellows with hoods on," White put in.

"He was convinced we had sheets out there in the car," Jack said.

Did any of the guest lecturers belong to any extremist groups? Pugh wanted to know.

"To my knowledge, no," Jack said. But he hadn't asked the university professor, the retired college administrator, the newspaper reporter about the organizations to which they belonged. He didn't think he had that right. They were doing him and the college a favor by participating in the course.

Linker told the group that he didn't know what his findings might be.

"I'm in a little bit of a quandary in that I have an obligation to these students," he said. "I contracted with them that I would provide a certain service and they would pay a certain fee. I am not the kind of person who will break a contract without some just cause. If I felt like the allegations were true, I'd probably say that's it. But if I don't find that to be true then I've got to evaluate...got to be sensitive of people we serve.

"We do have some sensitivity issues that I've got to deal with somewhere down the line.... To a certain element of society the very sight of a Confederate flag is offensive, the very question of slavery is offensive. Whether you agree with it, whether you like it, whether you don't, that's an issue. You've got your rights, but I'll have to look at some of this."

He would be going to Atlanta for a meeting this weekend, Linker said, and it would be the latter part of next week before he could get around to considering the information he was gathering. He promised a quick decision.

Pugh warned that groups on each side of this issue were no doubt eager to exploit it and suggested that it would be helpful if everybody withheld comments to reporters until the investigation was complete. Anything might be misinterpreted, he noted, and went on to mention a favorite observation: *I never had to explain something I never said.*

Jack found that amusing. Explaining something he never said was exactly the situation in which he found himself.

On the following Sunday, December 6, the *News & Record* published a lengthy article by Paul Muschick saying that several area community colleges were reviewing their policies on community service classes because of the controversy about RCC's Civil War course, which it claimed had been cancelled in "mid-session." The article went on to explain how such courses were chosen at several colleges.

Two days later, Doug Clark, editorial page editor of the *High Point Enterprise*, published a column attacking the SCV and the ad that appeared in the *Enterprise* and *News & Record*.

"The Sons of Confederate Veterans should stick to re-enactments of Civil War battles. That way, they can stage a victory now and then. When they engage in debate they only repeat Pickett's Charge." (The SCV does not stage re-enactments.)

In their ad, he wrote, the instructors had denied that anybody had taught that blacks were happy or satisfied under slavery.

"Why this was 'outrageous allegation...fabricated journalism...race baiting...irresponsible—and potentially libelous—reporting.'

"Hogwash...."

The following Sunday, four weeks after its original article about the RCC course, the *News & Record* devoted its opinion section to slavery. The package of stories was headlined: *THE **REALITY** OF SLA-VERY*.

The main article was written by Loren Schweninger, the UNCG history professor, who, Feinsilver falsely claimed, had been cited by the RCC instructors as endorsing their views. Schweninger was director of the Race and Slavery Petitions Project at UNCG, which collected and archived petitions to government agencies across the South concerning race, slavery, and free blacks. He also was co-author with acclaimed African-American historian John Hope Franklin of Duke University of the book *Runaway Slaves*, which was to be published by Oxford University Press in spring, 1999. A selection from the book was included in the package of articles.

Schweninger wrote that the "angry debate" about the RCC course "is a perfect example of how our sound-bite culture simplifies and distorts history." The class' assumptions "that slaves were content and that the Civil War was fought to defend the noble cause of states' rights is doing an injustice to historical reality," he wrote.

Schweninger's assumptions of the class' assumptions also were doing an injustice to historical reality, however, for they were assumptions that he obviously had not investigated.

Another article in the package was by James D. Steele, an African-American associate professor of political science at A&T University. It was headlined: *Romanticizing slavery days robs African-Americans of humanity*.

Steele referred to the supposed teaching that slaves were satisfied with their lives. "Why is it so hard for some to acknowledge the fact that slavery...was wrong;" he asked, "and why is it difficult to accept that those who supported slavery were on the wrong side of history and morality?"

Jack, who stated in class that slavery was wrong, believed that the purpose of these stories was to keep the controversy alive and to put pressure on Linker to permanently banish the course.

Ten days had passed since the students and instructors met with Linker and Pugh, and they still were wondering about the fate of their course. Most were not optimistic. They had no way of knowing that events were about to swing in their favor.

Twenty

Larry Linker and his trustees asked the law firm representing the college for legal opinions on several issues, and the firm's report, signed by Alan Pugh, was delivered on Monday, December 14, the day after the *News & Record* published its package of stories about "the reality of slavery."

Under the mandates of academic freedom, Pugh wrote, RCC had the right to examine and approve the contents of the course and to decide whether it should be taught. It also could refuse a course that "would be offensive to the generally accepted standards of the community or a segment thereof."

But Pugh found "no evidence whatsoever that any statements were made, or any material disseminated...that would rise to that level. Indeed, there is no evidence at all that the students, all adults, were taught or received any material that any rational person could conclude was inflammatory or insulting in any way to any person or group."

Nobody, he said, had been misled "as to the structure, plan, outline of the course, or the material to be presented."

Indeed, Pugh noted, responses from the students showed that the classes "exceeded their expectations as to detail, comprehensive examination of the period, critical analysis of the material, and freedom to challenge and debate the subject matter."

"After an examination of the allegations contained in Mr. Feinsilver's articles in the *News & Record*, we have concluded that he made a deliberate attempt to mislead his readers as to the nature, purpose, and content of the course," Pugh wrote.

"His statements included the course 'teaches that most black people were happy under slavery and that tens of thousands of black men fought for the Confederacy because they believed in the Southern cause.' That statement was false."

It also was false, he said, that instructors extrapolated that slaves were satisfied with their lives.

"Much of Mr. Feinsilver's articles contained negative comments about the course from individuals in various organizations or in academia which could only have been elicited in reaction to a deliberate, mendacious, misrepresentation by Mr. Feinsilver of both the content and conduct of the course.

"The Greensboro *News & Record* in its headlines, captions, and photographs deliberately exploited the negative reaction and comments of civil rights and anti-defamation leaders based on Mr. Feinsilver's false characterization of the course to them. This course was characterized as 'controversial.' It indeed became controversial because of the deceptive information conveyed by the newspaper and its reporter to those interviewed and to the paper's own subscribers and readers.

"Moreover, the *News & Record* and its reporter failed to follow the accepted practice in responsible journalism of providing reporting balance to their readers. For example, not one word was mentioned of the class where instructors and students discussed the vehement opposition to secession, slavery, and the war in Randolph County itself. The paper made no mention that students learned that Randolph County voted against secession nine to one, rebelled against Confederate conscription, and aided the underground railroad to protect fugitive slaves.

"However, in the context of public officials, public figures, and public institutions, the law of libel does not protect RCC against irresponsible journalism or even outright lying. Lies, in order to be actionable, must be made maliciously or in wanton and willful disregard of the truth. In this matter, the reporter cleverly and deviously took interviews, whether in context or not, with instructors made outside the classroom and conveyed to the public that such statements were being made in the classroom.

"In summary, the articles were irresponsible, deliberately conveyed a misleading and negative impression of the course, the college and Randolph County. The articles gratuitously hurt the reputation of the college and maligned entirely innocent students and instructors. Nonetheless, the article would not in our view support an action for libel by the college.

"Finally, we advise that RCC is contractually bound to authorize the completion of the course. It is also our view that the content, subject matter and academic integrity of this course as presented fully justifies it being offered in the future."

• • •

Pugh's report left Linker little room to do anything other than to allow the course to continue. That had been his instinct all along. He instructed Cathy Hefferin to prepare a statement for the press that the class would go on, and she did that the following day. But when Linker shared the findings with the college's crisis consultant, Rick Amme, complications arose.

Amme knew that it was rare for a news operation to cling to a mistake. Reporters had to face editors when questions were raised about accuracy. They had to defend their information.

"I found it really hard to believe that the newspaper would continue these stories, stand by them, if it didn't feel it had something," Amme recalled. "The reporter in me said, 'This doesn't add up. Something is missing here.'"

If Linker chose to allow the course to proceed, he would have to give reasons for doing so, presumably from the law firm's opinion, and that only could be seen by the *News & Record* as a challenge to present more damaging material, if it had it, or to attempt to dig up more.

"It's ill advised to...challenge a newspaper publicly," Amme said. "I think it's just not smart. You tweak the nose of a reporter and news operation at your peril."

His suggestion was that they try to find out what information the newspaper had before Linker reached a decision that could prove to be embarrassing later.

Amme knew Van King, the *News & Record* publisher. They occasionally covered the same events when both were reporters in the seventies.

"I said, 'Let me call Van and see what it is he knows.'"

Linker considered that a reasonable approach.

"It's a good thing you called us," Amme remembered King telling him, "because you've saved your client a lot of embarrassment."

"Van said, 'We've got it, Rick. We've got the story. We've got this, and we've got more.' Or words to that effect. The implication of the conversation was that if we deny this, then the newspaper will have no other recourse than to bring more out."

Amme conveyed this conversation to Linker and suggested that they meet with King and his editors to try to find out what they had. Linker agreed, and the meeting was set for 10 a.m. Wednesday, December 16. Linker and Cathy Hefferin met Amme at the newspaper's offices in Greensboro. Metro editor Tom Corrigan and city editor Ed

Williams also were present.

Linker later remembered their reception as "very cordial."

"We didn't demand retractions or this that and the other," he said. "We expressed that this was a serious situation."

He told about the ordeal the college had been through and went on to make several points: that Feinsilver hadn't attended the class on which he based his provocative charges; that Hefferin had called Feinsilver's editor more than a week before the first story to report students' fears that he wasn't going to present the class fairly; that Feinsilver hadn't given college officials a chance to respond to his claims.

"They basically listened," Linker recalled.

But that changed when he brought up inaccuracies in Feinsilver's reporting.

"I was probably pretty hard on Ethan's coverage," he said.

Hefferin joined in the criticism. She had gone through the articles marking all the parts she knew to be wrong, including the false quote attributed to her, and Feinsilver's later misquotes of what she had told him. But when she began pointing these out, she said, King interrupted.

"They basically just disagreed with everything we said," she remembered. "They just didn't see it the way we saw it. They said the way he presented it was fine. They completely backed him up. I saw the futility of going through the whole article. I just stopped."

"Van King was cordial right to the end," Linker recalled, "and then I saw that he was perfectly capable of playing hardball."

King brought out a folder from which he took several pages highlighted in yellow. He identified it as a handout from the course. It actually was Herman White's lesson plan, but Linker, Hefferin and Amme didn't know that.

As Hefferin later recalled, King was "saying that they didn't use everything they could have used, that there were other things that could be damaging."

As an example, he read aloud an item from the lesson plan:

> There seemed to be a fatality lurking in certain spots....It wasn't long before Mr. Reb made his whereabouts known, but he was so covered with leaves that no eye could discern him. Our sharpshooter drew a bead on him and something dropped, that something being a six-foot nigger whose weight wasn't less than 300 pounds.

This was one of three examples from period documents that White had included in his lesson plan to show that blacks had fought for the Confederacy. It was from the diary of Private John W. Haley, of the 17th Maine Infantry, which appeared in the book *The Rebel Yell and Yankee Hurrah*, edited by Ruth L. Silliker, and published by Down East Books of Camden, Me.

King let Amme look at the handout but said he couldn't allow them to take it.

"I had the sense we all had a sort of deer-in-the-headlights look," Amme recalled. "Jeez, they've got it. They do have something."

The meeting ended quickly, and afterward, Amme, Linker and Hefferin sat in the newspaper's parking lot in the Crown Victoria the college provided for Linker talking about what happened. All were aware that there could be only one reason why King chose the selection he read—because it contained the word "nigger." The implication was clear.

"They're going to shove this stuff back in our faces," Amme said. "All they have to do is start rolling quotes out and putting them in the paper."

All had seen what happened when that word was introduced in the O.J. Simpson trial. Could they risk allowing it to be connected to RCC?

"They were saying, 'We really could use this material,'" Linker recalled. "Reality began to set in on me. I don't even think of black-mail, but...."

Linker had little doubt that if he allowed the class to continue, the *News & Record* would continue to go after RCC, but this time on an even dirtier level.

"I had to ask, is this a fight the college wanted to fight?" Amme recalled. "Did it want to put its reputation on the line? I thought not. The press really doesn't give a damn about your reputation. They want a story."

He thought that the college had to cut itself free from the course as quickly as possible.

"Dr. Linker and I still weren't sure," Hefferin said. "I was just wondering what context that came from. Anything can be taken out of context and sound terrible. I wasn't convinced. I wanted to see a copy of that handout myself."

So did Linker. Before parting with Amme to return to the campus, he decided to try to get copies of all the materials passed out during the course before making a decision.

Later, newsroom sources said that Feinsilver's editor, Lex Alexander, gloated to reporters that day about the meeting with RCC officials. Faced with the newspaper's evidence, he claimed, they had been sent "whimpering back to Randolph County with their tails between their legs."

As soon as she got back to her office, Hefferin called Rhonda Winters to see if she could get copies of the handouts. Winters called one of the students, Louise Canipe, who immediately drove to the Archdale campus with the notebook Jack handed out on the first night, a notebook now fat with all the materials the students received. Winters delivered the book to Linker that afternoon.

Jack was unaware of the meeting between college officials and the *News & Record*'s publisher and top editors. The day after the meeting was his sixtieth birthday. He and Annie Laura went to his mother's for a traditional birthday dinner. Jack was not a cake person, so his mother always made him a chocolate pie.

Jack seemed to be in low spirits, his sister, Betsy, noticed. He didn't eat much. But she had a special present for him. Usually, she gave him a Civil War book for his birthday, and another a week later for Christmas. But this year she had found in her attic the old family radio, a table-top Crosley, that they listened to as children. She had it refurbished and put back into playing condition. Jack loved old things. She knew he would recognize this immediately.

"He was so thrilled," she said. "I told him this would be his birthday and his Christmas present for the next five years."

Linker would find that the word "nigger" appeared only twice in Herman White's lesson plan, both times in excerpts from the Maine private's diary, once used as evidence of disdain by northerners of both blacks and whites in the South, again as one of three period documents cited to show that blacks actually fought for the Confederacy.

In neither case was it an inappropriate use, Linker thought, simply part of an historical document. But he was concerned about the tone of White's lesson plan because of its references to "Yankee" and "abolitionist myths and lies." He also had read White's letters to the editor in the *News & Record* and *High Point Enterprise*, and an article about him in the Asheboro *Courier-Tribune*, as well as hearing his comments at the meeting with instructors. White had a stridency in his views that was not apparent in Jack, Linker thought, and he considered him a potential "wild card."

If he were going to risk the college's reputation, he wanted to see the tape of White's class so he could know for certain what White said and did.

"If I was going to take on Goliath, I wanted to have all the ammunition I could get," he said.

He called Rahlo Fowler and asked if he could see the tape. Fowler said he'd have to get back to him.

Fowler conferred with Jack and with national commander Patrick Griffin. At that time, Griffin recalled, the SCV was considering lawsuits against the college, the NAACP, the *News & Record*, and perhaps other newspapers. He had sent the tapes to the Rutherford Institute in Charlottesville, Va., which helped the SCV with its successful lawsuit to allow its logo on Maryland license tags, in the hope the institute would advise them. It would not be a good idea, Griffin thought, to hand over evidence to somebody they were considering suing until they had to. Fowler called Linker to say that the tapes could not be made available at present. Later, he would acknowledge that this probably was a mistake.

"Right up until that point," Linker later said, "that class would have had a chance of continuing."

More was pressuring Linker than was apparent to those outside the college. An accrediting team from the Southern Association of Colleges and Schools was due at the campus in the spring, and preparing for their inspections required vast amounts of extra work. Several weeks of work already had been lost because of the controversy. Now Linker was facing what he saw as a clear threat from the *News & Record* to expand and extend the ordeal that it had thrust upon the college, and he feared it could even endanger accreditation.

"The media keeps churning it out, churning it out," he said. "How do you fight that?"

Rick Amme's position remained solid: drop the course and move on; otherwise face the consequences of how allowing the course to continue would be presented.

"I had to ask, 'Do you want to stake the college's reputation on a course taught by the Sons of Confederate Veterans? That's how it's going to be portrayed," Amme said. "If you fight the good fight, take the long haul and hang in there, you may die. Can you afford to hang in there and fight?"

If the class continued, Amme said, so would protests from the NAACP, along with news stories, nasty editorials and columns. The *News & Record*, feeling challenged, might very well carry through on King's implied threat to publish the excerpts from the lesson plan containing the word "nigger." All of this could prompt demonstrations, which would generate even more unwanted and damaging attention. And there was the announced civil rights commission hearing to think about.

"I know it was a very, very hard decision for Dr. Linker to make," Cathy Hefferin said. "We went back and forth, back and forth. It really didn't matter which way you went, you were going to get criticized."

All of his staff recognized that Linker was under great pressure. Later, he said he felt like a ball in a pinball machine, being dizzily banged from side to side.

"You wake up at two in the morning and this is on your mind," he said. "You drive to work and it's on your mind. The pressure, it's there constantly."

No pressure was coming from his board of directors, however. "I think Larry had a lot of internal pressure, self-imposed," said chairman Jerry Tillman. "I think his head was saying one thing and his heart was saying another."

The Christmas break was looming, and Linker wanted to put this behind him before that, so the college wouldn't have to start a new year dealing with it.

"We had this one twenty-five-hour class, ten or eleven students, and that was paralyzing the whole operation," Linker said. "If you've got a malignancy, nip it off and keep going. You just can't keep taking a beating over a small part of your program."

Linker informed his staff that he would be dropping the course.

"I was in a no-win situation from day one," he later explained. "Did I like what I had to do? No. I did what I felt like I had to do to move this college on. Somehow we had to put this behind us."

Rhonda Winters had been keeping up with all that was happening on the main campus. She sensed the inevitable result and felt a personal obligation to warn Jack about what was coming.

She knew Jack had trusted all along that if he didn't criticize the college and depended on the truth, he would be allowed to continue the course.

She called and said she wanted to talk to him on a personal basis.

She didn't want to do it on campus, and didn't want anybody else to know about it. They agreed to meet at Fairfield Plaza, a shopping center on South Main Street in High Point. Jack got into her car to talk.

"I said, 'Jack, I'm telling you this as a friend,'" Winters recalled. "'The college wants nothing to do with you. You've got to realize they're going to cancel this course and they're not going to offer it again.' He didn't have much to say. He never showed how he felt. He just thanked me. He said, 'I appreciate you telling me that.'"

After returning from the meeting with the newspaper's publisher and editors, Cathy Hefferin wrote another press release just to be prepared. This one announced that the class would be dropped. She faxed it to Rick Amme that evening, and he sent it back with changes the following morning. That statement would go back and forth several times over the next few days, each time with changes, as the debate continued and Linker wavered over his decision. When the decision was made, Hefferin and Amme still had a problem: what reason would be given for cancelling the course?

They settled on lack of balance. But rewrites of the statement continued almost until the time of the press conference.

This was the final version:

> Following an investigation of press allegations about RCC's noncredit self-supporting course on the Civil War entitled "North Carolina History: Our Role in the War for Southern Independence," I have decided to stand by my original decision to cancel the one remaining class, and we will not offer the course again.
>
> After interviewing participants and examining course materials, I believe that the instructors and students think the content was sincerely and honestly presented and academically appropriate. However, I also believe that a part of the course material—especially when taken out of context—can be disputed and construed as offensive.
>
> Content that can be seen as controversial should not be of concern when presented from a balanced perspective. This particular Civil War course, however, was taught from a confederate perspective which was openly stated from the beginning. That is where the problem lies. Because the class was presented from a particular point of view, its content

can be challenged. For that reason, I cannot allow the class to resume. The college will refund the tuition of the students.

To prevent a recurrence of this misunderstanding, Randolph Community College has strengthened its method of approving self-supporting community service courses. We now require a more detailed course outline prior to approval at the vice president level.

Our goal now is to put this matter behind us and resume building on Randolph Community College's 36-year reputation for excellence.

Hefferin called the press conference for Monday afternoon, December 21. Only a single TV crew, from channel 45 in Winston-Salem, and two newspaper reporters showed up. Feinsilver was not one of them. The *News & Record* was represented by Eric Dyer.

Jack learned about the cancellation when he received Linker's statement on his fax machine shortly before the press conference. Not long afterward, reporters began calling to ask his response. He told them that the students got viewpoints from the North as well as from the South, and that he was mainly disappointed for the students who wouldn't get to have their last class.

The *News & Record* buried Dyer's brief article in a single column on page B-2 the following morning. It began with this paragraph:

A Civil War course that drew controversy over its discussion of slavery will not be offered again, Randolph Community College officials said Monday.

No mention was made of slaves being happy, satisfied, or contented, or of tens of thousands of blacks fighting for the Confederacy. The article contained only one of the newspaper's previous misrepresentations.

"Among other things, the course used a more than 50-year-old survey of former slaves, a majority of whom reported having good experiences as slaves." The survey White quoted was of recent derivation. The slave narratives on which it was based, however, were more than sixty years old.

Steve Huffman interviewed Linker by telephone and asked his feelings about the media attention.

"It's more of a hurt than an anger," Huffman quoted Linker in the *High Point Enterprise* the following morning. "I love this college deeply. This is like someone saying something about your wife or mama or kid."

Norman Hines of Asheboro's *Courier-Tribune*, the other newspaper reporter at the press conference, called Richie Everette, the Randolph County NAACP president, for his response.

"I appreciate Dr. Linker's bold statement," Everette said. "The emphasis of Confederate ideas is one of slanted interpretation. The course has a thin veil of hatred towards blacks, Indians, Jews and 'Yankees.'"

Earlier, Everette had said that the heritage of the SCV was one of hatred toward Yankees and blacks. Now he was saying that the course itself carried that "veil," and he had added Indians and Jews to the list of those about whom the course supposedly was spreading hatred. Both Jack and Herman White had spoken only favorably of native Americans, however, and no mention of Jews was made in the course, although the large Jewish communities of the South's major cities were, for the most part, strong supporters of the Confederacy, and many Jews served in its armed forces. Jack spoke commendably in class of Judah P. Benjamin, described as the most brilliant legal mind in the South, who had served as the Confederacy's attorney general, secretary of war, and secretary of state, although he didn't mention that he was Jewish. Descendants of Benjamin, he noted, lived in Greensboro. Everette later said that he included Jews because somebody told him that Feinsilver was Jewish.

Students learned of Linker's decision from news reports. Most expected it, feeling that Linker already had knuckled under to the NAACP, and it reinforced their sense of betrayal by the college.

Some thought that Linker's stated reason for dropping the course was contrived, absurd on its face. North Carolina was a Confederate state; any presentation of its history during the war was inherently Confederate. All history was presented from a point of view, Dedra Routh later noted. If the college offered a course on the civil rights era, would the Ku Klux Klan get equal time?

The students thought they had been misrepresented and abused by the *News & Record* and other newspapers, the NAACP, the college, and the U.S. Commission on Civil Rights.

Johnnie Branch summed up their feelings in a letter to the editor of the *High Point Enterprise* published more than two weeks earlier on December 6.

"We would never try to offend any person or group, and if all these journalists who wrote such scathing accounts about us and our history class were actually sitting in on the classes, they would know this is true.... The only people whose civil rights have been violated are the teachers and students of the history class at RCC."

The college mailed copies of Linker's statement to students along with refund checks on the same day as the press conference.

Tom Corns sent back his check with a letter:

> *I sincerely enjoyed the classes...and found them extremely professional and factual.*
>
> *I am returning your check and respectfully request that you fulfill your end of the contractual obligation and allow me to complete this class. I sincerely believe that accepting your check would be an act of cowardice. For your information,* Webster's Dictionary *defines cowardice as a lack of courage when faced with opposition.*

Corn's response was an early indication that the controversy Linker hoped to put behind him wasn't going away.

"The pounding didn't stop," Linker said later. "It just changed gears."

Part IV

Aftershocks

Carlyle said, "a lie cannot live." It shows
that he did not know how to tell them.
—**Mark Twain**

Twenty-one

Asked to define Jack as a person, Anita White tells a story. She had been diagnosed with a rare form of cancer and was a patient in High Point Regional Hospital. For two weeks she hadn't been able to eat or sleep. Her husband, Ronald, sat by her bedside every night.

Early in the morning hours one night as she lay awake and her husband snoozed in his chair, she looked out the narrow window and thought she saw a dove fly by. She was on the sixth or seventh floor, and she wondered why a dove would be there at this time of night.

Then she saw another. She crawled to the window to see what was happening and realized that she hadn't seen doves but huge snowflakes. They soon settled into a steady snowfall, and she stayed at the window watching, mesmerized by its beauty. In the distance she could see the lights of the Krispy Kreme doughnut shop. Krispy Kreme doughnuts originated in nearby Winston-Salem. They were a local delight and had been for as long as she could remember. She loved them hot from the fryer, when they practically melted in her mouth. She could almost envision the "Hot Now!" sign glowing in the Krispy Kreme window. Suddenly, for the first time in two weeks, she felt hunger.

Dawn came with six inches of snow on the ground. High Point usually ground to a standstill with that much snow. The streets were practically deserted. At about eight, Jack called to find out how she was doing. She told him about the doves she thought she had seen, and how the Krispy Kreme sign had beckoned.

Thirty minutes later, Jack and Annie Laura, bundled in heavy coats, walked into her room, big smiles on their faces, Jack carrying a boxful of hot Krispy Kremes.

"That's the kind of person Jack Perdue was," she says.

White met Jack when both were beginning careers in real estate.

White had gone to work for a mortgage lender, and part of her job was to make cold calls, a prospect that terrified her.

On her first call, she remembered getting almost to the door of the real estate agency eight or nine times and turning back to her car before she finally built courage enough to open that door. She failed to notice that beyond the door was a step down. She made her entrance tripping and sprawling onto the floor. Jack, who only recently had taken his first real estate job at the small agency in Archdale, was the person who rushed to help her.

"I don't think I've ever known anybody who was more of a gentleman," she said, "one of the few totally honest people I've ever known."

As their careers grew, they became close friends, the kind who could talk about almost anything. White could call Jack pig-headed, and sometimes he even would grin in acknowledgement.

Jack's integrity was what impressed White most about him. She remembered him telling people starting out in real estate, "Never do anything that would tarnish your integrity or cause anybody to question your ethics." After he became an appraiser and White needed an appraisal on her own house, Jack told her to find somebody else. Their friendship would make it a conflict of interest for him to do it.

White knew that Jack was teaching the Civil War course at RCC and knew that he was excited about it, but he hadn't mentioned his concern about the reporter who had shown up. She didn't know about Feinsilver's first article until a friend told her about it a couple of days after it appeared and faxed it to her. She was shocked by it and knew that Jack had to be hurting because of it. She called to see how he was doing.

"I knew immediately you don't tease him on this," she said, recalling their conversation. "This is a serious issue. It just cut him to the bone that his integrity was questioned."

She sensed that this was something he wasn't ready to talk about.

"He bottled things up and went over it and over it and over it in his mind," she said.

She didn't see Jack until a day or so after his birthday, December 17, when they met for lunch at a restaurant in High Point. At that point, the decision to cancel the class had not been announced.

"He was quieter," she recalled. "He was troubled. He was hurt. He was angry. He was losing weight. There was a lot of change in him. I was concerned about him. He wouldn't talk a lot about it. At first, he wouldn't talk about it at all."

She finally did get him to talk about it, though, and he had a few choice words for newspapers and how dishonest they were. He told her about the lies that had been written, and said he could prove they were lies.

"You know I'm not that stupid," he said. "I've got every class on tape."

"He wanted to keep that class going," she said, "and he would fight to keep it open. Everything he had said in that class was found in textbooks. It was part of history. He felt about it like he did about the battle flag. People died under that flag, he said, and it shouldn't be forgotten, shouldn't be banished because it's something we don't want to see, or hear, or think about."

White was worried about her friend when they parted. She could see in his face the toll all of this had taken. She didn't think he looked well.

Jack had trouble keeping up with all the dastardly deeds of which he had been accused in newspapers and other publications, all the derogatory labels with which he had been branded. He had been accused of teaching pseudo-history, pro-Confederate propaganda, historical fiction, lies, nonsense, prattle, absurdity, idiocy, hearsay history, fraudulent and morally bankrupt history. He had been charged with expressing hatred toward blacks, Jews, Indians and "Yankees," of spreading racist propaganda and obscenity, of prostituting truth to benefit disgraced forebears, of desecrating sacred soil, and stealing dignity from dead slaves. He had been repeatedly compared to neo-Nazis teaching that the Holocaust never happened, and to Bull Connor turning vicious dogs and fire hoses on civil rights demonstrators. He had been proclaimed to be on the wrong side of history and morality, a supporter of slavery, a member of a hate group, "an organization that celebrates the carnage, rape and murder of black people." Questions had been raised about whether he was evil, stupid, or had totally lost his mind. He had been called a crank, a cracker, a neo-Confederate and a Neanderthal.

Nobody saw the effect this had on him more than Annie Laura. Her arrival home from work each afternoon was ritual. Lady would hear her car before she turned into the driveway and announce her arrival with a bark. Jack and Lady would be waiting at the back corner of the house, near the basement entrance, when Annie Laura got out of the car. Lady would be twitching with excitement, rushing to be petted. Jack would greet her with a welcoming hug and kiss.

But after the excitement, anger and pressure of dealing with the daily assaults in the press had faded, and Jack was waiting for Linker to make his decision, Annie Laura would arrive home from work and find nobody waiting for her. Lady would be whining inside the basement entrance, and Annie Laura would find Jack sitting at his desk, his shoulders slumped, staring at the computer screen.

"Don't I get a hug?" she would ask plaintively, and he would stir from his stupor and try to pretend that nothing was wrong.

"When I came home in the evening I saw a different person than I saw before all of this started," Annie Laura remembered. "He was quieter. He didn't want to talk. He held it all in. It was eating away at him on the inside. It was there and it was gnawing away.

"The most important thing in the world to that man was his good name. His name was smeared all over the world, and he couldn't do anything about it."

Later, Annie Laura would marvel at photos made of Jack before Feinsilver's first article and afterward. In those made afterward, the light was gone from him, the spirit missing. The usual twinkle in his eye and the mischief of his grin were no longer to be seen. Solemnity overwhelmed him.

His sister, Betsy, saw the change, too. "He was quieter," she said. "He was eating less."

He always had brooded about things that bothered him, she knew, but she never had seen him like this.

"People were being critical of his integrity and his honor and his good name, and with Jack those were all important things."

Those closest to Jack knew that he was overwhelmed with a sense of helplessness to correct the injustices done to him and others by the *News & Record* and other media. He deeply resented that a newspaper could besmirch people and institutions with lies, spread those lies throughout the world, never allow the victims a fair opportunity to give their side, then blithely move on, leaving the wreckage and misery for others to deal with, never looking back, never acknowledging what it had done, never taking responsibility, never being held accountable.

His only option was to sue for libel, and he was considering that, had already called a couple of lawyers. But he knew that would be a long and difficult route. Libel law made the chances for success slim, at best. The Landmark Corporation, which owned the *News & Record*, had vast resources, could drag the matter out for years, building huge legal fees. A lawsuit could take control of his life, drain his finances and his energies, and allow the newspaper to continue hurting him.

Jack tried to keep his troubles from his children and mother, not wanting to worry them. His daughter, Laura, didn't know about any of this until she, her husband, Keith, and their son, Kenny, came from Rock Hill, S.C., for their Christmas visit. Laura was astounded when she learned all that had been going on.

She deeply resented that her father had been made to appear racist. Her parents had reared her and her brothers to respect all people, she said, and she never had seen racial prejudice in them.

Jack did his best to make Christmas the happy time it always had been for him and his family. Annie Laura bought him a special edition book on a Confederate weapons collection that had been donated to the Greensboro Historical Museum. Among his gifts for her was one that she would cherish—a videotape of the original version of *South Pacific*, the movie he'd taken her to see on their first date. What made it even more special was its wrapping: a note Jack had written in red ink.

"It's hard to believe that it's been almost four decades since a skinny little girl in a sexy red dress hoodooed me into taking her to a movie that I had already seen twice...." There was more, but it was so personal that Annie Laura chose not to reveal it.

She didn't mention to Jack that she actually had worn the red dress to church on the morning after their first date. That dress, she knew, always had a mind-numbing effect on him.

Twenty-two

Larry Linker made it through Christmas with no new turmoil about the course, but before the month was out he realized that the outcry wasn't going away. It just was taking a different path—and a far more personal one for him.

On December 30, Annette Jordan of the *Courier-Tribune* in Asheboro wrote in an editorial page column that she was dumbfounded by Linker's statement that the course was not proper because it was taught from a Confederate perspective.

"Whatever happened to freedom of speech and free exchange of ideas?" she asked. "If there's one place in the world where people can debate and hold varying opinions, it should be the academic world....

"Axing a course because it's based on a particular viewpoint is hypocritical—especially if the same can be said about other courses at RCC."

She brought up two from the current catalog: "Contemporary Issues Facing Families," and "Creating Racial Unity." She would bet they came with strong, particular viewpoints, she wrote, noting the publicly expressed views on race by Chuck Egerton, one of the instructors of the racial unity course.

"Just because a topic is not on today's politically correct list is no reason to snuff it out," she said. "That list changes daily—today it's white conservative beliefs. Tomorrow your pet topic may be on it."

The following day brought another publication affecting the direction of the controversy.

On December 16, the author of this book mailed an open letter to *News & Record* publisher Van King, questioning the integrity of

Feinsilver's reporting. The letter suggested King tell readers how Feinsilver "came to this story, what his motivations and reporting techniques were, and who and what were the sources that prove his stories to be true...."

Copies of the letter were sent to all area news organizations, but only one took note of it. That was the *Rhinoceros Times*, a lively, conservative alternative weekly newspaper distributed free in Guilford County. Founded in 1991, the *Rhino*, as it was called, was named for a local bar where its iconoclastic editor, John Hammer, conceived it as a newsletter. The *Rhino* often broke important news stories that the *News & Record* ignored and was frequently critical of the *News & Record*'s liberalism, it's failure to offer a local conservative voice, and its editorial attacks on area conservatives. The Rhino had grown rapidly, sapping much of the *News & Record*'s advertising, and rivaling it in readership in Guilford County.

On December 31, the *Rhino* published the open letter, evoking criticism of the *News & Record* and bringing calls and letters of encouragement to Jack, some urging him to sue.

The day after the letter to King appeared, the *Courier-Tribune* published a column by Talula Cartwright, an Asheboro resident who was a senior faculty member at the Center for Creative Leadership in Greensboro. The column lauded Linker for banishing the course.

"Experienced leaders...know how to recognize and deal with these important media events safely," she wrote. "Executive training classes actually teach strategies for these situations...."

Linker, she said, "knew the stakes. He knew he had to act quickly, and he did. He acted decisively to save the reputation of the college, to protect its academic integrity, even though the course was not in the academic area. He held the high ground...."

The column began a new wave of criticism of Linker, producing several letters of rebuttal. One, from Becky Bowman of Siler City, echoed Jordan's column, "Whatever happened to that wonderful American right of intellectual freedom and the open debating of ideas and opinions?"

RCC, she wrote, "risks its reputation far more by squelching controversial subjects...."

Bowman recalled former UNC President Bill Friday's stand against the speaker ban law in the '60s.

"...He knew that it was his duty to protect the integrity of the campuses as places of intellectual freedom. He was not about to be bullied by special interest groups, the media or the legislature. He never tried to 'cover his own derriere' under the guise of protecting the reputation of the university."

Another letter, by the author of this book, asked what had become of "the notion that courage is the first quality of leadership?"

Linker's decision "was not just a signal failure of leadership," it said, "it was cowardice, plain and simple."

Linker, it went on, had set the college on a dangerous path.

"What class will go next? How can he appease one offended group...without appeasing all others equally? How can his teachers know from moment to moment whether something they say may offend somebody and they might find their classes closed and themselves dangling in the wind? Where does it end?...."

Linker should reinstate the course or resign, the letter concluded. Failing either, he should be removed by trustees.

This letter brought others of agreement, one from Dedra Routh.

"Yes, yes, yes," she wrote to the suggestion that Linker resign or be removed.

"I have read letter after letter, people spilling their guts about the terrible atrocities committed in our classroom. Ludicrous; this entire controversy was simply created! I know, I was there."

She had taken the course, she said, because she was a Civil War buff, had begun researching her ancestors who served in the war, none of whom were slave owners, and hoped the class would give insight into why they fought. It had, she said, and she praised Jack for presenting facts fairly.

"We never intended to offend," she wrote. "History is full of many offenses and if we continue to hush the echoes of the past, then I feel we shall surely lose our way...."

Darla Barber, one of Jack's lecturers, a frequent instructor at RCC, wrote to Linker on January 8. After his meetings with instructors and students, she said, she had great faith that he would see the truth and do the right thing. But she'd never felt so betrayed.

"Now I see that the meeting with you was all just a sham. You had already judged us 'guilty as charged.' You sat in that meeting lying TO us just like Feinsilver lied ABOUT us."

His decision, she wrote, "made us guilty of a 'crime' we did not commit.... It seems in this world, lately anyway, the bad guys always win. Congratulations."

Linker later acknowledged that he was stung by the criticism, especially by the calls for his removal. "I had over a forty-year career. I had given almost my whole life to this place. I had never heard the thought uttered that I should be relieved of my duties. If I'd made the worst decision possible on this one thing, is that a basis for condemning your whole life? Did it hurt? Yes, it hurt."

Linker had been planning to retire this year. But now he decided that he would stay longer. He knew he had the backing of his trustees, and he didn't want to give the impression that he was being pressured into leaving.

Feinsilver's reporting created a schism in the *News & Record*'s newsroom. Some veteran reporters were concerned about its accuracy. They became even more dubious when they attempted to discuss the matter with top editors, who wouldn't answer direct questions about it.

"They just wanted it to go away," said one.

Some younger staff members were supportive of Feinsilver and saw nothing wrong with his reporting, even after all the denials of its accuracy. They also were sympathetic because of the public criticism.

Early in January, Feinsilver was named the news department's employee of the month. The recipient was chosen by a committee of news staffers, and although supervisors could overrule the choice, they didn't, even though Feinsilver was on probation. When RCC officials, class members and instructors learned about the honor, they took it as an insult not only to them but to truth.

Change was about to descend again on the news department. On January 12, Van King named a new editor. As predicted, he chose from within this time, but it was neither metro editor Tom Corrigan, nor city editor Ed Williams, as many in the newsroom had feared. It was editorial page editor John Robinson, who was forty-six. Robinson, who declined to be interviewed for this book, came to the paper in 1985. He left the news operation in 1995 to spend two years instituting "team management" in the company, and many thought that a primary factor in landing him the top job.

Robinson's role in the controversy included approving (possibly writing) the editorial about it, as well as overseeing the editorial page columns, including that by UNC professor Harry Watson about the"right history" of the Civil War in North Carolina, and the publication of the package of articles on the "reality of slavery."

During the holiday period, Jack had come down with a bad cold that wouldn't go away. He rarely got colds, was almost never sick, hated going to doctors. Annie Laura tried to get him to go, but he kept putting it off. Rahlo Fowler had a cold at the same time and did see a doctor.

"Jack asked me, 'What did he say?'" Fowler remembered. "I said, 'Three hundred dollars.' Jack said, 'I don't believe I need a doctor that bad.'"

Jack still was coughing and wheezing when his aunt, Gail Snow, his mother's sister, died on January 17. She was buried beside her husband, Ned, at Lakeview Cemetery northeast of Greensboro four days later. Jack's maternal grandparents, Norris Fulton and Della Horner, were buried there as well, along with other family members. After the graveside service, Jack, Annie Laura, Betsy and other family members wandered through the cemetery looking at gravestones. Jack was being the genealogist, explaining who was who. Afterward, several people remarked to Betsy that Jack didn't look well. His color wasn't good, they said.

The course rose into the news again on January 21, when the RCC trustees met on campus. Larry Linker told the board that the controversy brought about the creation of a committee of administrators to review all community service courses.

"Any way you look at it," he said, "there will always be potential weaknesses. Any time information is taken out of context you can get into sensitive areas."

At this meeting, Chuck Egerton also presented the petition opposing the course that he announced during Linker's emotional meeting with the faculty in November. It bore ten signatures out of approximately 150 staff members.

"If reports from the press and directly from the teachers and students are true," Egerton told the trustees, "this class has presented a distorted historical perspective of slavery and the role of African slaves in the Civil War. Slavery was an African holocaust in America. To attempt to minimize the pain, suffering and death that enslavement caused departs from reality and only creates a greater rift between whites and blacks at a time when greater unity is needed."

The trustees accepted the petition without comment. After the meeting, Egerton told Norman Hines of the *Courier-Tribune*: "We are concerned with creating unity. It was out of concern and love for the college that we made the statement."

Board chairman Jerry Tillman also spoke to Hines about the course. "From the research I have seen," he said, there were things taken out of context. The college has suffered some from it and I think we should put it behind us."

Egerton soon would learn that the committee chosen to review community service courses had determined that the standards applied to the Civil War course also prohibited the racial unity course. He moved it to the public housing facility managed by his co-facilitator and fellow NAACP member Gloria Whack, but only a few people signed up for it, and even those attended sporadically, the author of this book among them. The course was not held again.

Some at RCC suspected that Egerton was the source of the controversy. Rashidi Zalika, the Randolph County NAACP chapter president, who changed his name from Richie Everette, was reluctant to talk about Egerton's role, but said that Egerton was not happy with the way he handled the matter. Egerton wanted him to take a stronger stand, he said, but he didn't take his advice.

"He didn't want that course there," Zalika said.

Egerton declined to answer questions. "I've put that to rest," he said. "I don't feel like commenting about it."

On January 27, the *News & Record* published another Feinsilver article that confirmed for many Randolph County residents his feelings about the area. It was about a coffee shop that opened in downtown Asheboro. Feinsilver began his reporting at a home-cooking restaurant, Dixie III, asking elderly customers if they knew what a biscotti was, or a scone, or a *cafe breve*. None did. He used this as the opening of his article, proof of the area's lack of sophistication.

He moved on to a Starbucks in Greensboro where he got college students to say that some out-of-state entrepreneur must have gotten Asheboro mixed up with Asheville if a coffee shop actually had opened there.

"Asheboro is so tragic," he quoted a Starbucks employee who once lived ten miles from the town. "It's just not up to date. They're so...out of it."

Feinsilver described Asheboro as a place "where virtually the only art and live music are found in schools or through one government-sponsored arts agency...where drive-through dominates the restaurant scene...where magazines about guns, wrestling and cooking" were the reading alternatives.

The article provoked several letters to the editor, two of which were published. One was from Philip Shore, executive director of the Randolph Arts Guild. He pointed out that the guild received only twenty percent of its support from the state, county and city. The rest was privately raised. Feinsilver, Shore wrote, "demonstrated a lack of awareness of the ingredients to the community soup in which he has the honor to serve," going on to refer to him as a "crouton stuck to the side of the bowl.... All he sees is bleak horizon."

The other letter was from Ross Holt, who later in the year would become president-elect of the North Carolina Library Association. Feinsilver, he wrote, was a reporter who sought the negative. "Like a sour Midas every story he touches seems to turn bitter."

Although there was nothing wrong with magazines about guns and wrestling, Holt wrote, "as a librarian I can attest that the reading tastes of local residents are rich and varied."

Feinsilver's "contemptuous manner" with his sources and Randolph County, "suggests an acceptance of 'small-town' stereotypes and a failure to look deeper that is not conducive to good journalism," Holt wrote. "The number of us who have tried cheerfully to help him, but who will no longer talk to him, is growing. It's as if he resents being shipped off to what he perceives as a backwater, and has a barrel of ink at his disposal to take it out on the rest of us."

One letter that didn't appear was from George Gusler, executive vice president of the Asheboro/Randolph Chamber of Commerce, who had been quoted in the article. Gusler detailed the positive things he'd told Feinsilver that he didn't include.

"In the end I must question why this article was ever written," Gusler wrote. "What was the point? Was it to determine what it takes to make a local coffee shop successful or was it just to portray a very positive community in an extremely negative manner?"

Gusler sent a copy of his letter to Van King, who called him about it.

"He defended the article," Gusler remembered. "He told me he had read it and didn't glean from it the same things I did. I suggested he go back and read it again."

A few days afterward, Gusler said, he got a call from Feinsilver, who was angry that he had complained to his bosses. "He said it was his job to report as he saw fit and not my place to call his hand on that. I said, 'You write what you write and I can counter it as I see fit.' He left some hard feelings here. He made a lot of enemies in a short period of time."

The *Courier-Tribune* regularly ran a poll in its on-line edition asking for opinions on current events. The question and responses also appeared on the editorial page in the print edition. The question posted on Friday, January 29, was whether the RCC course should have been cancelled.

Only a few responses came in the first couple of days, editor Ray Criscoe reported in a column on Sunday, February 7. "Then, in one 24-hour period, more than 200 responses rolled in, or about one every seven minutes."

The paper's webmaster, Evan Jones, questioned some of the respondents to find out what was going on. He discovered that people were passing the question along to friends, who were responding, then urging their friends to respond. Many were members of the SCV, the United Daughters of the Confederacy, and other pro-South groups.

One, Steve Lynn of Lexington, Ky., read the original story about the course in his hometown newspaper, the *Herald-Leader*. "One of our local columnists wrote a scathing article on the 'facts' of the course," Lynn told Jones. "I must admit that when I first read the story, I thought the people teaching the course must have been close-minded idiots. Later, however, I learned that the controversial part of the story was fabricated.... Unfortunately, none of the newspapers were interested in that part of the story."

To this point, the paper had received 301 responses from twenty-seven states, Canada and England. All but twelve said the class shouldn't have been cancelled. Of the twelve, five were unsure. Chriscoe promised to publish all the responses from area residents, along with a sampling of others, but the newspaper offered only three on this day.

In his column—headlined, *The controversy that won't die*—Chriscoe also wrote that many white Southerners, himself included, "want to believe our ancestors were more than evil, white slave owners. We know today enslaving other human beings is wrong, and they should have known then. But other traits my ancestors wore—determination, grit, loyalty, sense of family among them—continue to help distinguish the South. And it's because of those traits that I am, and have always been, proud to be a Southerner, and I'm not going to apologize for it."

This episode, Chriscoe said, never should have reached such epic proportions. Feinsilver's original story shouldn't have been published without proof that its claims were true and without reactions from instructors, students and RCC officials. (Yet, the *Courier-Tribune* published the AP version of the story on the day after it appeared in the *News & Record*, and Larry Linker was irritated that the local paper did so without calling him to confirm its accuracy.)

Of Linker's cancellation of the course, Chriscoe wrote: "You have to wonder if he wasn't pressured. That's one reason I haven't joined the call for his resignation, because I don't think we know the full story yet. Plus, I hate to see a career tossed away over one questionable decision."

Over the next three weeks, responses to the *Courier-Tribune* poll appeared regularly, twice almost filling full pages. They excoriated Linker and Feinsilver and said that both should be fired. They denounced RCC and the *News & Record*. They raised questions of censorship, free speech and academic freedom and related the cancellation of the course to suppression in Nazi Germany and Soviet Russia. They decried political correctness, assaults on Southern heritage, and intimidation by the U.S. Commission on Civil Rights.

In cancelling the course, wrote Bill Ward of Matthews, N.C., Linker cast "a quality of illumination much like a cross burning in a cow pasture, which produces more dark shadows than enlightenment."

"RCC has put forth the proposition that history should be a pre-packaged bowl of 'politically correct' pablum spoon-fed to students," said Don Thore of Hopewell, Va. "A college should teach students how to think, not what to think."

"Perhaps we should explore a course to determine if the modern slaves of political correctness are 'happy,'" suggested James R. Campbell, of Stoneville, N.C.

The poll's final tally wouldn't come until February 25, nearly three and a half months after Feinsilver's first article appeared, when the *Courier-Tribune* published four replies. All said no to cancelling the course. Out of 381 responses, only ten said it should have been stopped. Eight were unsure.

David Melton of Winchester, Va., had the final say. "We are poorer for this irrational decision."

• • •

The *News & Record* ignored the continuing controversy it created. It did not report the calls for Linker to resign or any of the massive outpouring of criticism of him, the college, Feinsilver and the *News & Record*. Neither did it report the petition Chuck Egerton presented to the RCC trustees.

"The *News & Record* quit," Linker said. "They just quit."

But the newspaper was about to be forced into taking notice again.

Roger McCredie of Asheville took a strong interest in the course from the time he read about it in his local paper on November 16. A former journalist, McCredie was an executive with an advertising and public relations firm, as well as an SCV brigade commander. (He later would become chairman of the North Carolina Heritage Coalition and national heritage officer of the SCV.) He also was working on a book tentatively titled *The Whipping Boy: The South and Contemporary America*, and he saw the class as fodder for it.

McCredie didn't know Jack, but he thought that he had blown "a silver-platter opportunity to get our position before the American public" by not talking to the news media early on, and he said so in a lengthy memo to national commander Patrick Griffin on November 21, with suggestions for dealing with the uproar.

"The media," he wrote, "having once again made us out to be thinly-disguised racists suffering from Old South nostalgia, have now moved on to other things; it is essential to recapture their attention and regain this lost opportunity."

Gathering material for his book, McCredie interviewed several people involved in the controversy. He even called Feinsilver, presenting himself as a writer and not telling him of his SCV connections. Although he got little useful information, McCredie said that he did get him to talk about his feelings about the story and his expectations for it.

"It was like he was very proud of himself," McCredie recalled. "He wanted me to know how resourceful he'd been. He told me he expected things to go much further, and he was really looking forward to the civil rights commission coming."

The last news reports about the planned hearing said it would be in February. On February 4, McCredie called the office of the commission's chairperson, Mary Frances Berry, to find out a date for it. An assistant to Berry told him that the hearing had been dropped, he recalled.

McCredie called Feinsilver to tell him that the commission wouldn't be coming.

"He sounded just like a kid who had an adult renege on a promise," McCredie remembered. "He said, 'They're not? But they promised!'"

On the following day, the *News & Record* published Feinsilver's report that the course no longer was on the agenda. The hearing had been pushed back to April, he wrote, but would deal with other matters. (Actually, the hearing never would be held.)

State committee chairman Wyatt Kirk felt that the committee had over-reacted, the article reported.

Feinsilver's description of the course was far milder than in his first article. This time he wrote that it "differed from mainstream historians' teachings in its claims about former slaves' attitudes and the number of people who had willingly fought for the Confederacy...."

Nothing appeared about slaves being happy, satisfied, or contented, or of tens of thousands fighting for the Confederacy because they believed in its cause.

Twenty-three

Jack's and Annie Laura's thirty-seventh wedding anniversary would be Wednesday, February 10, but they decided to celebrate the weekend before.

Jack went every year to a relic show in Salisbury where he searched for arrowheads, Confederate buttons, other Civil War paraphernalia, and whatever else might fit into his collections or catch his fancy. (In his basement he even had charred remains of a Civil War blockade runner that he'd dug out of the coastal muck near Southport.) Annie Laura sometimes found reasons not to go to the show. But this time she told him that she would go if he would take her to see the new gallery of her favorite artist, Bob Timberlake, at Lexington, which was on the way.

Years earlier, Jack had bought Annie Laura a signed, limited edition Timberlake print called "Daisies." He bought it on condition that they wouldn't frame it until she dropped twenty-five pounds. The print was still in its cardboard folder beneath their bed, and getting it framed had become a standing joke between them.

At the relic show on Saturday morning, Jack and Annie Laura shopped for each other's anniversary gifts. She bought him four hand-made, walnut display cases for his collectibles. He bought her a green, cathedral glass bottle and a hat-pin holder that was more than a century old. The hat-pin holder was hand-painted with violets.

Both Annie Laura and Jack loved violets. They never mowed their grass in spring until the wild purple and white violets that grew there had bloomed out. Every February, they searched the woods behind their house for the first mottled sprouts of the dogtooth violet, their harbinger of spring. They had found one just this morning, and it had brightened their moods, a forecast of the pleasures—and later for Annie Laura, the happy memories—that this day would bring.

After leaving the relic show, they spent much of the afternoon at the Timberlake gallery, and Jack was certain that Annie Laura would have stayed half the night if the place had remained open. While at the gallery she checked on the current values of past prints and, after seeing what "Daisies" was now worth, she made a new vow to diet her way to a frame for it.

But she put off the diet until after Sunday dinner. Jack's mother was cooking in honor of their anniversary, and Annie Laura knew she'd bake chocolate pie.

Jack finally had gotten over his cold, and his sister, Betsy, thought his mood also had improved. He appeared to be overcoming the troubles of the past three months.

"I thought he seemed less stressed than he had seemed in a long time," she said.

Betsy would remember vividly the moment when Jack and Annie Laura left that day.

"He gave me a hug and went out the door carrying his half a chocolate pie, and he turned around and gave me his little grin and I thought he was going to be okay."

Jack still wasn't free from RCC. Complications pursued him. They went back to the first night of the course. That usually was when continuing education instructors signed contracts. But Jack had a problem.

He wanted all the money to go to the SCV for the essay contest. If it came to him, taxes would have to be paid, leaving less for the contest. He didn't sign. Instead, he talked to Rhonda Winters about it the next day. When Winters took the problem to Marcia Daniel, she got back word that a teaching contract couldn't be made to an organization, only an individual. Jack, however, declined to sign. It would take too much money from the essay contest, he said, and that was why he wanted the SCV to co-sponsor the course from the beginning.

An impasse resulted, even as the course continued. Weeks passed with no resolution. Then Winters had an inspiration. Nothing in the inflexible rules said how much an instructor had to be paid. She prepared a contract that paid Jack only ten dollars, an amount that would not affect his taxes. At the bottom, in a section marked "special instructions," she noted that an additional $338.50 was to be paid to the Frazier Camp. She presented this contract to Jack on October 30, and he signed it three days later.

But in January, Winters was instructed to get Jack to sign a revised contract, one that made no mention of the SCV. The college, she thought, wanted no evidence in its files of any relationship with the group. Winters knew that Jack wouldn't sign. She had no choice, however, but to present it to him. Although he took it, he made clear that he had no intention of signing.

The college wanted to clear the course from its records and acknowledge the students' participation with certificates even though they hadn't been allowed to finish it. But that was not possible without Jack's attendance records. He held onto those.

Early in February, the college relented. If Jack would sign his attendance sheets, Winters told him, RCC would abide by the contract he signed.

Jack put the signed attendance sheets in the mail on Tuesday, February 9.

That night, Jack and Annie Laura attended the monthly SCV meeting at Jamestown Library. As usual, Annie Laura joined the women of the Confederate Order of the Rose in preparing the pre-meeting meal. She made gingerbread with cherry sauce in anticipation of Valentine's Day. Jack always bragged that the Frazier Camp ate better than any SCV group.

The speaker on this evening was Bill Moore, director of the Greensboro Historical Museum, whose topic was the museum's recently acquired collection of Confederate firearms, 152 muskets, rifles and carbines, the finest such collection known to exist. It had belonged to a California doctor, John Murphy, a Virginia native, and his wife Isabelle. They had friends in Greensboro and came to the museum during a visit with them. After the death of his wife, Murphy decided that his collection should be exhibited in the city where Confederate troops stacked their weapons to end the war.

The exhibit was being prepared but would not open for another nine months, although Moore, who recognized Jack's expertise on the gunmakers of Guilford County, had given him a private look at the collection.

Jack and Moore chatted after the meeting, and Moore said that he was researching the end of the war in Greensboro. That had been the topic of Jack's last class, which he wasn't allowed to teach. He had some of the materials with him, and he gave Moore a sheet of fascinating facts that he'd uncovered.

Fifty-five people turned out for this meeting, and Jack was pleased because attendance and membership were growing. As usual, he and Rahlo Fowler were the last to leave. They stayed to make certain that everything was back in order in the library. Fowler locked the west door, Jack the east. Annie Laura had gone on home in her own car. Jack and his closest friend said goodnight in the parking lot.

"Jack, that was another good program, another good meeting," Fowler remembered telling him.

"I thought it went pretty well," Jack said. "I'll give you a call in the morning."

Several people asked Jack about the RCC course that night. Were there any developments? Had the national office said anything about possible lawsuits? Had he made arrangements for the final class? He hadn't been able to tell them anything.

Jack told Annie Laura about that after he got home.

She remembered that the last thing he said to her before they went to bed was that he absolutely had to set a date to hold that final class. He owed it to the students, he said, and he felt bad that this much time had passed and he still hadn't gotten around to it. He was thinking of having it as part of the next SCV meeting

They were in bed, as always, by eleven. Jack kissed Annie Laura, told her that he loved her, and she said that she loved him, too. Tired from a long day, both went quickly to sleep.

Annie Laura always slept lightly. Almost any sound roused her. Whenever Jack began to snore, she was instantly awake. She'd jab him with an elbow. He'd roll onto his side with a snort and burrow back to silence into his pillow. She'd return to sleep.

At a little before five, she was awakened by Jack's snoring. She jabbed him, but he didn't react. Then she realized that this was not his normal snoring sound. It seemed more like a gurgle. She sat up and turned on a little lamp on a bedside table.

Suddenly, Jack took two or three quick, desperate breaths, and Annie Laura realized that something was wrong. She jumped up and turned on the overhead light, rousing Lady from her slumber on the foot of the bed. She ran to Jack's side and shook him but got no response. Then she realized that he'd stopped breathing.

"I was shaking him," she remembered, "I was shaking him and shaking him and I couldn't get him to do anything. And I started yelling at him. I was saying, 'Jack Perdue, don't you die on our anniversary! Don't you dare die on our anniversary! You can't do this!"

From that point, all that ensued would become a blur of frenzied activity that she would relive over and over in days to come. She remembered grabbing the phone and dialing 911. She remembered frantically telling the dispatcher, "My husband's not breathing! I can't get him to breathe!" She remembered him asking, "Can you do CPR?" and she crying, responding, "No!" Later, she would feel so foolish, because she had taken a CPR class at Jack's instigation, but in her panic she couldn't remember.

"I'll tell you what to do," the dispatcher said.

She recalled him instructing her to get Jack onto the floor, and she tried, tugging hopelessly on him. "I couldn't move him. I couldn't budge him," she said, and she told that to the dispatcher. Just leave him where he was, the dispatcher said calmly, and instructed her in breathing into his mouth and performing chest compressions, and as she started, the training came back. She kept forcing her breath into him, pressing his chest and pleading with him not to leave her.

It seemed that only three or four minutes passed before she heard sirens, and then people were at the door and she had to run to let them in. The EMTs hurried in with their satchels and went to work on Jack with their special equipment, their sophisticated techniques, the experience that made them seem unruffled in even the most frantic and trying situations.

By this time other people were crowding into the house—sheriff's deputies, firemen, rescue squad members. Lady, upset and scared, was barking angrily. The EMTs wanted her out of there.

Then the phone rang, and John Deuterman, the next-door neighbor, awakened by all the commotion on this normally quiet cul-de-sac, was asking, "Annie Laura, do you need help?"

And she said, "Yes, yes, I need help." Deuterman hurried over with his wife-to-be, Lynn, and she calmed Lady and took her next door, away from all the people and excitement.

Annie Laura got on the phone to Charlie and Heidi Parnell, her employers at the Old Mill of Guilford, who had been like another set of parents to her and Jack. They seemed to get there instantly, as if they had flown like angels, and that was what they were when Annie Laura saw their concerned faces and felt their loving embraces. She also called Rahlo Fowler, told him that Jack had stopped breathing as he slept, and that the EMTs were working on him, and he, too, dressed and headed to his friend's side.

But before Fowler could get there, the EMTs realized their efforts were hopeless. Jack was dead when they arrived, and nothing could bring him back. They already had loaded his body into the ambulance and left for Moses Cone Hospital in Greensboro by the time Fowler arrived.

Fowler and the Parnells remained with Annie Laura through the morning, helping however they could. Lots of phone calls had to be made, lots more answered, but Annie Laura wanted to call her children, her sister Frances, and Jack's sister Betsy. They were the most difficult calls she ever had to make, she said later.

She especially dreaded calling her sister, who, she knew, was still grieving so deeply over the loss of her husband, Jim, only eleven months earlier. She didn't know if she'd be able to get out the words.

Jack's friend, Anita White, was awakened by the phone and heard Annie Laura crying, trying to say something.

"What's wrong?" she asked. "What's wrong?"

"He's dead, he's dead," Annie Laura said, "Jack's gone."

Only a little later did White, herself now distraught, realize that Annie Laura thought she was talking to her sister but had dialed her number by mistake.

Louise Canipe, the eldest student in the RCC course, attended the SCV meeting the night before, her second visit. She had been so angered by the cancellation of the course, and after seeing no effect from the letters she wrote, she felt obligated to do something to remedy the wrong. Seeking the companionship of others who felt as she did, and who might collectively muster the power to do something, was all that she could think to do. At the meeting, she spoke to Annie Laura about Jack.

"He acts as if he's doing okay," she remembered telling her. "She said, 'Oh, he acts that way, but he's really having a hard time.'"

One of the women who had helped serve the meal at the meeting called Canipe early the next morning to tell her of Jack's death. Later, Canipe couldn't remember who that was, because she'd been so distressed at the news. But she had no doubt about one thing.

"I think most of us will always believe that what happened to this class caused his death," she said.

She called the Archdale campus of RCC to pass on the news to Rhonda Winters.

Winters was about to leave for work when her phone rang and she heard the voice of her assistant, Carol Nunn.

"I've got bad news," Nunn said. "You need to know this before you get here. Louise Canipe called and said that Jack Perdue died of a heart attack this morning."

"I said, 'Damn, the bad guys win again,'" Winters recalled. "Then I totally broke down."

Winters didn't drive directly to her office in Archdale. She went instead to the Asheboro campus to tell Marcia Daniel.

"I lost it in her office, too," she said. "I was so upset. I said, 'I am ashamed of how the college treated this man, never once stood behind him, never believed him. We helped to destroy this man.' She didn't have a whole lot to say. She asked me, 'Do you want to leave before I tell Dr. Linker?' I said, 'I don't want to see Linker.'

"I knew that Jack was fighting so hard behind the scenes to right a wrong, to get his good name back, and with his death it would never happen now."

When Winters got to her office, she found Jack's attendance records in the morning's mail and broke down again.

Charlie, who lived in Boone, where he was a columnist for an alternative newspaper, was the first of the children to arrive home. Charlie was close to his father, although he did not share some of his political views or his great affinity for the Civil War and his devotion to the South. Both loved the Atlanta Braves, though, and the sports teams of UNC, and regularly watched games together with frequent whooping and shouting.

Charlie spent weekends with his parents because he had a part-time job in High Point. The first thing he did after comforting his mother was to walk to the head of the driveway and lower to half-staff the Confederate battle flag that Jack flew there.

Later, Charlie handled calls from the hospital about the possible use of his father's organs. Jack was an organ donor, but Annie Laura had been so distraught that she hadn't thought to tell that to the EMTs. Most of his organs were not usable, but his corneas and some skin were harvested.

• • •

A medical examiner called late in the morning and Annie Laura talked to her. The doctor wanted to know if Jack had any health problems, if he had complained of pains in his chest or arm. Annie Laura told her about the cold that wouldn't go away and how ten or twelve years earlier, Jack had suffered chest pains and had gone to several specialists who'd found nothing wrong and had written it off to stress, but he'd had no symptoms since. Had he been under stress recently? the doctor wanted to know. Annie Laura told her about the Civil War course, all that developed from it, and how deeply it troubled Jack.

"I told her all of that," she remembered, "and she said, 'Well, you know, stress can kill people.' She told me it was just amazing the number of men in North Carolina who had heart disease that went undetected until they died."

Only weeks earlier, the *News & Record* proclaimed that the whole world was waiting to hear from Jack, but now the newspaper's editors decreed that his death was not news. Some reporters objected, saying it would be unconscionable for the paper to fail to report his death after making him the object of worldwide attention and derision, pointing out that the paper frequently wrote news stories about the deaths of people who were much less prominent than Jack and whose contributions to Guilford County were far fewer and less important.

The editors stuck to their decision. Jack's family paid to have an obituary put into the *News & Record* so that friends and acquaintances could know of his death. Among the survivors listed was Lady. The *Courier-Tribune* of Asheboro would be the only newspaper to report Jack's death as news.

Jack's funeral was at two p.m., Friday, February 12, at the Guilford College Chapel of Forbis and Dick Funeral Home in Greensboro. The chapel was packed.

Joe Bryant, a Baptist minister married to Jack's distant cousin, Liz, who had become a close associate in his family research, opened the service with a prayer.

Then he called on his wife for a remembrance. Liz Bryant told how she'd taken refuge in genealogy after the death of her parents, how that had led her to Jack, and how happy each had been to find somebody "as crazy about genealogy" as the other. Jack had come to seem like a brother to her, she said. She'd lost her own brother twenty years earlier. "I needed a brother and God sent me a brother."

She recalled how she had telephoned Jack after suffering a stroke in 1995.

"The minute I heard his voice I started crying," she remembered. "He said, 'Now, Liz, if you're expecting sympathy from me, you're not going to get it.'"

He needed her in this research, he told her, and he was not going to let her leave him now.

"He said, 'It's happened, now get over it and live with it.'"

That shocked her back to reality, she said.

"I said, 'I'll keep trying,' and that's what I did."

Later, she said, Jack told her, "Friends you can choose, family you can't, but if I could have chosen you for family I would have."

That was how she felt about Annie Laura, as well, she said. Both she and Jack were special people.

"I promised Annie Laura I wouldn't start weeping," she said. "If I start weeping, she might, and Jack doesn't want us to weep. Jack would want us to say, 'So it's happened, now get over it and live with it, and folks, that's what we've got to do.'"

As Liz Bryant left the pulpit, Annie Laura rose from her pew and enveloped her in a long embrace.

Joe Bryant spoke of Jack's love for Annie Laura, his children, grand-children, and the rest of his family.

"Kinfolks were important to Jack," he said. "He wanted to know who was a part of his family.... He had an insatiable desire to fulfill in finding his roots."

Jack loved history and teaching, Bryant said, loved the South of history and the South of today, loved the SCV, loved his work, liked cemeteries, old tombstones, flags, muzzle loaders, ceremonies....

"But most of all he just liked people."

He called Jack "a vibrant person," and "a true gentleman from the South," who "gave more than he ever took from this life, far more."

Stan Clardy, who traveled throughout the South performing as a guitar-strumming Civil War troubadour, sang "Amazing Grace," and a song of his own composition that seemed appropriate for Jack, "Dixie Burns in My Heart."

Herman White, dressed in his re-enactor's uniform, spoke of the great void that Jack left and went on to bring up the controversy about the Civil War course.

"There were those that recently tried to smear the reputation and good name of Jack Perdue," White said. "However, I want Ethan Feinsilver, I want the Greensboro *News & Record* and the N—double A—CP and all other parties that had a part in that effort to know and to understand that they were never worthy even to carry his shoes."

He paused. "If I was in church, I'd expect you to say, 'Amen,'" and several did.

"I'm serious about that. And I'm not saying that in a mean spirit or a wrong attitude. I'm saying it because they tried to smear the man who had more character than all of them put together."

Some people of character would die before they'd break their principles, White noted, and Jack was such a man.

"Too many people want to do the expedient thing. That's why you get courses cancelled, because there are people who don't have enough character to stand if it might cost them their jobs...."

"No matter how much people may say, no one—and I mean no one—that knew Jack Perdue and the principles that he lived believed any of the libelous and racist statements that were made against this dear man. He was honest. He wouldn't have taught anything that was dishonest or not correct, nor would he have permitted it."

White acknowledged that he was the one who taught the class that had been used "to assassinate Jack Perdue's character."

"But it was a lie. They invented it.... I'm going to tell you they don't have a good name. Jack Perdue had a good name. And he had a good name until he died."

White closed with a prayer thanking God for Jack's life, a blessing, he said, to all who knew him.

At the end of the service, as a recorded string-band version of "Dixie" played, the honor guard of Confederate re-enactors assembled and marched to the chapel entrance behind their commander, Rahlo Leonard, who carried the tin containing Jack's ashes. Leonard later would say that this was one of the greatest honors of his life.

As the doors opened, a great gust of wind swept suddenly into the chapel. Thunder rumbled and roiling black clouds dumped a sudden torrent of rain that streaked indoors.

This had been an unusually warm day for early February, the temperature near seventy, but before the long funeral procession wound through the stormy downpour northward along Highway 68, past the Old Mill of Guilford, on to Stokesdale and into "Perdue Country" in Rockingham County, stopping finally at the little family cemetery near Oak Level Baptist Church that Annie Laura had spotted in the undergrowth on that sunny Saturday in May nearly six years earlier, the temperature had dropped thirty degrees.

People pulled on coats and sweaters and huddled, shivering, under umbrellas around the stones that marked the unknown graves of Jehu Jackson Perdue, and his brother-in-law, John C. Perdue, both of whom had died early in the Civil War.

A small rectangular hole had been dug in the red earth to accommodate the tin containing Jack's ashes. It was covered with a green tarp. The first flag of the Confederacy, the stars and bars, and the third, final, Confederate flag flapped in the gusty wind from staffs beside the stones.

A minister with a sharp northern accent, Jeff Palmer, conducted the graveside service. He spoke of grief, of the love Jack had for Annie Laura and his family, and read a passage from a poem by Edgar Guest that another minister had read when Jack and Annie Laura dedicated their new home to God and to love in 1965.

Palmer joked about his accent and said that although he had been born in California, he had grown up in the North. He told how he had become friends with Jack after moving to North Carolina in 1992. "Jack affectionately referred to me as 'Yankee,'" he said to laughter, but both had come to realize that they had a common heritage.

"Even though I came from the North, I came to revere many of our Southern leaders," Palmer said. "Men like Robert E. Lee, who really had a personal relationship with his God through Jesus Christ. Men like Stonewall Jackson, who many do not know used his own money to begin a Sunday school for young black boys who couldn't even write or read the English language, to teach them so they could learn the Bible.

"I came to respect Jack's passion for what he believed in, to leave a legacy of his heritage to his family, the people he cared for. Sometimes I wonder if a passionless life is really worth living. Jack had a lot of passion."

Through the brief service, the honor guard of ten re-enactors stood in two ranks, unprotected from the weather, their faces streaked with rain, each with one hand holding his musket at rest, the other covering the muzzle to keep out the water. The men were from different units and had only a few minutes to rehearse together. They were worried about whether they could successfully fire three rounds of tribute in these conditions.

After Palmer finished a brief prayer committing Jack's soul to God and his ashes to the earth on which his forebears lived and died, Rahlo Leonard ordered the honor guard to load.

"High elevation!" he called, and the men swung the muskets to their shoulders. "Aim! Fire!"

Three times the orders were given, and three times the muskets roared simultaneously. Later, one of the re-enactors, Jay Callaham, who had assisted with the RCC course, recalled how relieved and proud the honor guard had been.

"No misfires, no hangfires, no early fires, no rattle of musketry, just three crisp, clean volleys. I'm sure Jack was pleased."

"Pre-zent A-a-arms!" Leonard ordered as a uniformed bugler began playing taps.

Some students in Jack's course didn't learn of his death until too late to attend the funeral.

Joan King found out when she spotted his obituary in the *High Point Enterprise* after getting home from work Friday afternoon. "I said, 'Oh, my god, that's Jack.' I was very upset."

Like other students, she had little doubt that the *News & Record* articles and the events they brought about contributed to his death.

"I'm sure it would have caused me a lot of mental and emotional distress. If he didn't have blood pressure problems when that began, I'm sure he did afterward. That's a lot for a person to have to go through. It was a very frustrating experience for all of us, very sad in a way, the whole thing, especially after Jack died."

Nancy Boyles also learned of Jack's death from the obituary in the *Enterprise*.

"The way it happened and when it happened, I felt like all of this was just too much for him," she said. "That was my first thought. It was just such a shame."

Dedra Routh was stunned when she picked up the *Courier-Tribune* in her driveway Friday afternoon and saw the article about Jack's death on the front page.

"I stopped in my tracks," she recalled. "I started bawling. I read it again. I couldn't believe my eyes. I was beyond words. The one person I had kept thinking about was Mr. Perdue and how this was going to hurt him and by cracky if it didn't kill him."

Routh had been hoping that Jack would hold the last class. She had been busy tracking her Civil War ancestors and she had so much she wanted to tell him, so many questions she needed to ask.

"I hated to call him because he had been through so much," she said.

Jack had helped her confirm in class that one of her great, great, great grandfathers, Stokes Hopkins, had been at Appomattox. She wanted to find a family connection to Gettysburg, and she had done that. Another of her great, great, great grandfathers, Ashley Muse, who served in the 26th N.C. Regiment, had been killed there on the first day. She was eager to tell Jack about it and hoped that he could help her learn where Muse was buried.

"I was chomping at the bit to go to their graves and let them know I'm acknowledging them," she said, "that finally somebody knows about them."

But now she never would get to tell Jack, never would have his help again. "It just tore me up," she said.

When Jack's sister Betsy got home that chill and rainy evening, she was surprised to see that the first pink blossoms had appeared on one of the small February-blooming, fragrant shrubs called *Daphne adora* in her back yard. She knew how much her brother loved flowers, and on his birthday ten months later she would buy a *Daphne adora* and plant it by his grave, where it would thrive, blooming each year about the time of Jack's death.

One person who could not be present for the funeral was Billy Joe Hill, whom Jack and Annie Laura made family before they had children. Hill dropped out of High Point College to join the Army, but he returned later to get his degree, and afterward went to work for the U.S. Department of State. He since had served in embassies all over the world, had married while in Thailand, had risen to the highest civil service rank, and was now in Seoul, South Korea. Whenever he was back in this country, he made a point to see Jack and Annie Laura, and they had a big family reunion. But it had been several years since he and his wife, Dang, had been able to come to Jamestown. Laura, who still thought of Billy Joe as an older brother and kept in regular touch, e-mailed him about her father's death.

"I'm still shocked and deeply saddened," Billy Joe wrote to Annie Laura.

Jack's influence had guided him through life, he said, and he was sure that Jack was proud "that I didn't turn out so bad after all."

"Who knows where I might have wound up if I hadn't met you two and if you hadn't had the kindness to take care of a delinquent kid who was always headed into more trouble than anything else. Anyway, I'm sure glad you guys came along when you did. It seems like only yesterday when I was staying with you, riding the bike you gave me to Oakdale Cotton Mill and Laura was sitting in a little bucket on top of the kitchen counter. Gosh! That was the summer of 1969, 30 years ago. Anyway, it's getting late here and I guess I'm beginning to get maudlin so I better close for now.

"I want to say thank you for everything. You've really meant a lot to me and changed my life for the better...."

Twenty-four

Following Jack's funeral, Ed Julian, a friend from Franklinville in Randolph County, sent a letter to the editor of the *News & Record*.

The newspaper, he wrote, "may not have noticed that the man whose reputation it had done so much to smear with false witness, innuendo and bold lies had passed. Did it care how deeply it had wounded this man for trying to present an honest and complete account of our history? Did it realize how without justification were its attempts to paint him as some thoughtless bigot with no respect for others?

"I know that Jack Perdue took all this very personally, all the hurtful accusations, all the unfounded notoriety, all the repeated misstatement of the facts and all the stress that came with the outcry against him. I can only believe that the stress of that ill-conceived journalistic assault contributed to the ending of this good man.

"If the *N&R* had any real respect for freedom of speech, any respect for an individual's right to pursue happiness at no expense to others, or the right of a man not to have his good name defamed, it would slink out of town in shame for the role it played.

"There have been many cowards throughout the history of this nation who have used the bold false statement to incite the public to an abuse of good men, but not witch-hunters, nor the red-hunters of McCarthyism showed any more disregard for the truth or an individual's rights.

"The very least the *N&R* owes is an apology to the family of Jack Perdue. We realize by now that it does not have the combined simple strength of character to post a retraction or an apology for its mischief. As long as political correctness governs its editorial judgment, then good men should beware, lest they fall victim to its ill-used 'freedom of the press.'"

The *News & Record* did not publish Julian's letter, as it did not publish other letters about Jack's death. Julian's letter did appear, however, in the *Courier Tribune* in Asheboro.

A week after Jack's funeral, Ethan Feinsilver took leave of absence from the *News & Record* to be with his cancer-stricken father in Washington. Considering the criticism he had drawn and the restrictions under which he worked because of his probation, some in the newsroom thought he might use the leave to begin a search for another job and wouldn't return.

David Feinsilver died at home with his family on February 23, just thirteen days after Jack's death, only a couple of days after his son arrived to be with him, the same day that Ed Julian's letter appeared in the *Courier-Tribune*.

However, only three weeks after taking leave, Feinsilver returned to his job in the Randolph County bureau.

Rahlo Fowler carried through on Jack's plan to hold the final class. A condensed version was presented at the Jamestown Library at the next meeting of the Frazier Camp on March 9. Only five of the eleven students attended. Dedra Routh brought her husband and two children. A moment of silence in memory of Jack was observed, then all stood for the pledge of allegiance to the U.S. flag and salutes to the N.C. and battle flags. When everybody joined in singing "Dixie," Annie Laura cried.

Fowler reported that contributions to the heritage fund Jack started had been "tremendous" in the wake of his death, and that the fund had been named in his memory. He also reported that statewide the SCV's history essay writing contests for school students would be named for Jack.

"Jack felt it was very important that this day would come about, that this class would be held," Fowler said. He'd found Jack's notes and some of the materials from which he'd worked, and hoped he could present some of what Jack wanted them to know.

He went on to tell how Guilford County had voted overwhelmingly against secession, and how uncertain Jefferson Davis had been of his reception upon his arrival in Greensboro with his cabinet at the end of the war. He told about the confrontation between Davis and

General Joseph Johnston that resulted in the surrender of remaining Confederate forces. He described the last great parade of Confederate soldiers in Greensboro as they stacked their arms to fight no more, after Davis had fled on southward. He told, too, of mustering out troops in Greensboro and northern Randolph County.

"I would like you all to continue studying," Fowler said, closing the lesson. "I know that's what Jack wanted you to do."

Annie Laura stood to thank the students. "Jack loved that class," she said, and she wanted them to know that his obligation to them was one of the last things on his mind the night he died. Afterward, several of the students hugged her.

On April 13, more leadership changes were announced by the *News & Record*.

Sports editor Allen Johnson was named editorial page editor, filling the spot vacated in January by John Robinson when he became editor. Johnson was the first African-American to hold that job.

Linda Austin, a North Carolina native, became managing editor. Austin once had been business editor of the *Philadelphia Inquirer*, but at the time of her appointment was publisher and editor of a magazine marketed to high-tech professionals in Philadelphia.

Metro editor Tom Corrigan was named content editor of the Internet site. No mention was made of city editor Ed Williams, who, along with Corrigan, played a major role in the RCC controversy, but he soon was to become personnel recruiter, assigned to bring more minority employees into the newsroom, a job that previously hadn't existed. Business editor Mark Sutter was appointed city editor.

Another change in the newsroom staff was announced on Monday, May 24, but it didn't appear in the *News & Record*. It came to staff members in an e-mail from Mark Sutter:

> *Ethan Feinsilver has resigned from the paper. We wish him the best.*

Feinsilver's resignation came six months from the day that he arrived thirty minutes late for his meeting with Rhonda Winters and Cathy Hefferin at RCC's Archdale branch, the day that Feinsilver most likely underwent his lengthy interrogation by Ed Williams. Standard probation was six months. Word soon filtered through the newsroom that Feinsilver was given the option of resigning or being fired.

He later settled in Chapel Hill, where he became assistant to a fellow at the Frank Porter Graham Child Development Center and entered the graduate program at UNC.

That a Southern college was teaching that slaves were happy as the 21st century approached not only was still accepted as truth but appeared to be on the way to becoming part of the country's racial mythology.

Anthony Walton, an African-American writer, brought it up in a book review in the *Oxford American*, a Southern literary magazine.

"This false nostalgia has astonished me well into my adulthood," he wrote, "and I have come to think that it can express but one thing: an ongoing desire to hold down, and hold back, blacks; to turn back the clock. Can blacks and whites ever hope to find true reconciliation when the mythology of the one is so fundamentally offensive to the other?"

In late May, six months after the controversy erupted, the *High Point Enterprise* raised it again in an editorial about the release of the book *Runaway Slaves* by historians John Hope Franklin and Loren Schweninger, claiming that the book was proof of the falsehood of the "ridiculous notion" taught in the RCC course that slaves were happy, although the *Enterprise* had received numerous denials from students and instructors that this happened.

In October, during a speech at the University of Tennessee, Julian Bond, chairman of the board of the NAACP, also brought up the "happy slaves" course at RCC.

When matters involving the Confederacy were raised in the presidential race of 2000, and later in the selection of President George W. Bush's cabinet, articles appearing in the web magazine *Slate* provided a link to the article referring to the RCC view of slavery as "smiling, singing 'Sambos.'"

On Thursday, October 7, 1999, the *News & Record* entertained Randolph County community leaders at a breakfast at Asheboro Country Club to announce a new county edition, part of a major expansion.

A news bureau of nine people in a new office in downtown Asheboro would replace the single reporter who had covered the county from a small basement office. This move would prompt the *Courier-Tribune* to add a Saturday edition and become a morning newspaper.

News & Record publisher Van King, editor John Robinson, and editorial page editor Allen Johnson spoke at the event. Ross Holt, president-elect of the North Carolina Library Association, thought they seemed uncertain and ill at ease. They spoke from notes, without enthusiasm or spontaneity, frequently hesitating and stammering, he recalled.

Readers would see "increasing urgency, authority and depth" in the newspaper's reporting, King promised in a later article, with "fairness, accuracy and distinction," going on to say that the newspaper's purpose was to be the "most trusted" news source in the area. Some in this audience, however, had little faith in the *News & Record*'s willingness to report fairly and accurately.

At the end of the presentation, King offered to take questions. When nobody asked about the RCC controversy, he brought it up himself, saying he had expected questions, had prepared for them, and would go ahead and talk about it.

He told of reading Feinsilver's first article and telling his wife that this was going to be a big national story.

"He stood by the story," Holt recalled. "He said, 'Our story was accurate and the mischaracterization was by others in the media.' He said, 'If you look at it line by line, it's completely true.'"

Holt was surprised that King would bring this up among people with hard, first-hand experience with Feinsilver's reporting.

"It was pouring salt in open wounds," he said.

Larry Linker, still angry at the paper, declined an invitation to the breakfast, but Cathy Hefferin was there, and she was shocked to hear King defending as "completely true" what she knew to be false, things that she had told him to his face, only to have them ignored. Bringing this up in this setting was completely inappropriate, she thought.

"He just continued to say they stood behind the story and they felt they had presented an accurate portrayal of the class," she said.

She wanted to ask a question, but King didn't offer to take more.

Her question was this: Why is the reporter who wrote those articles no longer working for you?

(The *New & Record*'s push into Randolph County would prove to be less than successful. In the summer of 2001, all but two of the employees assigned to the news bureau were removed without public notice.)

• • •

After Jack's death, Rahlo Fowler took on the job of finding a law-yer to sue the *News & Record*, and possibly others, for libel. He later estimated that he talked with ten or more. Some were not familiar with libel law; some were too busy; some didn't want to take on so formidable an opponent. Then a friend, a lawyer who had worked with Fowler and Jack in saving Jamestown School, told Fowler that Joseph McNulty was the person to see.

McNulty, who was with the firm Tuggle Duggins & Meschan in Greensboro, had been a reporter for the *Greensboro Daily News*, prede-cessor of the *News & Record*, for seven years in the 1970s. He repre-sented former Greensboro Mayor Vic Nussbaum in a libel action against the *News & Record* over articles published in 1993 that implied that Nussbaum had used his influence as mayor to benefit his company, Southern Foods, in a land transaction with the city. Nussbaum claimed that the newspaper nearly had destroyed his reputation with a "bucket of misinformation" and a "host of slanted, distorted or manufactured quotes." Nussbaum didn't want money, only a prominently published retraction and apology, and he got it from Van King.

The national SCV office agreed to hire McNulty to determine whether a lawsuit was feasible, and Fowler turned over the tapes of the classes, news articles, and course materials for his analysis.

On October 7, 1999, McNulty sent a twenty-seven-page report to national commander Patrick Griffin. The advice it contained, Griffin later said, was not what he was hoping to hear.

McNulty concluded that a libel suit against the *News & Record* would be impossible to win. The SCV could not claim damage as an organization. Feinsilver had named only two SCV members who could be considered plaintiffs.

Jack was the center of the controversy, and clearly the person who suffered the most damage, but his case had died with him. Herman White was the other possible plaintiff. But under libel law, White would be considered a public figure, as would have Jack, requiring more strin-gent standards. He would have to prove malice on the part of Feinsilver and the *News & Record*, and that would be extremely difficult.

If the SCV proceeded, the tape of White's lecture would become evidence, and a jury was certain to include descendants of slaves. Would any jury, after hearing White's observations about "abolition-ist lies," his views about civil rights leaders, and his off-hand remarks about the biblical view of slavery, be likely to find on his behalf, even though he hadn't taught what Feinsilver claimed? McNulty thought not. Also, he pointed out, a trial would attract great media attention. Did the SCV want White and his unpredictable views to be the face it presented to the world?

"It is an axiom of the law that not all wrongs are actionable," McNulty wrote. "In our opinion, the tawdry journalistic trick played by Mr. Feinsilver and the *News & Record* is such a wrong."

Word went out to all members of the Frazier Camp to be certain to attend the January, 2000, meeting. Rick McCaslin, the High Point University professor who had been a lecturer in the RCC course, would be guest speaker, talking about his new book on Robert E. Lee. National commander Patrick Griffin also would be present with important news.

Griffin later said that his appearance before the Frazier Camp that night was the hardest thing he had to do during his term as commander.

The one great benefit he gained from this experience, Griffin told the group, was getting to know Jack. They had long telephone conversations, and both believed that the damage the *News & Record* wrought was actionable. The Rutherford Institute said that a reasonable case appeared to exist, although an experienced libel lawyer would be needed. He told of hiring Joseph McNulty and receiving his conclusions.

"The advice I got tells me that the chances of us winning are slim to none," he said. "This is a bitter pill for all of us. I didn't want to bring you this message."

McNulty sent a letter to the *News & Record* demanding retraction of its false claims, Griffin told the group, but Van King responded that no retraction would be made.

Griffin said he hoped a memorial could be established for Jack.

"A spirit like that you don't ever want to forget. What he did was right and it came from his heart. What he wanted to do was educate people and that really is what our purpose is."

Five weeks later, a week after the first anniversary of Jack's death, Annie Laura sat in her kitchen dinette beneath the framed print of Bob Timberlake's painting "Daisies." She'd never lost the twenty-five pounds, but she had it framed anyway. It was so bright and colorful, and it made her feel better seeing it every day.

Lady lay at her feet, her head in a plastic cone to prevent her from chewing sutures from recent surgery. She had been depressed after Jack's death and her health was failing.

"I don't know who's grieved more," Annie Laura said, "her or me."

February never had been an easy month for Annie Laura, and now it was a dreaded month of bitter memories. But the dog-tooth violets had come up in the woods behind her house a day earlier, she noted. "And I knew I could make it through."

Her daughter, Laura, spent several days with her the week before. On the anniversary of Jack's death, they recalled happy memories, retold funny family tales. They laughed at the clutter in Jack's office that Annie Laura still couldn't bring herself to face, remembering how he always talked about his "piling system," as he referred to the method of filing that only he could decipher. They went through his leather address book, giggling at the odd notes he made to himself. The book's binding still held the sweet aroma of Sir Walter Raleigh pipe tobacco, his favorite. It was Jack's essence, still with them.

Later that week, Annie Laura made a Valentine's Day wreath to put on Jack's grave. "I was sitting here, and I said to myself, 'Dammit, I ought to be baking him some cookies and here I am putting together a wreath." She had taken it to the cemetery the previous Saturday and brought back the Christmas wreath that she'd left two months earlier. The *Daphne adora* that Betsy planted by Jack's grave was blossoming a cheerful pink.

The past year had been anything but cheerful for Annie Laura.

"I get real mad sometimes and want to stomp and beat on walls and things like that," she said.

She remembered a day when Laura called to tell her that she'd been embarrassed because she'd started thinking about her dad at work and had broken down crying.

"I said, Honey, I've cried everywhere in town. I've cried at Pep Boys. I've cried at the mill. I've cried at the grocery store. You get to where you think you're cried out, and then you just cry some more. I do my crying at two o'clock in the morning a lot of times."

In December, Laura had given birth to a second child, Annie Laura's fourth grandson, Charlie, and that had been a bright spot.

"But it hurts me so much that these little boys aren't going to have a granddad to know," she said.

Only one, Liam, Lewis' older son, now four, might have memories of Jack. Liam, who lived in Virginia, had spent two weeks with his grandparents two summers earlier. Jack had taken him everywhere, and they had gotten very close. Liam called him Papa Jack. After Jack's death, Liam's mother, Jenny, told him that Papa Jack had gone to heaven. Liam picked out the brightest star in the sky and decided that was his grandfather.

"One night he was standing at the window watching the moon come up," Annie Laura said, "and he told his mother, 'Papa Jack's making it shine.'"

While Laura was home she told her mom that her dad once told her that he didn't think he'd live past sixty.

"I think Jack always thought he would die young," Annie Laura said. "He kept making me do things I didn't want to do, made me learn to do all kinds of things so I'd be able to take care of myself. I've been really glad about that, because everything you have breaks when your husband dies, not just your heart."

When she couldn't handle things, someone always was willing to help. Jack's friends from the SCV built a new deck on the back of her house and wouldn't let her pay a cent. She still attended every SCV meeting. They were such good people, she said, and were so much like family. To the most recent meeting she had taken her traditional gingerbread with cherry sauce for Valentine's Day.

Her sister, Frances, still grieving the loss of her own husband, had been her greatest help in getting through this year, Annie Laura said. Not a day passed that they didn't talk by telephone, often for hours on end, and neither of them even wanted to think about phone bills.

"We're getting better," she noted with a laugh. "We only talked three times yesterday."

There were things that they could talk about with each other that they couldn't talk about with anybody else.

"What gets us both," Annie Laura said, "here we are, we had our husbands to ourselves again and our kids educated. We could start doing things together again, could almost pay for everything. Now they're both gone and it's just really the pits."

Her life had changed so radically so suddenly, she noted, and there was so much that she missed. She would give anything, she said, to come home again from work and see Jack and Lady waiting for her near the back door, Jack grinning and Lady twitching with excitement.

"Oh, how I miss that hug every day," she said.

Then she laughed. "You wouldn't think you'd miss arguing, but I do. We all loved to argue. We argued just for the sake of arguing. I'd argue with my daddy. He said he was so glad when Jack came along and took over that chore from him. That's something I really miss. I don't have anybody to argue with anymore. I hate being right all the time."

• • •

Early in 2000, Larry Linker told the RCC board of trustees that they could begin the search for a new president. He would be retiring on June 30, a year later than he once had planned. He requested that no special event be held, but he and his family attended the college's annual retiree recognition reception on June 29, where Jerry Tillman, chairman of the trustees, cited his thirty-seven years of service and presented a rocking chair and a drawing of a lamp of learning.

"It's been a heck of a ride," Linker told those assembled, but he made no mention that the roughest part of that ride had been the ordeal the *News & Record* put him and the college through a year and a half earlier, causing him to delay his retirement.

He was named president emeritus and kept an office on campus at the RCC Foundation, where he intended to continue working without pay to raise money for the college.

By the second anniversary of Jack's death, Annie Laura's sense of loss, grief and loneliness had abated little.

"They say that acceptance gets easier after the third year," she said, "but I don't know."

She still believed that the strife brought by the *News & Record*'s false charges had been a major contributor to her husband's death, although she knew that never could be proved. Her feelings about Ethan Feinsilver, however, had softened.

"There was a time when I thought that if I could get my hands on him, I might have strangled him," she said. "I still don't have kind thoughts about that young man. What he did to everybody in that class was abominable, without even trying to find the truth. It's just sad that newspapers have come to that kind of reporting. They want to make news instead of reporting it. Yet I feel sorry for him, too."

She thought him unable truly to see or accept people whose views and experiences differed from his own. His reporting, she thought, was the result of an eagerness to believe stereotypes and an intolerance that produced willful ignorance. Sadder by far to her was that the *News & Record*, a newspaper she had read for all of her adult life, not only embraced and spread that intolerance and ignorance but continued to defend it in the face of truth.

Epilogue

Until Ethan Feinsilver fastened onto the RCC course, not in the memory of longtime former and present members of the news staff had the *News & Record* sent a reporter into a classroom to question the accuracy and authenticity of the teaching.

News & Record reporters don't independently choose the subjects they write about. They submit proposals to editors, who discuss them at meetings before they are approved.

Why did editors single out this course over all the courses presented at the many institutions of education within the newspaper's circulation area over many decades?

Their reason appears apparent.

Feinsilver showed up at the first class before he could have known anything about content. He and his editors obviously chose this course because it was co-sponsored by a camp of Sons of Confederate Veterans, an organization stereotyped by the news media, including the *News & Record*, as "racist" and a "hate group" for its devotion to Confederate history and defense of the battle flag.

If that was indeed the reason this course was picked, didn't the editors have an obligation first to determine if the SCV was what they assumed it to be?

Then, if they found valid cause to question the course, wouldn't reason demand that they assign a reporter with knowledge in the field and no bias to the subject or the people teaching it? Wouldn't it demand that they require the reporter to enroll, attend every class, and report about the content as a whole?

How else could it be fairly judged?

Yet, it was apparent to instructors and students that Feinsilver had little, if any, knowledge of North Carolina or Civil War history and obvious animosity toward the Confederacy, the SCV, the college, and them. He entered classes without permission, spent little time there, proclaimed the course "controversial" from the beginning, and showed no interest in any topic but slavery.

Why would *News & Record* editors allow this?

Feinsilver's attitude and questions convinced students and instructors that he believed he had happened onto a den of racists, if not overt, at least "secret." His editors had to think that as well. Editors also had to have approved the sensational, false and misleading articles that eventually were published, despite prior warnings from college officials and a class member that Feinsilver seemed to be interested only in creating controversy.

In committing the newspaper's resources to exposing this supposed "racism," *News & Record* editors not only set the newspaper on what essentially was a witch-hunt, they also set a trap in which they, in the end, could be caught.

From the beginning, *News & Record* editors took a defensive position about claims of inaccuracies in Feinsilver's first article and never backed away, no matter the evidence that accumulated.

No later than three days after the first article, they knew that Feinsilver hadn't attended the class that included blacks in the Confederacy. A day later, if not earlier, they knew by his own admission that he had no knowledge of an instructor teaching that most blacks were "happy" in slavery, that this was his opinion, presented as fact. They knew, too, that the only reason the worldwide media latched onto this story was because of that provocative claim.

At that point, the newspaper's responsibility to truth obligated it to retract the article, to reveal that its main premise was false, and that the reporter hadn't attended the class. Editors also had a duty to begin an investigation to give a thorough and honest report to readers.

But the *News & Record* did none of that.

Although class members and instructors were publicly saying that Feinsilver's articles were false, editors never called any of them to get their views.

Instead, they allowed a claim they knew to be false to stand as fact. And they continued to insist that it was true.

Why?

From the beginning, the editors and publisher declined to answer reporters' questions about Feinsilver's articles. In doing so, they left only speculation to provide answers.

One possibility for their actions is that Tom Corrigan and Ed Williams didn't fully inform publisher Van King to protect their chances of promotion. Some in the newsroom, however, think this unlikely.

Could corporate lawyers have advised King not to reveal certain facts to prevent fueling the possibility of libel suits? Former editors think this improbable as well.

A more frightening prospect is that the *News & Record* decided that the SCV and anybody associated with it weren't worthy of fairness and accuracy and deserved whatever treatment the newspaper inflicted upon them.

The libel case brought by former Greensboro Mayor Vic Nussbaum could have played a role. The retraction and apology by King provoked criticism and resentment within the newsroom and that could have prompted him to stand strongly behind the reporter in this incidence.

A more likely reason is simply that the editors and publisher would have been embarrassed to reveal four days into a growing national controversy that the article that created it—one of the rare *News & Record* articles to be picked up by the country's major newspapers and worldwide media—was false and had to be withdrawn.

Whatever the reasons, the newspaper's managers, while declining to answer questions, or to offer proof of Feinsilver's claims, continued to insist that his stories were fair and accurate even after forcing him out of his job.

As late as May, 2001, in a letter declining for a second time to be interviewed for this book, King held to that position.

"We conducted a review, and we were convinced our stories accurately portrayed what occurred," he wrote. "We stood by the stories then, and we stand by them now."

The flaws in Feinsilver's first article should have been apparent to any news editor. The sensational and provocative claims, the lack of attribution, the failure to say when and how these things had been taught, the dependence on unnamed "experts," "academics," and "observers," and the style and disorganization of the article were red flags that should have raised questions. Yet editors at newspapers all across the country, and around the world, including the *New York Times* and *Washington Post*, published that article, or portions of it, without question. Larry Linker was astounded that nobody from any news organization called the college to ask if the claims were true before presenting them as news.

The college's lawyer, Allen Pugh, thought that was due to the national media's eagerness to accept stereotypes, especially about the South. In this case, the stereotypes fit into a neat package: small Southern college; rural county; SCV members supposedly teaching that slaves were happy; NAACP and U.S. Commission on Civil Rights objecting. How could it not be racist and newsworthy?

Yet in accepting such stereotypes, the news media expose their great vulnerability, the reason for their inherent unreliability: interlocked and instantly connected, they are only as dependable as their weakest link.

The most dishonest or incompetent reporter in the tiniest backwater town can instantly spread devastating lies worldwide so long as he, or she, has access to a wire service and the lies are sensational enough to fit media stereotypes. And if the organization that supplies the lies decides, for whatever reasons, to stand behind them, they forever will be accepted as truth.

When Larry Linker called the Associated Press to question the accuracy of Feinsilver's first article, he was amazed that his word was not cause enough for the AP to look into its report. The *News & Record*, he was told, would have to retract or correct the article before the AP could do anything. He should call the *News & Record* if he had a complaint.

Later, Linker said that the ordeal he endured as a result of the *News & Record*'s articles was the most bizarre situation in which he'd ever found himself. If he'd read about it happening to somebody else, he would've had difficulty believing it, he said, because he couldn't imagine that something so unlikely actually could happen.

Feinsilver's first article, Linker said, started a media avalanche, and once it gained momentum nothing could stop it. It had to run its course, destroying reality, truth, decency, honor and whatever else was unfortunate enough to stand in its path.

It also permanently altered how Linker and others viewed the news media.

"I've long been a believer that the media are far too powerful," Linker said. "Now, I've seen the power, just what the media can do. This has tainted me. I'm far more skeptical. You can't believe what you read in the paper."

"I couldn't believe that the newspaper I read growing up in Davidson County had just flat lied to its readers," said RCC vice president Marcia Daniel, who later would take a job with the community college system. "I was angry about that and I was angry that they supported it. Probably today I'll read an article in the Greensboro paper and I'll think, *Well, I wonder what the true story is?"*

"It's made me more wary of the press," said RCC public relations officer Cathy Hefferin. "Personally, coming from a journalism background, the whole situation makes me ashamed of my profession. When it happens to you, it's a lot different."

Although they were denied their final class, students in the course got an unexpected educational bonus: a lesson in media irresponsibility.

"The press took this one article and just ran with it," said Joan King, who described Feinsilver's reports as "fabricated" and "yellow journalism." "No one bothered to investigate anything, didn't try to find out the truth. It was just amazing to me, left me with such a bad feeling about the press. They have the power and they can use it anyway they want to, and because it's in the newspaper a lot of people believe it."

"Unfortunately, in our country the media treat people as if they are stupid," said Hope Haywood. "A lot of people think if I read it in the newspaper, it's true. Well, it may not be."

Before Feinsilver's first article appeared, Louise Canipe wrote to his editor telling of his actions, warning of his intent, even spoke to his editor by telephone, only to be ignored. Afterward, she wrote to the *News & Record* denying the truthfulness of Feinsilver's articles, only to receive no response and never to see her letter published. She went to the *High Point Enterprise* to talk with editorial page editor Doug Clark about his editorials and column, asking how he got his information and how he could be so certain about what went on in their class. That, too, was without effect.

"I felt like I was doing all of this and I was just making a nuisance of myself," she said. "I wasn't getting anywhere. They wouldn't listen, no matter what you said. They didn't want to hear the truth. They were going to make it the way they wanted it and that was that."

On December 15, 1998, as the students waited to learn what would become of the course, the *Courier-Tribune* of Asheboro published an AP article with which they could identify. It reported that a study by the American Society of Newspaper Editors found that eighty percent of adults believed that newspapers overdramatized and used sensational stories because they were deemed exciting, not because they were important. Sensationalism, garbled grammar, and misquotes were "chief reasons for the decline of credibility in newspapers," the study concluded. Seventy-five percent of adults were concerned about the reliability of stories with anonymous sources.

The article went on to say that the public thinks that reporters are out of touch with reality, and that people who had first-hand experience with reporters and editors were among the news media's strongest critics.

Author and sociologist John Shelton Reed, who had been quoted about the course, was unaware of the effect of Feinsilver's articles until he spoke at the Frazier Camp two months after Jack's death.

"When people are being abused by corporations or the government," he later wrote to the author of this book, "they can sometimes look to the press for sympathy, but when it's the press that's doing the abusing, it's hard to know where to turn."

Students and instructors in the course felt that they had been thrust into a world turned upside down. They were faced with a newspaper crusading against free expression, the U.S. Commission on Civil Rights seeking to deny them the fundamental rights granted by the First Amendment, and a college closing the classroom door to them.

They clearly were victims of censorship, yet no public officials, no academic groups, no university presidents came to their aid. No students demonstrated on their behalf. The American Civil Liberties Union took no notice; neither did any other groups charged with protecting America's freedoms. No editorial writers decried this denial of free speech and academic freedom. Only a single columnist, Annette Jordan of Asheboro's *Courier-Tribune*, expressed concern.

To the students and instructors it was apparent that the suppression of certain views and even of history itself had become acceptable so long as some groups were apt to take offense, even if the offense was not based in reality.

And what happened to them surely would have a chilling effect in the future. Would any community college president ever again risk offering an adult-education course on the history of the Civil War in North Carolina?

The ultimate effect of the actions by the *News & Record*, the NAACP, the U.S. Commission on Civil Rights, and Randolph Community College was not only to subdue free expression, but to create racial division and ensure ignorance.

Dedra Routh expressed the students' feelings about their experience.

"This is the United States of America," she said. "We should be able to go to any class, read any book. This shouldn't be happening in this country."

•   •   •

Larry Linker estimated actual costs from the *News & Record*'s articles to be more than $100,000 for RCC, including attorney and consultant fees, employee hours, and other charges. Damage to the college's reputation would take years to determine.

Rahlo Fowler said the costs to the SCV were about $30,000, including attorney fees, advertising bills, travel and other expenses.

Dedra Routh applied herself to family research after the aborted course and discovered that she had numerous ancestors who served in Confederate forces, including several who fought at Gettysburg. In the spring of 2000, she, her husband, Dan, and their sons, Tristan and Devin, went to Gettysburg and walked Willoughby Run, the creek where her great, great, great grandfather, Ashley Muse, died in the fight for Cemetery Ridge on the first day of battle.

She couldn't find where Muse was buried, but she kept searching. She learned that the bodies of many Confederate dead at Gettysburg had been disinterred and returned to their home states, some brought to Oakwood Cemetery in Raleigh.

In March, 2001, she and Dan went to Oakwood Cemetery in the hope of finding that Muse was there. They didn't, but Dan happened upon the grave of a Civil War veteran named Barney H. Hopkins. Could he be one of the great, great, great uncles Dedra's mother told her about on the night Jack taught about finding Confederate ancestors? She called her father, James Cranford, as soon as she got home, and he verified that Hopkins was indeed her ancestor.

Hopkins, Dedra discovered, was a sergeant with the 38th North Carolina Regiment, which had been at Gettysburg, although she hadn't yet established whether he was with his unit at that time. He survived the war, however, and died in a veterans home in Raleigh in 1922.

This was the first grave of her Confederate ancestors that Routh had found, and she wanted to keep her pledge to honor their service. On May 5, 2001, the Saturday before Confederate Memorial Day, she returned to Oakwood Cemetery with her husband, sons, and father. She brought flowers to decorate the grave; her father carried a battle flag. Her eldest son, Tristan, fifteen, lugged his bagpipes to the gravesite, and Dedra cried when he played "Amazing Grace."

"Mr. Perdue lives on in me," she said a few days later. "He really does. Just the energy to keep delving, to keep trying to find out about the Civil War and the people who fought in it and what they believed and what they felt. He gave that to me. He spurred me on. That's what that class was about."

Afterword

At the risk of appearing sanctimonious, I found it easy after researching this book to understand why so many people detest journalists and hold newspapers and other news media in contempt, as many surveys have shown.

Editors defending dishonest, sensational reporting and ignoring its consequences...reporters presenting opinion as fact and molding stories to fit their piques and political preferences...editorial writers and columnists mistaking invective and name-calling for commentary and doing little or no research before loosing their diatribes...reporters and editors willingly accepting a highly politicized government commission as an appropriate forum for determining truth and deciding which views of history are "correct"...corporate news media seeking the easy, the obvious, the tawdry—all disgusted me and made me ashamed for my profession.

But as disturbed as I was over these findings, as distressed as I became about the future of journalism, as despairing as I remain about transgressions of the First Amendment to prevent self-serving offense, I was even more troubled by another aspect of this story: the willingness, even eagerness, of the media to exploit race and keep people divided for no greater purpose than controversy.

That came home to me literally when I interviewed Randolph County NAACP president Rashidi Zalika, formerly Richie Everette. I didn't know him. We agreed to meet at the library in Asheboro. I'd seen his photograph in the local newspaper several times and was sure I'd recognize him.

"I'm easy to pick out," I told him, "I'll be the tall, skinny, ugly one."

He laughed. "Oh, I know you," he said. "I'll tell you how when I see you."

We sat across a table from each other in a quiet corner of the library. He smiled and told me that a person dear to me and my family said hi. She once was married to my son's best friend, who for nearly a quarter century has been like a second son to my wife and me.

"How do you know her?" I asked, surprised.

"My wife is her sister," he said. "I saw you at the wedding but I didn't get a chance to speak."

We also attended a funeral together at a tiny country church. It was for another of his wife's sisters who died young.

We ended up talking for more than three hours, and the first thirty minutes focused on family. I greatly admire his wife's parents, who got their many children through college on unending work and textile mill salaries.

As we talked about Zalika's own background, I was struck by how much he had in common with Jack: a concern for heritage, love of place, home and family, even shared political views.

"I wish you could have gotten to know Jack Perdue better," I told him. "I think you might have liked each other."

"I wanted to," he said. "I intended to take that course."

It wasn't his desire for the course to be dropped, he told me, although other NAACP officers wanted that. Yet he publicly had lauded Larry Linker's decision. He had labeled the Sons of Confederate Veterans as a hate group without knowing Jack or any of the other members involved in the course. He later described the course as having a thin veil of hatred toward blacks, Yankees, Jews, and native Americans, although that wasn't so.

Nothing racial had come up in the class he attended. I wondered how he could come to such conclusions after acknowledging that he had been treated courteously and had heard and seen nothing offensive.

He sensed those things, he said, in part because he expected them. Just as the instructors and students viewed him with suspicion because of his sudden appearance so late in the course after their experience with Feinsilver, he, too, saw them with mistrust that caused him to accept what he anticipated finding, even though he didn't see or hear it.

To understand that, he said, I had to be able to see it through his eyes, his experiences. And that wasn't possible.

Here we sat, strangers, with people we loved in common, and so much else, yet divided by the irrelevancy of skin color and a complicated past that transformed the present into different realities for both of us.

"How are we ever going to overcome this?" I asked. "How are we ever going to be able to accept each other just as people?"

He had no answer, and neither did I.

We walked out together and stopped on the sidewalk to say farewells.

"So do you think that Feinsilver held out the race bait and we bit?" he said.

"I do."

He nodded.

We shook hands, wished each other well, and went our separate ways.

ML

3/02